PRENTICE HALL

SCIENCE EXPLORER

Integrated Science
Laboratory Manual

Student Edition

PRENTICE HALL
Needham, Massachusetts
Upper Saddle River, New Jersey
Glenview, Illinois

Safety Reviewers

W. H. Breazeale, Ph.D.
Department of Chemistry
College of Charleston
Charleston, South Carolina

Ruth Hathaway, Ph.D.
Hathaway Consulting
Cape Girardeau, Missouri

Field Testers

Tom Barner
F. A. Day Middle School
Newton, Massachusetts

Nikki Bibbo
Russell Street School
Littleton, Massachusetts

Rose-Marie Botting
Broward County School District
Fort Lauderdale, Florida

Tom Messer
Cape Cod Academy
Osterville, Massachusetts

Carol Pirtle
Hale Middle School
Stow, Massachusetts

Pasquale Puleo
F. A. Day Middle School
Newton, Massachusetts

Anne Scammell
Geneva Middle School
Geneva, New York

PRENTICE HALL
Needham, Massachusetts
Upper Saddle River, New Jersey
Glenview, Illinois

Student Edition ISBN 0-13-436369-8
3 4 5 6 7 8 9 10   06 05 04 03 02 01 00

Laboratory Investigations

© Prentice-Hall, Inc.

TABLE OF CONTENTS *(continued)*

To prepare yourself to work safely in the laboratory, read over the following safety rules. Then read them a second time. Make sure you understand and follow each rule. Ask your teacher to explain any rules you do not understand.

Dress Code

1. To protect yourself from injuring your eyes, wear safety goggles whenever you work with chemicals, flames, glassware, or any substance that might get into your eyes. If you wear contact lenses, notify your teacher.
2. Wear an apron or coat whenever you work with corrosive chemicals or substances that can stain.
3. Tie back long hair to keep it away from any chemicals, flames, or equipment.
4. Remove or tie back any article of clothing or jewelry that can hang down and touch chemicals, flames, or equipment. Roll up or secure long sleeves.
5. Never wear open shoes or sandals.

General Precautions

6. Read all directions for an experiment several times before beginning the activity. Carefully follow all written and oral instructions. If you are in doubt about any part of the experiment, ask your teacher for assistance.
7. Never perform activities that are not assigned or authorized by your teacher. Obtain permission before "experimenting" on your own. Never handle any equipment unless you have specific permission.
8. Never perform lab activities without direct supervision.
9. Never eat or drink in the laboratory.
10. Keep work areas clean and tidy at all times. Bring only notebooks and lab manuals or written lab procedures to the work area. All other items, such as purses and backpacks, should be left in a designated area.
11. Do not engage in horseplay.

First Aid

12. Always report all accidents or injuries to your teacher, no matter how minor. Notify your teacher immediately about any fires.
13. Learn what to do in case of specific accidents, such as getting acid in your eyes or on your skin. (Rinse acids from your body with plenty of water.)
14. Be aware of the location of the first-aid kit, but do not use it unless instructed by your teacher. In case of injury, your teacher should administer first aid. Your teacher may also send you to the school nurse or call a physician.
15. Know the location of the emergency equipment such as fire extinguisher and fire blanket.
16. Know the location of the nearest telephone and whom to contact in an emergency.

Heating and Fire Safety

17. Never use a heat source, such as a candle, burner, or hot plate, without wearing safety goggles.
18. Never heat anything unless instructed to do so. A chemical that is harmless when cool may be dangerous when heated.
19. Keep all combustible materials away from flames. Never use a flame or spark near a combustible chemical.
20. Never reach across a flame.
21. Before using a laboratory burner, make sure you know proper procedures for lighting and adjusting the burner, as demonstrated by your teacher. Do not touch the burner. It may be hot. Never leave a lighted burner unattended. Turn off the burner when not in use.
22. Chemicals can splash or boil out of a heated test tube. When heating a substance in a test tube, make sure that the mouth of the tube is not pointed at you or anyone else.
23. Never heat a liquid in a closed container. The expanding gases produced may shatter the container.
24. Before picking up a container that has been heated, first hold the back of your hand near it. If you can feel heat on the back of your hand, the container is too hot to handle. Use an oven mitt to pick up a container that has been heated.

Using Chemicals Safely

25. Never mix chemicals "for the fun of it." You might produce a dangerous, possibly explosive substance.

26. Never put your face near the mouth of a container that holds chemicals. Many chemicals are poisonous. Never touch, taste, or smell a chemical unless you are instructed by your teacher to do so.

27. Use only those chemicals needed in the activity. Read and double-check labels on supply bottles before removing any chemicals. Take only as much as you need. Keep all containers closed when chemicals are not being used.

28. Dispose of all chemicals as instructed by your teacher. To avoid contamination, never return chemicals to their original containers. Never pour untreated chemicals or other substances into the sink or trash containers.

29. Be extra careful when working with acids or bases. Pour all chemicals over the sink or a container, not over your work surface.

30. If you are instructed to test for odors, use a wafting motion to direct the odors to your nose. Do not inhale the fumes directly from the container.

31. When mixing an acid and water, always pour the water into the container first then add the acid to the water. Never pour water into an acid.

32. Take extreme care not to spill any material in the laboratory. Wash chemical spills and splashes immediately with plenty of water. Immediately begin rinsing with water any acids that get on your skin or clothing, and notify your teacher of any acid spill at the same time.

Using Glassware Safely

33. Never force glass tubing or a thermometer into a rubber stopper or rubber tubing. Have your teacher insert the glass tubing or thermometer if required for an activity.

34. If you are using a laboratory burner, use a wire screen to protect glassware from any flame. Never heat glassware that is not thoroughly dry on the outside.

35. Keep in mind that hot glassware looks cool. Never pick up glassware without first checking to see if it is hot. Use an oven mitt. See rule 24.

36. Never use broken or chipped glassware. If glassware breaks, notify your teacher and dispose of the glassware in the proper broken-glassware container.

37. Never eat or drink from glassware.

38. Thoroughly clean glassware before putting it away.

Using Sharp Instruments

39. Handle scalpels or other sharp instruments with extreme care. Never cut material toward you; cut away from you.

40. Immediately notify your teacher if you cut your skin when working in the laboratory.

Animal and Plant Safety

41. Never perform experiments that cause pain, discomfort, or harm to animals. This rule applies at home as well as in the classroom.

42. Animals should be handled only if absolutely necessary. Your teacher will instruct you as to how to handle each animal species brought into the classroom.

43. If you know that you are allergic to certain plants, molds, or animals, tell your teacher before doing an activity in which these are used.

44. During field work, protect your skin by wearing long pants, long sleeves, socks, and closed shoes. Know how to recognize the poisonous plants and fungi in your area, as well as plants with thorns, and avoid contact with them. Never eat any part of a plant or fungus.

45. Wash your hands thoroughly after handling animals or a cage containing animals. Wash your hands when you are finished with any activity involving animal parts, plants, or soil.

End-of-Experiment Rules

46. After an experiment has been completed, turn off all burners or hot plates. If you used a gas burner, check that the gas-line valve to the burner is off. Unplug hot plates.

47. Turn off and unplug any other electrical equipment that you used.

48. Clean up your work area and return all equipment to its proper place.

49. Dispose of waste materials as instructed by your teacher.

50. Wash your hands after every experiment.

These symbols alert you to possible dangers in the laboratory and remind you to work carefully.

Safety Goggles Always wear safety goggles to protect your eyes in any activity involving chemicals, flames or heating, or the possibility of broken glassware.

Lab Apron Wear a laboratory apron to protect your skin and clothing from damage.

Breakage You are working with materials that may be breakable, such as glass containers, glass tubing, thermometers, or funnels. Handle breakable materials with care. Do not touch broken glassware.

Heat-Resistant Gloves Use an oven mitt or other hand protection when handling hot materials. Hot plates, hot glassware, or hot water can cause burns. Do not touch hot objects with your bare hands.

Heating Use a clamp or tongs to pick up hot glassware. Do not touch hot objects with your bare hands.

Sharp Object Pointed-tip scissors, scalpels, knives, needles, pins, or tacks are sharp. They can cut or puncture your skin. Always direct a sharp edge or point away from yourself and others. Use sharp instruments only as instructed.

Electric Shock Avoid the possibility of electric shock. Never use electrical equipment around water, or when the equipment is wet or your hands are wet. Be sure cords are untangled and cannot trip anyone. Disconnect the equipment when it is not in use.

Corrosive Chemical You are working with an acid or another corrosive chemical. Avoid getting it on your skin or clothing, or in your eyes. Do not inhale the vapors. Wash your hands when you are finished with the activity.

Poison Do not let any poisonous chemical come in contact with your skin, and do not inhale its vapors. Wash your hands when you are finished with the activity.

Physical Safety When an experiment involves physical activity, take precautions to avoid injuring yourself or others. Follow instructions from the teacher. Alert the teacher if there is any reason you should not participate in the activity.

Animal Safety Treat live animals with care to avoid harming the animals or yourself. Working with animal parts or preserved animals also requires caution. Wash your hands when you are finished with the activity.

Plant Safety Handle plants in the laboratory or during field work only as directed by the teacher. If you are allergic to certain plants, tell the teacher before doing an activity in which those plants are used. Avoid touching harmful plants such as poison ivy, poison oak, or poison sumac, or plants with thorns. Wash your hands when you are finished with the activity.

Flames You may be working with flames from a lab burner, candle, or matches. Tie back loose hair and clothing. Follow instructions from the teacher about lighting and extinguishing flames.

No Flames Flammable materials may be present. Make sure there are no flames, sparks, or other exposed heat sources present.

Fumes When poisonous or unpleasant vapors may be involved, work in a ventilated area. Avoid inhaling vapors directly. Only test an odor when directed to do so by the teacher, and use a wafting motion to direct the vapor toward your nose.

Disposal Chemicals and other laboratory materials used in the activity must be disposed of safely. Follow the instructions from the teacher.

Hand Washing Wash your hands thoroughly when finished with the activity. Use antibacterial soap and warm water. Lather both sides of your hands and between your fingers. Rinse well.

General Safety Awareness You may see this symbol when none of the symbols described earlier appears. In this case, follow the specific instructions provided. You may also see this symbol when you are asked to develop your own procedure in a lab. Have the teacher approve your plan before you go further.

I, _____ , have read
(please print full name)

the Science Safety Rules and Safety Symbols
sections on pages v–vii of this manual,
understand their contents completely, and agree
to demonstrate compliance with all safety rules
and guidelines that have been established in each
of the following categories:

(please check)

☐ Dress Code

☐ General Precautions

☐ First Aid

☐ Heating and Fire Safety

☐ Using Chemicals Safely

☐ Using Glassware Safely

☐ Using Sharp Instruments

☐ Animal and Plant Safety

☐ End-of-Experiment Rules

_____
(signature)

Date _____

© Prentice-Hall, Inc.

Name _____ Date _____ Class _____

Recognizing Laboratory Safety

◆ Pre-Lab Discussion

An important part of your study of science will be working in a laboratory. In the laboratory, you and your classmates will learn about the natural world by conducting experiments. Working directly with household objects, laboratory equipment, and even living things will help you to better understand the concepts you read about in your textbook or in class.

Most of the laboratory work you will do is quite safe. However, some laboratory equipment, chemicals, and specimens can be dangerous if handled improperly. Laboratory accidents do not just happen. They are caused by carelessness, improper handling of equipment, or inappropriate behavior.

In this investigation, you will learn how to prevent accidents and thus work safely in a laboratory. You will review some safety guidelines and become acquainted with the location and proper use of safety equipment in your classroom laboratory.

◆ Problem

What are the proper practices for working safely in a science laboratory?

◆ Materials *(per group)*

science textbook
laboratory safety equipment (for demonstration)

◆ Procedure

Part A. Reviewing Laboratory Safety Rules and Symbols

1. Carefully read the list of laboratory safety rules listed on pages v and vi of this lab manual.

2. Special symbols are used throughout this lab book to call attention to investigations that require extra caution. Use page vii as a reference to describe what each symbol means in numbers l through 8 of Observations.

Part B. Location of Safety Equipment in Your Science Laboratory

1. The teacher will point out the location of the safety equipment in your classroom laboratory. Pay special attention to instructions for using such equipment as fire extinguishers, eyewash fountains, fire blankets, safety showers, and items in first-aid kits. Use the space provided in Part B under Observations to list the location of all safety equipment in your laboratory.

© Prentice-Hall, Inc.

RECOGNIZING LABORATORY SAFETY (continued)

◆ Observations

Part A

1. _____
_____
_____

2. _____
_____
_____

3. _____
_____
_____

4. _____
_____
_____

5. _____
_____
_____

6. _____
_____
_____

7. _____
_____
_____

8. _____
_____
_____

© Prentice-Hall, Inc.

RECOGNIZING LABORATORY SAFETY *(continued)*

Part B

_____
_____
_____
_____
_____

◆ Analyze and Conclude

Look at each of the following drawings and explain why the laboratory activities pictured are unsafe.

1. _____
   _____
   _____
   _____

2. _____
   _____
   _____
   _____

3. _____
   _____
   _____
   _____

RECOGNIZING LABORATORY SAFETY *(continued)*

◆ Critical Thinking and Applications

In each of the following situations, write *yes* if the proper safety procedures are being followed and *no* if they are not. Then give a reason for your answer.

1. Gina is thirsty. She rinses a beaker with water, refills it with water, and takes a drink.

_____

_____

2. Bram notices that the electrical cord on his microscope is frayed near the plug. He takes the microscope to his teacher and asks for permission to use another one.

_____

_____

3. The printed directions in the lab book tell a student to pour a small amount of hydrochloric acid into a beaker. Jamal puts on safety goggles before pouring the acid into the beaker.

_____

_____

4. It is rather warm in the laboratory during a late spring day. Anna slips off her shoes and walks barefoot to the sink to clean her glassware.

_____

_____

5. While washing glassware, Mike splashes some water on Evon. To get even, Evon splashes him back.

_____

_____

6. During an experiment, Lindsey decides to mix two chemicals that the lab procedure does not say to mix, because she is curious about what will happen.

_____

_____

Name _____ Date _____ Class _____

Following Directions

1. Read all of the following directions before you do anything.

2. Print your name, last name first, then your first name and middle initial (if you have one), at the top of this page.

3. Draw a line through the word "all" in direction 1.

4. Underline the word "directions" in direction 1.

5. In direction 2, circle the words "your first name."

6. In direction 3, place an "X" in front of the word "through."

7. Cross out the numbers of the even-numbered directions above.

8. In direction 7, cross out the word "above" and write the word "below" above it.

9. Write "Following directions is easy" under your name at the top of this page.

10. In direction 9, add the following sentence after the word "page": "That's what you think!"

11. Draw a square in the upper right corner of this page.

12. Draw a triangle in the lower left corner of this page.

13. Place a circle in the center of the square.

14. Place an "X" in the center of the triangle.

15. Now that you have read all the directions as instructed in direction 1, follow directions 2 and 16 only.

16. Please do not give away what this test is about by saying anything or doing anything to alert your classmates. If you have reached this direction, make believe you are still writing. See how many of your classmates really know how to follow directions.

Defining Elements of a Scientific Method

Laboratory activities and experiments involve the use of the scientific method. Listed in the left column are the names of parts of this method. The right column contains definitions. Next to each word in the left column, write the letter of the definition that best matches that word.

_____ **1.** Hypothesis

_____ **2.** Manipulated Variable

_____ **3.** Responding Variable

_____ **4.** Controlling Variables

_____ **5.** Observation

_____ **6.** Data

_____ **7.** Conclusion

A. Prediction about the outcome of an experiment

B. What you measure or observe to obtain your results

C. Measurements and other observations

D. Statement that sums up what you learn from an experiment

E. Factor that is changed in an experiment

F. What the person performing the activity sees, hears, feels, smells, or tastes

G. Keeping all variables the same except the manipulated variable

Analyzing Elements of a Scientific Method

Read the following statements and then answer the questions.

1. You and your friend are walking along a beach in Maine on January 15, at 8:00 AM.

2. You notice a thermometer on a nearby building that reads $-1°C$.

3. You also notice that there is snow on the roof of the building and icicles hanging from the roof.

4. You further notice a pool of sea water in the sand near the ocean.

5. Your friend looks at the icicles and the pool and says, "How come the water on the roof is frozen and the sea water is not?"

6. You answer, "I think that the salt in the sea water keeps it from freezing at $-1°C$."

7. You go on to say, "And I think under the same conditions, the same thing will happen tomorrow."

8. Your friend asks, "How can you be sure?" You answer, "I'm going to get some fresh water and some salt water and expose them to a temperature of $-1°C$ and see what happens."

◆ Questions

A. In which statement is a **prediction** made? _____

B. Which statement states a **problem**? _____

C. In which statement is an **experiment** described? _____

D. Which statement contains a **hypothesis**? _____

E. Which statements contain **data**? _____

F. Which statements describe **observations**? _____

Performing an Experiment

Read the following statements and then answer the questions.

1. A scientist wants to find out why sea water freezes at a lower temperature than fresh water.

2. The scientist goes to the library and reads a number of articles about the physical properties of solutions.

3. The scientist also reads about the composition of sea water.

4. The scientist travels to a nearby beach and observes the conditions there. The scientist notes the taste of the sea water and other factors such as waves, wind, air pressure, temperature, and humidity.

5. After considering all this information, the scientist sits at a desk and writes, "If sea water has salt in it, it will freeze at a lower temperature than fresh water."

6. The scientist goes back to the laboratory and does the following:
   a. Fills each of two beakers with 1 liter of fresh water.
   b. Dissolves 35 grams of table salt in one of the beakers.
   c. Places both beakers in a freezer at a temperature of $-1°C$.
   d. Leaves the beakers in the freezer for 24 hours.

7. After 24 hours, the scientist examines both beakers and finds the fresh water to be frozen. The salt water is still liquid.

8. The scientist writes in a notebook, "It appears that salt water freezes at a lower temperature than fresh water does."

9. The scientist continues, "I suggest that the reason sea water freezes at a lower temperature is that sea water contains dissolved salts, while fresh water does not."

◆ Questions

A. Which statement(s) contain **conclusions**? _____

B. Which statement(s) contains a **hypothesis**? _____

C. Which statement(s) contain **observations**? _____

D. Which statement(s) describe an **experiment**? _____

E. In which statement is the **problem** described? _____

F. Which statement(s) contain **data**? _____

G. Which is the **manipulated variable** in the experiment? _____

H. What is the **responding variable** in the experiment? _____

LABORATORY SKILLS CHECKUP 5

Identifying Errors

Read the following paragraph and then answer the questions.

Andrew arrived at school and went directly to his earth science class. He took off his cap and coat and sat down at his desk. His teacher gave him a large rock and asked him to find its density. Realizing that the rock was too large to work with, Andrew got a hammer from the supply cabinet and hit the rock several times until he broke off a chip small enough to work with. He partly filled a graduated cylinder with water and suspended the rock in the water. The water level rose 2 cm. Andrew committed this measurement to memory. He next weighed the rock on a balance. The rock weighed 4 oz. Andrew then calculated the density of the rock as follows: He divided 2 cm by 4 oz. He then reported to his teacher that the density of the rock was .5 cm/oz.

◆ Questions

1. What safety rule(s) did Andrew break?

_____

_____

2. What mistake did Andrew make using measurement units?

_____

_____

3. What should Andrew have done with his data rather than commit them to memory?

_____

_____

4. What is wrong with the statement "He next weighed the rock on a balance"?

_____

_____

5. Why is "4 oz" an inappropriate measurement in a science experiment?

_____

_____

6. What mistake did Andrew make in calculating density?

_____

_____

SKILLS LAB 1   **LABORATORY INVESTIGATION**

How to Use a Microscope

◆ Pre-Lab Discussion

As you explore the natural world in science labs, you will be doing something you do every day—making observations. You use your senses to make observations, but sometimes your senses need help. For several labs in this book, you will be using a microscope to examine organisms and objects that are too small to be seen with the unaided eye. Refer to Figure 1 throughout this lab and other labs that use a microscope.

When you view an object through a microscope, you place the object on a glass slide. The slide may be either a dry-mount or a wet-mount slide. In a dry-mount slide, the object to be examined is placed on the slide and covered with a small square of plastic called a coverslip. In a wet-mount slide, a drop of liquid is placed over the object before being covered with a coverslip. In this investigation, you will learn how to correctly prepare a wet-mount slide and how to observe an object under the microscope.

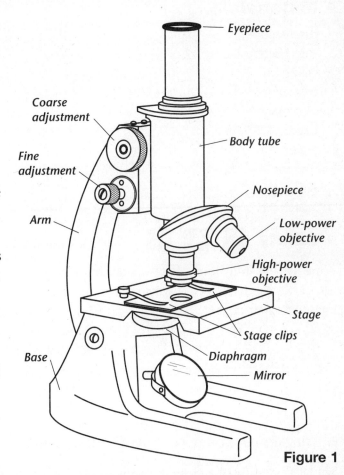

Figure 1

1. When you carry a microscope, why should you carry it with one hand on the arm of the microscope and the other hand under the base?

_____

_____

_____

2. Why should you hold a microscope slide by its edges?

_____

_____

HOW TO USE A MICROSCOPE *(continued)*

◆ Problem

How do you prepare an object to be viewed under the microscope, and how do you use the microscope to observe the object?

◆ Materials *(per group)*

microscope
microscope slide
coverslip
newspaper
scissors
plastic dropper
water
forceps
paper towel

◆ Safety   *Review the safety guidelines in front of your lab book.*

Wipe up any spills immediately. Handle slides with care to avoid breakage. Tell the teacher if a slide breaks. If your microscope has a mirror, do not tilt it directly toward the sun. Eye damage can occur if direct sunlight is used as a light source.

◆ Procedure

1. Cut a small letter "d" from the newspaper and place it in the center of a clean microscope slide so that it is in the normal reading position.

2. Using the plastic dropper, carefully place a small drop of water over the letter.

3. Place one side of a clean coverslip at the end of the drop of water at a 45° angle. See Figure 2. Use forceps to carefully lower the coverslip over the letter "d" and the drop of water. Do not press on the coverslip. It should rest on top of the water. Try not to trap any air bubbles under the coverslip because these will interfere with your view of the specimen. If you have trapped air bubbles, make a new wet-mount slide.

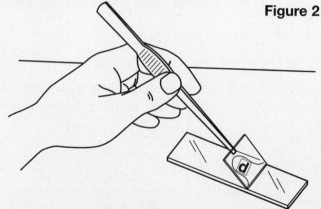

Figure 2

4. Absorb excess water by touching a folded piece of paper towel to the water that comes out around the edges of the coverslip.

© Prentice-Hall, Inc.

HOW TO USE A MICROSCOPE *(continued)*

5. In Observations, draw a picture of the letter "d" just as you see it on the slide, without the aid of the microscope.

6. Place the slide under the clips on the stage of the microscope. Position the slide so that the letter "d" is directly over the center of the stage opening.

7. Turn the nosepiece so that the low-power objective is facing downward, toward the slide. Use the coarse-adjustment knob to slowly lower the low-power objective until it almost touches the slide. **CAUTION:** *To prevent damage to the microscope and the slide, do not let the lens actually touch the slide.*

8. Tilt the mirror and adjust the diaphragm until you get the best light for viewing the specimen. **CAUTION:** *Do not aim the mirror at direct sunlight.*

9. Looking through the eyepiece, use the coarse-adjustment knob to slowly raise the lens until the letter comes into view. **CAUTION:** *To prevent damage, do not lower the coarse adjustment while looking through the eyepiece.*

10. Use the fine-adjustment knob to focus the letter clearly. You should only need to turn the knob one-quarter of a turn or less.

11. Look at the objectives and the eyepiece of your microscope. Then answer question 1 in Observations.

12. Find the total magnification power of your microscope by multiplying the magnification of the eyepiece lens by the magnification of the objective lens you are using. Then answer questions 2 and 3 in Observations.

13. In Observations, draw a picture of the letter "d" as viewed through the microscope. Record the magnification you are using.

14. While looking through the eyepiece, move the slide to the left. Notice which way the letter seems to move. Now move the slide to the right. Again notice which way the letter seems to move.

15. Switch to the high-power objective lens by revolving the nosepiece so that the high-power lens clicks into place. **CAUTION:** *The high-power objective is longer than the low-power objective; it may easily touch and damage the slide. Look at the side of the microscope when switching to the high-power objective to make sure it clears the slide.* Using the fine-adjustment knob only, bring the specimen into focus.

16. In Observations, draw a picture of the letter "d" as seen with the high-power objective lens. Record the magnification you are using.

HOW TO USE A MICROSCOPE *(continued)*

◆ Observations

1. What is the magnification of each objective of your microscope? What is the magnification of your eyepiece?

_____

_____

2. What is the total magnification power using the low-power objective?

_____

_____

3. What is the highest magnification of your microscope?

_____

_____

Letter "d" Without Microscope   **Low-Power Objective**   **High-Power Objective**

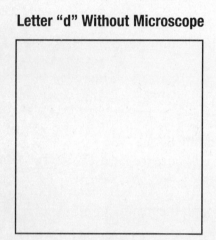
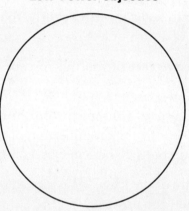
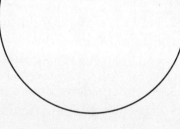

Magnification: _____   Magnification: _____

◆ Analyze and Conclude

1. How does the letter "d" as seen through the microscope differ from the way a "d" normally appears?

_____

_____

2. When you move the slide to the left, in what direction does the letter "d" appear to move?

_____

© Prentice-Hall, Inc.

HOW TO USE A MICROSCOPE *(continued)*

3. When you move the slide to the right, in what direction does the letter "d" appear to move?

_____

4. How does the ink that was used to print the letter differ in appearance when you see it with the unaided eye compared with the way it appears under the microscope?

_____

_____

_____

5. Briefly explain how to make a wet-mount slide.

_____

_____

_____

_____

_____

◆ Critical Thinking and Applications

1. Why should you always use the low-power objective lens to locate objects mounted on the slide first, even if you want to observe them with the high-power objective lens?

_____

_____

_____

_____

2. Suppose you were observing an organism through the microscope and noticed that it moved toward the top of the slide and then it moved right. In what directions did the organism actually move?

_____

_____

_____

_____

HOW TO USE A MICROSCOPE *(continued)*

◆ More to Explore

New Problem What do other objects look like under a microscope?

Possible Materials Small, common objects or thin pieces of material to observe. Consider which materials you should use from the previous part of this lab.

Safety Follow the safety guidelines in the lab.

Procedure Write your procedure on a separate sheet of paper. Have the teacher approve of your procedure and your list of objects to observe.

Observations Draw what you see when using the microscope. Record the magnifications you used.

Analyze and Conclude Evaluate the objects you observed. What objects worked well? What other kinds of objects would you choose?

_____

_____

_____

SKILLS LAB 2   **LABORATORY INVESTIGATION**

How to Use a Balance

◆ Pre-Lab Discussion

The ability to measure accurately the mass of an object is an important skill in the science laboratory. You can use a triple-beam balance to measure mass. As you can see in Figure 1, the balance has several parts. The pan is the flat surface on which you place the object to be measured. The three beams show the mass of the object. Notice that each beam has a different scale. The scale of the middle beam is from 0–500 grams and measures an object to the nearest 100 grams. The scale of the beam in back is from 0–100 grams and measures an object to the nearest 10 grams. The scale of the beam in front is from 0–10 grams and measures an object to the nearest tenth of a gram.

Notice that each beam carries a weight called a rider. You find the mass of an object by placing it on the pan and moving the riders until the pointer on the right of the balance stays pointed to zero.

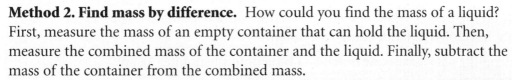

There are three ways you can use the triple-beam balance to find mass:

Method 1. Measure mass directly. Place the object on the pan and move the riders until the pointer points to zero. Add up the numbers on the beams where the riders are positioned to find mass.

Method 2. Find mass by difference. How could you find the mass of a liquid? First, measure the mass of an empty container that can hold the liquid. Then, measure the combined mass of the container and the liquid. Finally, subtract the mass of the container from the combined mass.

Method 3. Measure out a chemical substance. Suppose you need to obtain 50 g of a powdered chemical. How could you do it? First find the mass of a piece of paper or empty container that will hold the chemical. Then, add this amount to the desired mass of the chemical and preset the riders to this number. Finally, add the chemical to the paper a little at a time until the pointer points to zero.

In this investigation, you will learn how to measure accurately the mass of various objects by using the three methods described above.

1. What does it mean when the pointer of the balance reads "zero"?

_____

_____

HOW TO USE A BALANCE (*continued*)

2. Suppose a rock is balanced on a triple-beam balance. The riders on the three beams point to 60 g, 300 g, and 3.5 g. What is the mass of the rock?

_____

◆ Problem

What is the proper way to use the triple-beam balance to measure the mass of different objects?

◆ Materials (*per class*)

triple-beam balance small scoop
100-mL graduated cylinder table salt
3 different small, solid objects 200-mL beaker
weighing paper

◆ Safety *Review the safety guidelines in the front of your lab book.*

◆ Procedure

Before you measure the mass of any object, be sure that the riders are moved all the way to the left and that the pointer rests on zero. If necessary, slowly turn the adjustment knob until the pointer rests on zero. This is called zeroing the balance.

Part A: Measuring Mass Directly

1. Place a small, solid object on the balance pan. The beams will rise and the pointer will point above zero.

2. Move the rider on the middle beam one notch at a time until the pointer drops and stays below zero. Move the rider back one notch.

3. Move the rider on the back beam one notch at a time until the pointer again drops and stays below zero. Move the rider back one notch.

4. Slide the rider along the front beam until the pointer stops at zero. The mass of the object is equal to the sum of the readings on the three beams.

5. Record the mass to the nearest tenth of a gram in Data Table 1.

6. Remove this object and repeat steps 1–5 twice, using two other solid objects.

Part B: Finding Mass by Difference

1. Find the mass of an empty 250-mL beaker. Record the mass in Data Table 2.

2. Using the graduated cylinder, obtain 50 mL of water.

3. Pour the water into the beaker and find the mass of the beaker and water. Record the mass in Data Table 2.

HOW TO USE A BALANCE *(continued)*

Part C: Measuring Out a Chemical Substance

1. Place a piece of weighing paper on the balance pan and find its mass. Record the mass in Data Table 3.

2. Add 5 g to the mass of the weighing paper and move the riders to this number.

3. Obtain a sample of table salt from the teacher. Using the scoop, add a small amount of salt at a time to the paper on the balance until the pointer rests on zero. Record the total mass of the weighing paper and salt in Data Table 3.

4. Dispose of the table salt in the container provided by the teacher.

◆ Observations

Data Table 1

Object	Mass (g)

Data Table 2

Mass of Empty Beaker (g)	Mass of Beaker with 50 mL of Water (g)

Data Table 3

Mass of Weighing Paper (g)	Mass of Weighing Paper and Table Salt (g)

◆ Analyze and Conclude

1. What is the mass of 50 mL of water? How did you find this mass?

   _____

   _____

2. Which rider on the balance should always be moved first when finding the mass of an object? Why?

   _____

   _____

3. What is the mass of the largest object your balance is able to measure?

   _____

4. What is the mass of the smallest object your balance is able to measure accurately?

   _____

5. After using your balance, how should it always be left?

   _____

   _____

HOW TO USE A BALANCE *(continued)*

◆ Critical Thinking and Applications

1. Suppose you did not zero the balance before finding the mass of an object. How might that affect your measurement?

_____

_____

2. In this lab, you found the mass of 50 mL of water. Calculate the mass of 1 mL of water. (Do not use the balance.)

_____

_____

3. Describe how you could find the mass of a certain quantity of milk that you poured into a drinking glass.

_____

_____

_____

_____

4. If you were baking a dessert and the recipe called for 250 g of sugar, how could you use the triple-beam balance to obtain this amount?

_____

_____

_____

_____

◆ More to Explore

Design a balance that finds mass by comparing the mass of a known object to the mass of an unknown object. Study the triple-beam balance used in this activity and think about how you could balance two or more objects. Construct your balance and use it to find the mass of an object. How could you improve your balance?

© Prentice-Hall, Inc.

How to Use a Balance

A - 1   **LABORATORY INVESTIGATION**

Developing a Classification System for Seeds

◆ Pre-Lab Discussion

Suppose you discovered a plant or an animal that no one had ever seen. What would you call it? Where would you even begin?

To simplify the identification and naming of organisms, scientists have developed a system of classification. The classification system groups similar animals, plants, and other organisms. There are seven major levels of classification. The broadest group is a kingdom. Kingdoms contain phyla (singular *phylum*), classes, orders, families, genera (singular *genus*), and species. Organisms of the same species have the most characteristics in common.

In this investigation, you will develop a system of classification for seeds.

1. Why do scientists classify organisms into groups?

_____

_____

_____

2. How is evolution related to classification?

_____

_____

_____

◆ Problem

What characteristics can be used to classify seeds?

◆ Materials *(per group)*

paper cup containing seeds
2 hand lenses
tray
metric ruler
scrap paper

◆ Safety *Review the safety guidelines in the front of your lab book.*

Keep seeds in containers at all times to prevent accidents. Do not eat the seeds.

© Prentice-Hall, Inc.

DEVELOPING A CLASSIFICATION SYSTEM FOR SEEDS *(continued)*

◆ Procedure

1. Get a cup containing seeds. Carefully pour the seeds onto the tray. **CAUTION:** *Immediately pick up any seeds that drop on the floor.* Use a hand lens to examine the seeds carefully. Answer question 1 in Observations.

2. Think about what characteristic you could use to divide all the seeds into two large groups. Remember, each group must contain seeds with similar characteristics.

3. Sort the seeds into two piles, based on the characteristic that you selected. On scrap paper, note the characteristics that you choose.

4. Working with one of the two large groups, divide the seeds in that group into two smaller groups based on another characteristic. Record the characteristic as in Step 3.

5. Continue to divide the seeds into smaller groups by choosing and recording new characteristics. Eventually, you should have only one seed left in each group.

6. Repeat steps 4 and 5 with the other large group.

7. In Observations, draw a diagram that shows how your classification system works.

8. Compare your classification system with those of other groups in your class. Answer questions 2–4 in Observations.

◆ Observations

Diagram of Seed Classification

© Prentice-Hall, Inc.

DEVELOPING A CLASSIFICATION SYSTEM FOR SEEDS (continued)

1. What are some of the characteristics of your seeds?

_____

_____

2. How many groups are in your classification system?

_____

_____

_____

3. Compare the final classification system you have with those of other groups using different characteristics. Do they differ or are they the same? What different characteristics did they use?

_____

_____

_____

◆ Analyze and Conclude

1. What characteristics did you find most useful for classifying the seeds?

_____

_____

2. Explain why your final classification groups differed or were the same as those of other groups.

_____

_____

3. How does a classification system help you understand organisms?

_____

_____

_____

4. How is this investigation similar to the way in which scientists classify organisms?

_____

_____

_____

_____

© Prentice-Hall, Inc.

DEVELOPING A CLASSIFICATION SYSTEM FOR SEEDS *(continued)*

◆ Critical Thinking and Applications

1. Could you have classified your seeds using another system? Give a reason for your answer.

_____

_____

2. Could you have classified each characteristic in groups of three or more types at each step? Do you think more groups would make choices harder or easier? Give a reason for your answer.

_____

_____

_____

_____

3. Suppose you wanted to classify all the birds that came to a particular area of a pond during a spring day. What are some of the characteristics that you would use to classify the birds?

_____

_____

4. When classifying organisms, do you think that it is better to go from general characteristics to specific characteristics or from specific characteristics to general characteristics? Give a reason for your answer.

_____

_____

_____

◆ More to Explore

Make a list of five or more household appliances. Combine your list with a class-mate's. Then separately devise classification systems for the combined list of appliances. What characteristics did you use to classify these items into groups? Did your classmate come up with the same classification system?

© Prentice-Hall, Inc.

A-2   **LABORATORY INVESTIGATION**

Eubacteria That Dine on Vegetables

Members of the Eubacteria kingdom are among the most numerous organisms on Earth. If a microscopic bacterium is in the right temperature range and has enough moisture and food, it can reproduce rapidly. In 24 to 48 hours, it can multiply so often that its offspring form a visible colony.

In this investigation, you will witness this explosive growth as you grow eubacteria on common vegetables.

◆ Pre-Lab Discussion

1. How are the cells of eubacteria different from those of other organisms?

_____

_____

2. Name the two kingdoms of bacteria. Where do these different kingdoms live?

_____

_____

_____

◆ Problem

What conditions do eubacteria need for growth?

◆ Materials *(per group)*

4 clear, resealable plastic bags
8 small pieces of masking tape
pen or pencil
2 slices of baked potato
spatula
2 cotton swabs
transparent tape
2 slices of baked yam

◆ Safety   *Review the safety guidelines in the front of your lab book.*

Do not open the plastic bags after placing the vegetables inside. Wash your hands thoroughly after handling the vegetables and plastic bags. Have the teacher dispose of the specimens at the end of the experiment.

EUBACTERIA THAT DINE ON VEGETABLES *(continued)*

◆ Procedure

1. Thoroughly wash four plastic bags with soap and water and rinse them thoroughly.

2. Put a masking-tape label on the outside of each bag. Write the following words on the four different labels: "A-Potato," "A-Yam," "B-Potato," and "B-Yam."

3. Predict where eubacteria might be living in your classroom. Give a reason for your predictions. Record your predictions in Observations. Compare your predictions with those of your classmates, and choose an area of your classroom that you will test for eubacteria. Have the teacher approve your choice before you continue.

4. Get two slices of baked potato. Use the spatula to pick up the slices. Take care that each slice has one side that touches nothing but the knife that cut it.

5. Put a potato slice with its untouched side facing up in a bag labeled "A-Potato." Seal the bag securely and tape the sealed edge shut.

6. Put the other potato slice with its untouched side facing up in a plastic bag labeled "B-Potato."

7. Rub a cotton swab on the area in your classroom where you think eubacteria might live. Then rub the cotton swab on the untouched side of the potato in bag B.

8. Seal the bag securely and tape the sealed edge shut. Set both potato bags in a warm place. Do not open them again. Your teacher will tell you where to dispose of the used cotton swab.

9. Repeat steps 4–8, using two baked yam slices.

10. Wash your hands when you're finished with the lab.

11. Observe the potato and yam slices daily for 5 days. DO NOT OPEN THE BAGS. Each day, draw both slices of each vegetable in the appropriate spaces in Observations and record your observations in the Data Table.

12. At the end of the fifth day, ask the teacher to dispose of the plastic bags and their contents.

◆ Observations

1. Predict where eubacteria might be living in your classroom. Give a reason for your prediction.

_____

_____

2. What area of your classroom will you test for eubacteria?

_____

© Prentice-Hall, Inc.

EUBACTERIA THAT DINE ON VEGETABLES *(continued)*

Vegetable 1: _____

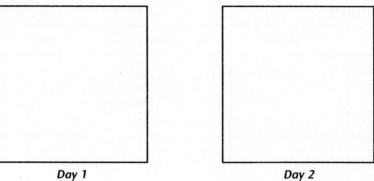

Day 1	*Day 2*	*Day 3*

Day 4	*Day 5*

Vegetable 2: _____

Day 1	*Day 2*	*Day 3*

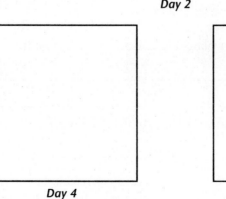

Day 4	*Day 5*

2

EUBACTERIA THAT DINE ON VEGETABLES *(continued)*

Data Table

Day	Date	Potato		Yam	
		A-Potato	**B-Potato**	**A-Yam**	**B-Yam**
1					
2					
3					
4					
5					

◆ Analyze and Conclude

1. Large groups of eubacteria may look shiny or like mucus. Which container(s) had the greatest growth of eubacteria? The least growth?

_____

_____

2. Do the organisms growing on the potato appear to be different from the organisms growing on the yam? Give a plausible reason for your results.

_____

_____

3. Why did you leave the slices untouched in the plastic bags labeled "A"?

_____

_____

EUBACTERIA THAT DINE ON VEGETABLES *(continued)*

◆ Critical Thinking and Applications

1. Early biologists grew eubacteria on freshly cut slices of vegetables. They considered the inside of a vegetable to be sterile, or free of microorganisms. How did the eubacteria get on your vegetables?

_____

_____

_____

2. Why was it important to thoroughly wash and rinse the plastic bags before placing the vegetable slices in them?

_____

_____

_____

3. Why did you use a spatula instead of your hand to transfer the vegetable slices into the plastic bags?

_____

_____

_____

4. Suppose you repeated this investigation, but this time you left the plastic bags labeled "A" open for a few minutes before sealing them. What do you think you might observe? Why?

_____

_____

_____

_____

_____

5. What methods can you suggest for keeping vegetables unspoiled for a long time?

_____

_____

_____

_____

_____

© Prentice-Hall, Inc.

EUBACTERIA THAT DINE ON VEGETABLES *(continued)*

◆ More to Explore

Try this activity with other vegetables, such as boiled carrots or cooked fresh beets. Sample other areas of your classroom where you think eubacteria might be living. Have the teacher approve your procedure before you carry out the investigation. Do your results resemble results found in this lab?

2

A - 3   **LABORATORY INVESTIGATION**

Comparing Protists

◆ Pre-Lab Discussion

Protists are organisms that have nuclei and live in wet environments, such as ponds, oceans, and the bodies of larger organisms. Other than that, protists don't have much in common. For example, some live independently as separate cells; others form colonies of many unattached cells. Plantlike protists are autotrophs—organisms that can make their own food. Animal-like protists and funguslike protists are heterotrophs—organisms that cannot make their own food.

In this investigation, you will observe and compare three common protists: amebas, euglenas, and paramecia.

1. Protists are eukaryotes. What does that mean?

_____

2. Name three different protist structures that aid in movement.

_____

_____

◆ Problem

How are protists similar? How are they different?

◆ Materials *(per group)*

3 plastic droppers   microscope
ameba culture   piece of cotton
microscope slide   euglena culture
3 coverslips   paramecium culture
paper towel

◆ Safety   *Review the safety guidelines in the front of your lab book.*

Do not use the same droppers for different cultures. Always use both hands to pick up or carry a microscope. Hold the microscope base with one hand and hold the microscope arm with your other hand. Handle glass slides carefully. Don't handle broken glass. Wash your hands thoroughly after the lab.

◆ Procedure

1. With a plastic dropper, place a drop of the ameba culture on the slide.

2. Make a wet-mount slide by gently laying the coverslip over the drop of ameba culture.

COMPARING PROTISTS (*continued*)

3. Touch a piece of paper towel to the edge of the coverslip to blot up any excess liquid. See Figure 1.

4. Place the slide on the stage of the microscope. Use the low-power objective to bring an ameba into focus. Have the teacher check to see that you have an ameba in focus.

5. Switch to the high-power objective. **CAUTION:** *When turning to the high-power objective, always look at the objective from the side of your microscope. Don't let the objective hit the slide.*

6. Use the fine-adjustment knob to bring the organism into sharper focus. **CAUTION:** *Never focus the high-power objective with the coarse-adjustment knob. The objective could break the slide.*

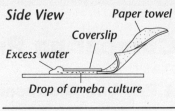

Side View

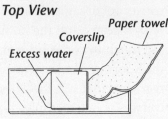

Top View

Figure 1

7. Observe an ameba and draw what you see in Plate 1 in Observations. Label the nucleus, cell membrane, cytoplasm, food vacuole, and pseudopods. Record the microscope magnification that you used below your sketch.

8. Carefully clean and dry the slide with a paper towel.

9. Separate a few strands of cotton and place them on the slide. The cotton strands will help slow down the euglena. Using a clean dropper, add a drop of the euglena culture to the strands of cotton.

10. Repeat steps 2–6 with the drop of euglena culture.

11. Observe a euglena and draw what you see in Plate 2 in Observations. Label the nucleus, cell membrane, cytoplasm, eyespot, flagellum, and chloroplasts. Record the microscope magnification you used below your sketch.

12. Carefully clean and dry the slide.

13. Separate a few strands of cotton and place them on the slide. Using a clean dropper, add a drop of the paramecium culture to the strands of cotton.

14. Repeat steps 2–6 with the drop of paramecium culture.

15. Observe a paramecium and draw what you see in Plate 3 in Observations. Label the cytoplasm, cell membrane, cilia, nucleus, contractile vacuole, food vacuoles, oral groove, and gullet. Record the microscope magnification you used below your sketch.

16. Clean and dry the slide once again. Return all the materials to the teacher. Wash your hands when you're finished with the lab.

◆ Observations

1. Describe the shape of the ameba.

_____

2. Describe the shape of the euglena.

_____

COMPARING PROTISTS *(continued)*

3. Describe the shape of the paramecium.

_____

4. Describe how an ameba moves.

_____

5. Describe how a euglena moves.

_____

6. Describe how a paramecium moves.

_____

7. What structures does the euglena have that the ameba and paramecium do not have?

_____

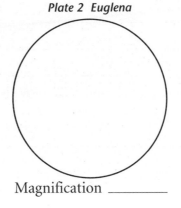
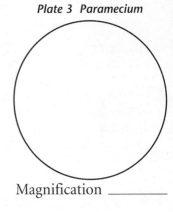

Plate 1 Ameba   *Plate 2 Euglena*   *Plate 3 Paramecium*

Magnification _____   Magnification _____   Magnification _____

◆ Analyze and Conclude

1. What structures do all protists have?

_____

2. Which protist has structures that are characteristic of both autotrophs and heterotrophs?

_____

3. Classify the three protists that you observed as animal-like, funguslike, or plantlike protists. Give a reason for your answers.

_____

_____

_____

COMPARING PROTISTS *(continued)*

4. Which is the slowest moving of the three protists?

_____

5. Why are some protists able to move faster than others?

_____

_____

_____

◆ Critical Thinking and Applications

1. Why is the eyespot an important structure in the euglena?

_____

_____

2. The paramecium has two types of cilia. One type covers its entire surface. The other is at the entrance to the gullet. How does the paramecium use each type?

_____

_____

_____

3. Certain cells in your body, such as white blood cells, move by ameboid motion. What does this mean?

_____

_____

◆ More to Explore

A paramecium has thousands of cilia that project through the pellicle—the covering that gives the paramecium its shape. These cilia beat with a wavelike pattern that keeps a paramecium moving smoothly in one direction. Write a hypothesis for how a paramecium will respond when it runs into objects that are in its path. Write a procedure you would follow to test your hypothesis. Have the teacher approve your procedure before you carry out the investigation. Describe how the paramecium responds. Did your results support your hypothesis?

© Prentice-Hall, Inc.

A-4

Investigating Stomata

◆ Pre-Lab Discussion

For an organism to live and grow naturally in any place, it must be adapted to the conditions of that place. A land plant, for example, must have adaptations that prevent it from drying out. A thick, waxy layer of tissue, called the cuticle, is one adaptation that prevents water loss. However, the cuticle also prevents exchange of oxygen and carbon dioxide with the environment. Photosynthesis cannot take place without this exchange of gases. Small openings, called stomata (singular *stoma*), allow gases to move into and out of the plant. Each stoma is surrounded by two guard cells that control the size of the opening. When these guard cells absorb water, the stoma opens; when the guard cells lose water, the stoma closes.

In this investigation, you will observe stomata in a land plant and in a floating water plant.

1. Why is photosynthesis important for plants?

_____

_____

2. What adaptations make it possible for plants to live on land?

_____

_____

_____

◆ Problem

How do the number and position of stomata differ in plants from different environments?

◆ Materials *(per group)*

leaf from a land plant
leaf from a floating water plant
scissors
microscope
2 slides
dropper
2 coverslips

INVESTIGATING STOMATA *(continued)*

◆ Safety   *Review the safety guidelines in the front of your lab book.*

Use caution in handling sharp scissors. Handle glass slides carefully. Do not let the microscope lens touch the slide.

◆ Procedure

1. Predict where stomata are on the leaf of a land plant. Give a reason for your prediction.

   _____

   _____

2. Select a land plant. With the lower epidermis (underside of the leaf) facing upward, bend and then tear the leaf at an angle as illustrated in Figure 1. This will reveal part of the thin, colorless, lower epidermis.

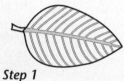 

Step 1   *Step 2*   *Step 3*

Figure 1

4

3. With the scissors, cut off a strip of the colorless tissue and make a wet-mount slide. Place the slide on the microscope stage and focus under low power. Locate the stomata. Switch to high power. Draw the stomata, the guard cells, and a few of the lower epidermis cells in Observations. Count the stomata seen in the field of vision under high power. Record your data in the Data Table. (Identify and record the name of your lab group in the first column of the Data Table. Record data only in the row for your group.)

4. Repeat Step 3, using the upper epidermis of the same leaf. Draw your observations. Count the stomata seen in the field of vision under high power and record your data.

5. Predict where stomata are on the leaf of a floating water plant. Give a reason for your prediction.

   _____

   _____

6. Repeat Step 3, using the lower epidermis of a leaf from a water plant. Draw what you see in Observations. Count the stomata in the field of vision and record this number in the Data Table.

7. Repeat Step 3, using the upper epidermis of a leaf from the water plant. Draw your observations and record your data.

8. Exchange and record data from other groups to complete your Data Table.

INVESTIGATING STOMATA *(continued)*

◆ Observations

Land Plant		Water Plant	

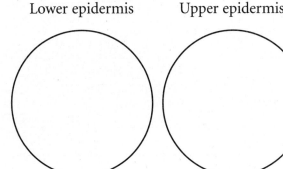
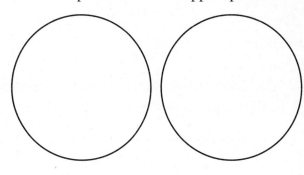

Lower epidermis   Upper epidermis   Lower epidermis   Upper epidermis

Data Table

Group	Land Plant: _____		Floating Water Plant: _____	
	Lower Epidermis	*Upper Epidermis*	*Lower Epidermis*	*Upper Epidermis*

◆ Analyze and Conclude

1. Is the class information more reliable than the information gathered by one group? Give a reason for your answer.

_____

2. Using data from the entire class, compare the number of stomata in the upper and lower epidermis of land plants.

_____

3. Using data from the entire class, compare the number of stomata in the upper and lower epidermis of water plants.

_____

INVESTIGATING STOMATA *(continued)*

◆ Critical Thinking and Applications

1. What advantage could the number of stomata and their location provide for land plants?

_____

_____

_____

2. What advantage could the number of stomata and their location provide for floating water plants?

_____

_____

_____

3. When do you think stomata are usually open—during the day or at night? Give a reason for your answer.

_____

_____

_____

4. How could you change the procedure you followed to improve the accuracy of the data?

_____

_____

_____

◆ More to Explore

New Problem Are stomata affected by a salt solution?

Possible Materials Consider which materials you can use from the previous part of the lab. What other materials might you need?

Procedure Develop a procedure to solve the problem. Keep in mind that, in osmosis, water moves from an area where it is concentrated to an area where it is less concentrated. Write your procedure on a separate sheet of paper. Have the teacher approve your procedure before you carry out the investigation.

Observations Keep records of your observations on a separate sheet of paper.

Analyze and Conclude Were more stomata open or closed in the salt solution? What might explain your results?

_____

_____

_____

© Prentice-Hall, Inc.

Investigating Hormones That Control Germination

◆ Pre-Lab Discussion

Tomato seeds usually germinate when exposed to moisture, oxygen, and a fairly warm temperature. Yet inside the tomato, where these conditions are met, seeds do not germinate. How do tomato seeds know when to develop and when not to develop?

Plants produce chemicals called hormones that control how the plants grow and develop. Only a small amount of hormone is needed to control plant processes such as the growth of the plant toward light.

In this investigation, you will explore the plant hormone that controls seed germination.

1. How can you tell if a seed is germinating?

_____

_____

2. Besides germination, what other processes do plant hormones control?

_____

_____

_____

◆ Problem

Do tomatoes have a hormone that affects seed germination?

◆ Materials *(per group)*

wide, shallow bowl   funnel
metal or wooden spoon   beaker
tomatoes (2 or more varieties)   glass-marking pencil
strainer   filter paper
plastic cup   4 plastic petri dishes
tap water   paper towel
brush

◆ Safety 🥼 🧤 🧦 🔥 *Review the safety guidelines in the front of your lab book.*

Handle glass objects carefully. If they break, tell the teacher. Do not pick up broken glass.

© Prentice-Hall, Inc.

INVESTIGATING HORMONES THAT CONTROL GERMINATION *(continued)*

◆ Procedure

1. Use a spoon to crush a whole tomato (variety A) in a bowl. Strain the crushed tomato and collect the liquid extract in a beaker. With a glass-marking pencil, label the beaker "Extract A" and set it aside.

2. Empty the pulp from the strainer onto a paper towel and blot the pulp to remove some of the moisture. Separate 20 seeds from the pulp and rub them gently with a paper towel to remove the jelly-like capsule from the outside of the seeds.

3. Clean the strainer. (Use a brush, if necessary, to remove the pulp.) Place the 20 seeds in the strainer and rinse with water. Empty the seeds out on a fresh paper towel and blot them dry.

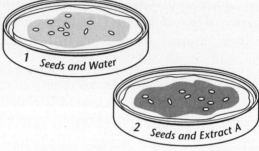

Figure 1

4. Label two petri dishes as shown in Figure 1. Line the petri dishes with filter paper. Place 10 seeds in each dish. Wet the filter paper in dish 1 with water; wet the paper in dish 2 with tomato extract. Cover the dishes.

5. Crush a different kind of tomato (variety B). Remove 20 seeds and wash them.

6. Line two more petri dishes with filter paper. Place 10 seeds in each petri dish.

7. Wet the filter paper in one dish with water. Label this dish 3. Wet the filter paper in the other dish with Extract A. Label it dish 4. Cover these two dishes.

8. Observe the seeds in the four dishes for several days, adding more water or tomato extract to keep the filter paper moist.

9. Each day record the total number of seeds that have germinated in each dish in the appropriate place in the Data Table.

◆ Observations

Data Table

Dish	Day 1	Day 2	Day 3	Day 4	Day 5	Day 6	Day 7	Day 8
1: Variety A with Water								
2: Variety A with Extract A								
3: Variety B with Water								
4: Variety B with Extract A								

INVESTIGATING HORMONES THAT CONTROL GERMINATION *(continued)*

◆ Analyze and Conclude

1. What is the purpose of dish 1?

_____

_____

2. What conclusion can you draw after observing the results in dishes 1 and 2? Do tomatoes contain a hormone that inhibits germination? Give evidence to support your answer.

_____

_____

_____

_____

3. What conclusions can you draw after studying the results in dishes 3 and 4? Does the juice from variety A inhibit germination of seeds from variety B? Give evidence to support your answer.

_____

_____

_____

_____

◆ Critical Thinking and Applications

1. Explain why some of the seeds in dishes 1 and 3 may not have germinated, even though they had all the necessary conditions for growth.

_____

_____

2. Explain why many seeds that do not contain hormones that inhibit germination might begin to germinate outside during late spring.

_____

_____

_____

3. What are three fruits and/or vegetables (besides tomatoes) that you think contain hormones that inhibit germination?

_____

_____

© Prentice-Hall, Inc.

INVESTIGATING HORMONES THAT CONTROL GERMINATION *(continued)*

◆ More to Explore

New Problem Is the hormone that inhibits the germination of tomato seeds a protein? (Hint: Proteins lose their effectiveness when boiled.)

Possible Materials Consider which materials you can use from the previous part of this lab. What else will you need?

Safety Be careful when boiling a liquid. Use a hot plate and pyrex beakers for heating. Use oven mitts to handle hot containers. Wear safety goggles and a lab apron.

Procedure Make a hypothesis that answers and explains the problem. Consider your data from the lab when developing your hypothesis. Make sure to keep a control to compare with the experimental dishes. Write your procedure on a separate sheet of paper. Have the teacher approve your procedure before carrying out the investigation.

Observations On a separate sheet of paper, make a data table to record your data.

Analyze and Conclude Is the hormone responsible for inhibiting seed germination a protein? Give a reason for your answer.

_____

_____

_____

5

© Prentice-Hall, Inc.

Observing Flatworms and Roundworms

◆ Pre-Lab Discussion

Flatworms have flat bodies and a body cavity with one opening. Most are parasites, living inside or on other organisms. Although most free-living flatworms live in the oceans, some live in fresh water or in soil.

Roundworms have long, cylindrical bodies that taper to a point at each end. There are more species of roundworms than any other kind of worm. They live in nearly every kind of moist environment, including forest soils, Antarctic sand, and pools of super-hot water. Like flatworms, some roundworms are parasitic and others are free-living.

In this investigation, you will observe some of the characteristics of parasitic and free-living flatworms and roundworms.

1. What are the three main groups of worms?

_____

_____

2. Why are earthworms important to farmers and gardeners?

_____

_____

◆ Problem

What are some characteristics of flatworms and roundworms?

◆ Materials *(per group)*

microscope
planarian slide
pork-tapeworm slide
vinegar-eel slide
trichina-worm slide

© Prentice-Hall, Inc.

OBSERVING FLATWORMS AND ROUNDWORMS *(continued)*

◆ Safety *Review the safety guidelines in the front of your lab book.*

Use both hands to carry a microscope. Hold the microscope base with one hand and the microscope arm with your other hand. Handle glass slides carefully.

◆ Procedure

Part A: Observing Flatworms

1. **CAUTION:** *Handle the slides carefully; they're breakable.* Use a microscope to look at a planarian slide under low magnification. Planarians are free-living, freshwater flatworms that have a definite head with a simple brain. Locate the two eyespots in the head region. They sense light. Find the mouth in the middle of the body on the ventral (belly) surface. Note a long tube, the pharynx, through which food moves from the mouth into the gastrovascular cavity. The gastrovascular cavity digests food and circulates it to the entire body. It also gets rid of waste.

2. Sketch a planarian under low power in the appropriate space in Observations. Label the eyespots, mouth, pharynx, and gastrovascular cavity. Record the magnification you used next to your sketch.

3. Tapeworms live as parasites inside the bodies of other animals. They attach themselves to the inner walls of their hosts and take in food through their skin. Examine a slide of a tapeworm under low magnification. Find the head. Note several suckers and the ring of hooks on the head. Behind the head is a narrow neck. The rest of the tapeworm's body is a string of nearly square sections that grow from the neck. The youngest sections are closest to the neck. These sections contain the male and female reproductive organs.

4. Sketch the tapeworm under low power in the appropriate space in Observations. Label the head, suckers, hooks, neck, young sections, and older sections. Record the magnification you used next to your sketch.

Part B: Observing Roundworms

1. A vinegar eel is a roundworm usually found in vinegar. Examine a slide of a vinegar eel under low magnification. Find the mouth at its anterior (head) end and the anus at its posterior (tail) end. Note the bulblike pharynx and long intestine. If the vinegar eel is female, eggs will be lined up in the uterus. If it is male, it will have a single testis.

2. Sketch the vinegar eel under low power in the appropriate space in Observations. Label the mouth, pharynx, intestine, anus, eggs (if female), and testis (if male). Record the magnification you used next to your sketch.

3. Examine a slide of a trichina worm. This worm is often found inside a hard capsule called a cyst. Such cysts are located inside the muscle tissue of the host.

4. Sketch what you see in the appropriate space in Observations. Label the trichina worm, cyst, and muscle tissue. Record the magnification you used next to your sketch.

© Prentice-Hall, Inc.

OBSERVING FLATWORMS AND ROUNDWORMS *(continued)*

◆ Observations

Planarian

Magnification: _____

Tapeworm

Magnification: _____

Vinegar eel (male)

Magnification: _____

Vinegar eel (female)

Magnification: _____

Trichina worm in muscle tissue

Magnification: _____

OBSERVING FLATWORMS AND ROUNDWORMS *(continued)*

◆ Analyze and Conclude

1. Identify two ways in which flatworms and roundworms differ in body structure.

_____

_____

_____

_____

2. How are flatworms similar to roundworms in body structure?

_____

_____

_____

_____

3. How are parasitic flatworms and roundworms able to survive without structures for locomotion?

_____

_____

_____

_____

4. Compare the nervous and digestive systems of the free-living forms of flatworms and roundworms with those of parasitic forms.

_____

_____

_____

_____

_____

◆ Critical Thinking and Applications

1. Why is the structure at the anterior end of the planarian body called an eyespot instead of an eye?

_____

_____

_____

_____

© Prentice-Hall, Inc.

OBSERVING FLATWORMS AND ROUNDWORMS *(continued)*

2. List two necessities that parasitic worms get from their hosts that free-living worms have to obtain for themselves.

_____

_____

_____

_____

_____

3. Why is it rare that an individual parasite kills its host?

_____

_____

_____

_____

_____

4. You have a new job as a product inspector in a large meat-packing company. Your first assignment is to inspect pork for trichina worms. You've been warned that if humans eat undercooked or raw pork that has a large number of trichina worms in it, a serious infection can result. What should you look for?

_____

_____

_____

_____

◆ More to Explore

New Problem Do planarians prefer to live in a light environment or a dark one?

Possible Materials List materials that you will be using in this experiment.

Safety Keep planarians in pond water at all times, so they will not be harmed. Always treat animals with great care. Use both hands to carry a microscope. Hold the microscope base with one hand and the microscope arm with your other hand. Handle glass slides carefully. Wash your hands after completing the investigation.

Procedure Hypothesize whether planarians prefer to live in a light environment or a dark one. On a separate sheet of paper, write a procedure you would follow to test your hypothesis. Have the teacher approve your procedure before you carry out the investigation.

Observations Make appropriate data tables and drawings.

OBSERVING FLATWORMS AND ROUNDWORMS *(continued)*

Analyze and Conclude

1. Was your hypothesis supported by your data? Why or why not?

_____

_____

_____

_____

2. Based on your experiment, what can you infer about where planarians live
in nature?

_____

_____

_____

_____

B-2   LABORATORY INVESTIGATION

Characteristics of Sea Stars

◆ Pre-Lab Discussion

The sea star, or starfish, is a spiny-skinned sea invertebrate in the echinoderm phylum. Echinoderms are animals whose bodies are usually covered with hundreds of small spines. Brittle stars, basket stars, sand dollars, sea cucumbers, and sea urchins are also echinoderms.

Sea stars live in coastal waters and on rocky seashores. They are predators that eat oysters, clams, snails, barnacles, and worms. Sea stars usually have 5 arms branching out from a central disk. Sun stars have 7 to 14 arms, however, and some sea stars have 15 to 24 arms. If an arm breaks off, the sea star can regenerate a new one.

In this investigation, you will examine the external structures of a sea star.

1. What does *echinoderm* mean, and why is it a good name for this phylum?

_____

_____

2. What characteristics are typical of echinoderms?

_____

_____

◆ Problem

How is the anatomy of a sea star adapted to sea life?

◆ Materials *(per group)*

wet paper towels
preserved sea star
dissecting tray
2 hand lenses

◆ Safety   *Review the safety guidelines in the front of your lab book.*

To prevent skin irritation, wear aprons and goggles during this investigation.

CHARACTERISTICS OF SEA STARS (continued)

Procedure

1. Put on safety goggles and a lab apron. **CAUTION:** *The preservative used on the sea star can irritate your skin. Don't touch your eyes or mouth while working with the preserved sea star. Keep a piece of wet paper towel handy to wipe your fingers after touching the star.* Rinse the sea star thoroughly with water to remove any extra preservative. Put the sea star, top surface up, in the dissecting tray. Notice that the sea star's body has 5 arms radiating from a central disk.

2. Using a hand lens, examine the skin on the top surface. Notice the many coarse spines that cover the entire top surface. The skin is spiny and irregular because parts of the endoskeleton protrude through the skin. Around the base of the spines are jawlike structures. They capture small animals and keep the skin free of foreign objects.

3. Use a hand lens to locate a spine and the jawlike structures around it. See Figure 1. Answer Observations question 1.

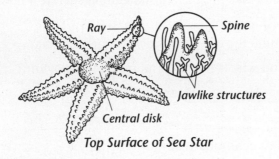

Figure 1

Ray — Spine

Jawlike structures

Central disk

Top Surface of Sea Star

4. Study the top surface of the central disk. Answer Observations question 2.

5. Locate a small red or yellow buttonlike structure on the top side of the central disk. This structure contains many tiny pores through which water enters the water vascular system. The water vascular system has water-filled canals that function primarily in movement and feeding.

6. Try to find the anus on the top surface of the central disk. The anus, which opens out from the intestine, lets solid wastes escape from the body.

7. In Observations, label the following structures on the top side of the sea star: central disk, arms, spines, and anus.

8. Turn the sea star over so that its bottom surface is visible. With the hand lens, examine the mouth, an opening in the middle of the central disk. Notice the small spines that surround the mouth. Many types of sea stars feed by pushing part of the stomach through the mouth. The stomach secretes enzymes that digest prey.

9. Find the groove that begins at the mouth and extends down the center of each arm. Find the small tube feet that line the groove. The tube feet are part of the water vascular system. A tube foot is a hollow, thin-walled cylinder with a bulb-like structure at one end and a sucker at the tip. Answer Observations question 3.

© Prentice-Hall, Inc.

B-2, Characteristics of Sea Stars

CHARACTERISTICS OF SEA STARS *(continued)*

10. In Observations, label the following structures on the bottom side of the sea star: groove, mouth, and tube feet.

11. When you have finished examining the specimen, follow the teacher's instructions for storing the sea star for further use. **CAUTION:** *Wash your hands thoroughly at the end of the lab.*

◆ Observations

Top Side of Sea Star

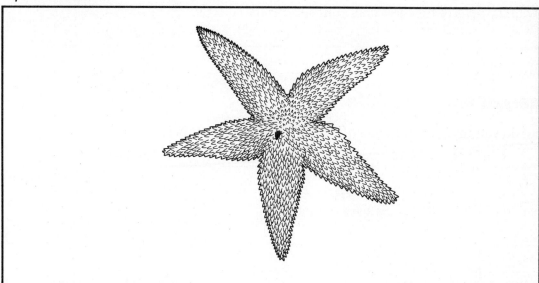

Bottom Side of Sea Star

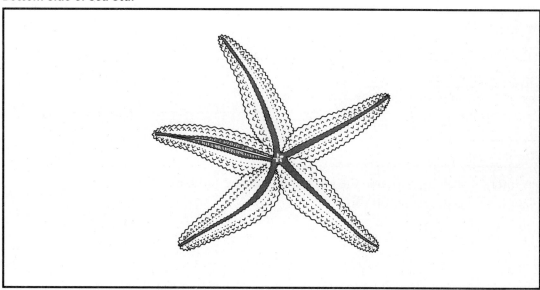

CHARACTERISTICS OF SEA STARS *(continued)*

1. Describe the appearance of a sea star's spines.

_____

_____

2. How does the number of spines in the central disk compare to the number of spines in the arm?

_____

_____

3. How many rows of tube feet does your sea star have?

_____

_____

◆ Analyze and Conclude

1. What do you think the function of a sea star's spines might be?

_____

_____

2. What kind of symmetry does a sea star have?

_____

_____

3. What do you think the tube feet might be used for?

_____

_____

4. How do you think a sea star might eat?

_____

_____

_____

_____

5. What internal structures enable the sea star to capture food and to move? Explain how the structures do this.

_____

_____

_____

_____

© Prentice-Hall, Inc.

CHARACTERISTICS OF SEA STARS *(continued)*

◆ Critical Thinking and Applications

1. Sea stars produce large numbers of eggs and sperm. Why is this production an adaptive advantage?

_____

_____

_____

_____

2. When a sea star pries open the shell of a clam or an oyster, the mollusk resists. Even if the shell opens only slightly, the sea star will get its meal. How does this happen?

_____

_____

_____

_____

_____

3. Because sea stars eat many clams and oysters, divers were hired to catch sea stars and chop them into pieces. After this, fishers found even more empty clam and oyster shells than before. Why did their plan backfire?

_____

_____

_____

_____

4. Can a sea star move equally well in any direction? Why or why not?

_____

_____

_____

_____

5. Many echinoderms, which are bottom dwellers as adults, have free-swimming larvae. What advantage do free-swimming larvae give to echinoderms?

_____

_____

_____

_____

CHARACTERISTICS OF SEA STARS *(continued)*

◆ More to Explore

New Problem Why do sand dollars, sea urchins, sea lilies, sea cucumbers, and brittle stars belong to the same phylum as sea stars?

Possible Materials List and gather the materials you will need. Decide which materials you could use from the previous lab.

Safety Wear aprons and goggles if working with specimens.

Procedure Write a hypothesis that includes those features that you think each of these organisms share. Write a procedure you would follow to test your hypothesis. Have the teacher approve your procedure before you carry out the investigation.

Observations Make drawings and record other observations on a separate sheet of paper.

Analyze and Conclude What characteristics do your observed animals share that place them in the same phylum as sea stars?

_____

_____

_____

Adaptations of Fish

◆ Pre-Lab Discussion

Fishes are vertebrate members of the phylum Chordata. The largest group of fishes has skeletons made of bones. The perch and the goldfish are bony fishes. Bony fishes exhibit many adaptations for life in water. All fishes are ectotherms. They live in water and have fins. Fins are fanlike structures used for steering, balancing, and moving. Most fishes obtain oxygen through gills and have scales. Scales are thin, hard, overlapping plates that cover the skin of fish.

In this investigation, you will observe the movement and behavior of a live goldfish. You will also identify the external parts of a perch.

1. Explain how a fish breathes.

_____

_____

2. What are the three major groups of fishes? Describe their characteristics.

_____

_____

_____

◆ Problem

How are the structures of fish adapted for life in water?

◆ Materials (per group)

large glass jar or beaker
water from an aquarium (to fill beaker)
fishnet
goldfish
paper towels
preserved perch
dissecting tray
probe
forceps
hand lens
microscope slide
medicine dropper
coverslip

© Prentice-Hall, Inc.

ADAPTATIONS OF FISH (continued)

◆ Safety 🏠 🥽 🧪 ⚒ ☠ 🔥 🐁

Review the safety guidelines in the front of your lab book.

Always treat living things with great care. Keep the goldfish in the aquarium water as much as possible. Do not use tap water directly from the tap. Tap water must be left at room temperature for at least 24 hours before placing fish in it. To prevent slips or falls, immediately wipe up any water spilled on the floor. To prevent skin irritation, wear aprons and goggles during Part B. Handle glass items carefully. Tell your teacher about any broken glass.

◆ Procedure

Part A: Observing the Behavior of a Live Fish

1. Fill a large glass or beaker three-quarters full with water from an aquarium.

2. **CAUTION:** *Keep the goldfish in the water as much as possible.* With a fishnet, carefully remove one goldfish from the aquarium. Immediately transfer the fish to the jar of water.

3. Observe the goldfish. Find the gills. Carefully watch the movements of the body, fins, and tail as the goldfish swims. Answer Observations question 1.

4. Use the labeled diagram of the perch on page 48 to find the goldfish's dorsal, caudal, pectoral, pelvic, and anal fins. Answer Observations question 2. Observe the function of each fin as the fish swims. Complete the Data Table on fins.

5. With a fishnet, carefully return the goldfish to the aquarium.

Part B: Examining the External Anatomy of a Fish

1. Put on safety goggles and a lab apron. **CAUTION:** *The preservative used on the perch can irritate your skin. Don't touch your eyes or mouth while working with the fish. Keep a piece of wet paper towel handy to wipe your fingers after touching the fish.* Rinse the perch thoroughly with water to remove any extra preservative. Dry the fish with paper towels. Position the fish in a dissecting tray with the head of the fish pointing left.

2. Observe the dorsal (back) and ventral (belly) surfaces. Answer Observations question 3.

3. Find the three regions of the fish's body: the head, the trunk, and the tail.

4. Find the nostril—one of two openings between the eye and the mouth.

5. Insert a probe into the mouth and carefully pry it open. Observe the teeth. **CAUTION:** *Do not touch the fish's teeth; they are very sharp.* Answer Observations question 4.

6. With a probe, carefully lift the protective bony cover away from the gills lying underneath. Observe the flat, scalelike bones that support the gill cover.

© Prentice-Hall, Inc.

ADAPTATIONS OF FISH *(continued)*

7. With forceps, carefully remove a single scale. Observe the scale with a hand lens. Notice the growth rings. As a fish grows, its scales grow. Each growth ring on the scale represents 1 year's growth. Answer Observations question 5. In Observations, draw a scale as seen under the hand lens. Label the growth rings on your drawing.

8. On the diagram in Observations, label the following parts of the external anatomy of a perch: head, trunk, tail, eye, nostril, mouth, upper jaw, lower jaw, gills, and scales.

9. When you have finished examining the fish, follow your teacher's instructions for storing the perch for further use. **CAUTION:** *Wash your hands thoroughly at the end of the lab.*

◆ Observations

Data Table

Fin	Function Choose from among the following: • Helps fish steer and stop • Keeps fish from rolling over • Propels fish through water • No apparent function
Anterior dorsal (on back near head)	
Posterior dorsal (on back near tail)	
Anal	
Caudal	
Pectoral	
Pelvic	

Perch Scale

© Prentice-Hall, Inc.

ADAPTATIONS OF FISH *(continued)*

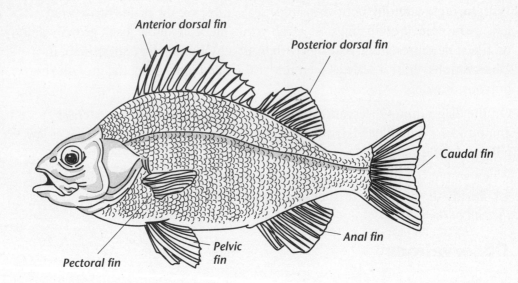

Anterior dorsal fin

Posterior dorsal fin

Caudal fin

Anal fin

Pelvic fin

Pectoral fin

3

1. Describe the motion of the fish as it swims.

_____

_____

2. How many fins does the goldfish have? Which fins occur in pairs?

_____

_____

3. Compare the color of the dorsal and ventral surfaces of the fish.

_____

_____

4. Describe the perch's teeth. Where are they in the mouth?

_____

_____

5. How old is your fish?

_____

_____

ADAPTATIONS OF FISH *(continued)*

◆ Analyze and Conclude

1. What is the shape of the fish's body? Why do you think this body shape is suited to living in water?

_____

_____

2. The fish has different colors on its back and belly. How do these different colors protect the fish from its enemies, both the birds in the sky above it and the sea organisms that live below it?

_____

_____

_____

3. How are the perch's teeth adapted to their function?

_____

_____

4. What structures on the perch make it adapted for life in water?

_____

_____

◆ Critical Thinking and Applications

1. While many invertebrates have an exoskeleton, or hard shell covering, vertebrates such as fish have an endoskeleton. How does the endoskeleton help the fish?

_____

_____

_____

2. The perch possesses a gas-filled internal structure called a swim bladder. What is the function of the swim bladder?

_____

_____

_____

_____

© Prentice-Hall, Inc.

ADAPTATIONS OF FISH *(continued)*

3. Certain species of fish that live deep in the ocean have chemicals in their skin that make them glow in the dark. How does this characteristic help these fishes survive in their environment?

_____

_____

_____

4. The perch fertilizes its eggs externally and leaves them exposed on underwater rocks. The guppy fertilizes its eggs internally and gives birth to live young. Which fish probably produces fewer eggs? Which species is likely to have a higher survival rate for its young?

_____

_____

_____

_____

_____

_____

3

◆ **More to Explore**

What does a fish skeleton look like? Obtain a fish from a grocery store. Boil the fish so that the flesh peels off easily. Or, if you prefer, cook the fish for dinner and carefully remove the meat so that the skeleton remains intact. Sketch and label the fish's skeleton.

B-4 LABORATORY INVESTIGATION

Adaptations of Birds

◆ Pre-Lab Discussion

Whether you are in an open meadow, a city park, or your own backyard, you are likely to hear the sounds of birds. There are many different bird species, and each has special adaptations to its environment. For example, birds can have different types of feathers. These feathers, which are actually modified scales, provide insulation and balance. Birds also have bills or beaks of various shapes and sizes. The shapes of bills are adaptations to the different kind of foods found in the birds' environment.

The feet of birds are also adapted to specific environments. In addition to walking and running, birds' feet are used for gripping and tearing food, climbing, and swimming. The shape and size of the feet determine how well a bird can perform these tasks within its specific environment.

In this investigation, you will examine how birds' bills and feet help them survive in their environment.

1. What are some types of food that birds eat?

_____

_____

2. In addition to eating, what are other functions of birds' bills?

_____

_____

◆ Problem

How have birds adapted to living in different environments?

◆ Materials *(per class)*

30 petri dishes
4 bags of different seeds or seedlike materials, such as
   sunflower seeds, popcorn, lima beans, or couscous
6 different hand tools
clock or watch with a second hand

◆ Safety   ✂ *Review the safety guidelines in the front of your lab book.*

Use caution in handling pointed or sharp tools. Keep seeds in containers at all times to prevent spills and accidents. Do not eat seeds. Wash hands after handling seeds.

© Prentice-Hall, Inc.

ADAPTATIONS OF BIRDS *(continued)*

◆ Procedure

Part A: Modeling Bills

1. **CAUTION:** *Handle pointed or sharp tools carefully.* There are several stations around your classroom. At each station you will find the following: a tool; four petri dishes, each filled with a different type of seed; and an empty petri dish. The tools will be used to model the effectiveness of different bill shapes in picking up seeds. Each station has a different tool-bill. Visit each station briefly and examine the different tool-bills and seeds.

2. Predict which tool-bill will work best to pick up each type of seed. Give a reason for your prediction.

   Seed 1 _____

   Seed 2 _____

   Seed 3 _____

   Seed 4 _____

   Predict which tool-bill will be the worst at picking up each type of seed. Give a reason for your prediction.

   Seed 1 _____

   Seed 2 _____

   Seed 3 _____

   Seed 4 _____

3. Go to one station and practice using the tool-bill to pick up the different seeds. Pick up one seed at a time. Each petri dish contains only one type of seed. Be sure not to mix the seeds in the petri dishes. Use either one or both hands to hold the tool-bill. Everyone in the group should practice using the tool-bill.

4. While a classmate times you, use the tool-bill to pick up as many seeds from the Seed 1 dish as you can within 30 seconds. Pick up only one seed at a time and place it into the empty petri dish. Count how many seeds you pick up within 30 seconds and record this number in Data Table 1 on the next page. When your time is up, return the seeds to the Seed 1 dish. Everyone in the group should take a turn at picking up as many seeds as possible from the Seed 1 dish.

5. Repeat Step 4 for the other three types of seeds at the station. Calculate the average number of seeds picked up by your group within 30 seconds for each type of seed. Record the averages in your data table.

6. Repeat steps 3–5 at each station. Record your data in Date Table 1.

© Prentice-Hall, Inc.

ADAPTATIONS OF BIRDS *(continued)*

◆ Observations

Part A

Data Table 1: Number of Seeds Picked up in 30 Seconds

Station Number _____   Tool _____

Student Name	Seed 1	Seed 2	Seed 3	Seed 4
1.				
2.				
3.				
4.				
Average Number of Seeds				

Station Number _____   Tool _____

Student Name	Seed 1	Seed 2	Seed 3	Seed 4
1.				
2.				
3.				
4.				
Average Number of Seeds				

Station Number _____   Tool _____

Student Name	Seed 1	Seed 2	Seed 3	Seed 4
1.				
2.				
3.				
4.				
Average Number of Seeds				

© Prentice-Hall, Inc.

ADAPTATIONS OF BIRDS *(continued)*

Station Number _____   Tool _____

Student Name	Seed 1	Seed 2	Seed 3	Seed 4
1.				
2.				
3.				
4.				
Average Number of Seeds				

Station Number _____   Tool _____

Student Name	Seed 1	Seed 2	Seed 3	Seed 4
1.				
2.				
3.				
4.				
Average Number of Seeds				

Station Number _____   Tool _____

Student Name	Seed 1	Seed 2	Seed 3	Seed 4
1.				
2.				
3.				
4.				
Average Number of Seeds				

ADAPTATIONS OF BIRDS (continued)

1. List the tool-bills in order of effectiveness at picking up each type of seed.
Begin with the most effective tool and end with the least effective.

Seed 1 _____

Seed 2 _____

Seed 3 _____

Seed 4 _____

2. Were some tool-bills more effective at picking up a certain type of seed than other
tool-bills? Name the tool-bills and which seeds they picked up more effectively.

_____

_____

_____

3. Were some tool-bills effective at picking up a variety of seeds? If so, name them.

_____

_____

Part B: Examining Bird Beaks and Feet

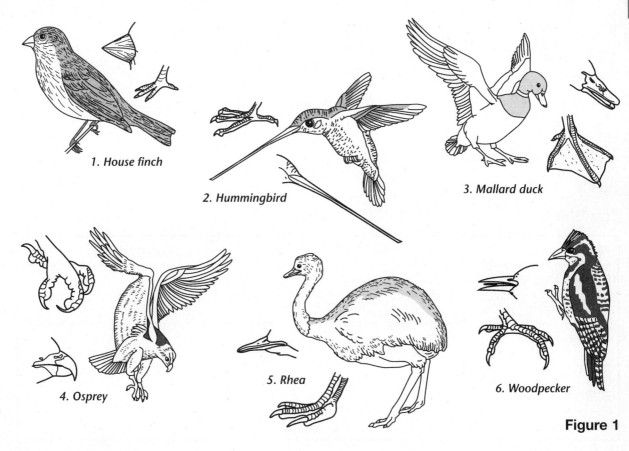

1. House finch

2. Hummingbird

3. Mallard duck

4. Osprey

5. Rhea

6. Woodpecker

Figure 1

© Prentice-Hall, Inc.

ADAPTATIONS OF BIRDS *(continued)*

◆ Procedure

Part B: Examining Bird Beaks and Feet

1. Examine and compare the shape and size of each bird's bill in Figure 1. Use the following list to infer the likely structure and function of the bill for each bird. Record this information in Data Table 2.

   - *Straight and pointed:* used as a chisel to drill trees
   - *Flat and broad:* used to strain algae and small organisms from water
   - *Massive and hooked:* used to tear flesh
   - *Short and stout:* multipurpose; used to eat insects, seeds, and small crustaceans
   - *Long, fine, pipelike tube:* used to obtain nectar from flowers

2. Examine and compare the feet of the birds in Figure 1. Use the following list to determine the number and position (front or back of the foot) of the toes and to infer the function of the feet for each bird. Record this information in Data Table 3 on the following page.

   - *Climbing foot:* four toes; two toes in front and two toes in back for support when climbing upward to prevent falling backward
   - *Grasping foot:* four toes; two in front and two in back; large, sharp curved claws
   - *Perching foot:* four toes; three front toes and one back toe that can hold onto a perch tightly
   - *Running foot:* two to three toes rather than four
   - *Swimming foot:* four toes; three in front and one in back; webbed feet that act as paddles

◆ Observations

Part B

Data Table 2

Bird	Structure of Bill	Function of Bill
1. House finch		
2. Hummingbird		
3. Mallard duck		
4. Osprey		
5. Rhea		
6. Woodpecker		

ADAPTATIONS OF BIRDS *(continued)*

Data Table 3

Bird	Number of Toes	Toe Positions	Function
1. House finch			
2. Hummingbird			
3. Mallard duck			
4. Osprey			
5. Rhea			
6. Woodpecker			

◆ Analyze and Conclude

1. How do your results for the tool-bills compare with your predictions? Give possible reasons for differences.

_____

_____

2. Based on the information you have gathered, describe what a bill that can effectively pick up and crack small seeds might look like.

_____

_____

3. If a bird has grasping feet and a large hooked bill, what might the bird eat? Explain your answer.

_____

_____

◆ Critical Thinking and Applications

1. Why would a woodpecker probably be unsuccessful at depending on small mammals for food?

_____

_____

2. What advantage might a bird that is able to eat a variety of seeds have over a bird that can eat only one type of seed?

_____

_____

© Prentice-Hall, Inc.

ADAPTATIONS OF BIRDS *(continued)*

3. A bird has been sighted in a mountainous area, where it lives at high altitudes and low temperatures. There are few, if any, trees and food sources are limited. Only sagebrush and some grass grow up through the mostly snow-covered land. Most likely, the bird would spend a lot of time on the ground, as does the ptarmigan, with three toes in front and a large toe in back for balance. What might a bird in this environment eat? What might its beak and feet look like? Explain your answer.

_____

_____

_____

_____

◆ More to Explore

Using the information below and the previous activity, draw the beaks and feet of the following birds in the spaces provided. If you like, use your imagination to draw the whole bird as well. To the left of each illustration, explain your drawing.

4

Bird A lives in a South American tropical forest and eats nuts, seeds, and fruit. This bird makes nests in holes in trees and has been seen gathering on a cliff of salty clay to lick minerals.

Bird B is a songbird that sits in the trees of India and Malaysia. This bird eats flower nectar as well as insects. Sometimes it hovers before tube-shaped flowers and reaches into them with its long tongue. But when it feeds from large blooms, it pierces the petals to reach the nectar at the base.

© Prentice-Hall, Inc.

B-5   LABORATORY INVESTIGATION

Family Life of Bettas

◆ Pre-Lab Discussion

Betta fish, also known as Siamese fighting fish, live in fresh water and originally came from Southeast Asia. These beautiful aquarium fish are usually red, blue, or turquoise. The males' colors become brighter when the fish are courting or get excited. Bettas do not get all their oxygen from water; they rise to the surface from time to time for air. They can live in containers without special pumps or filters.

In this investigation, you will select a male and a female betta fish, set them up in a container, and observe them to see if they will produce a batch of eggs that will hatch into tiny fish, called fry. During your investigation, remember that fish, like all other living organisms, must be handled with care. The containers that you will be using must be filled with tap water that has been sitting for at least 24 hours. The water should be changed once a week. Floating aquatic plants must be present when both male and female bettas are in the same container. The fish prefer low light, and the water should be kept between 21°C and 29°C (70°F and 84°F). Betta fish should be fed a pinch of food twice a day. Male bettas are extremely territorial and MUST be kept out of sight of one another.

1. What type of behavior is courtship—instinctive or learned? Explain your answer.

_____

_____

2. Betta males are very aggressive toward one another. What is aggressive behavior?

_____

_____

◆ Problem

What behaviors enable betta fish to reproduce?

FAMILY LIFE OF BETTAS *(continued)*

◆ **Possible Materials** *(per group)*

colored pencils
2 clean 2-liter soda bottles filled
    with aged water
1-gallon or larger container filled
    with aged water
aquarium gravel
floating clump of aquatic plants
betta food
male and female betta fish
hand lens

◆ **Safety**   *Review the safety guidelines in the front of your lab book.*

Wash your hands after handling the fish.

◆ **Procedure**

1. Read the entire lab before continuing your investigation.

2. Brainstorm with other students on how to use the materials to set up a container for your fish to live in. Have the teacher approve your plans before you set up these containers with your fish.

3. Place your male and female bettas in separate containers for one or two days. Sketch the fish in Observations and record their behaviors in the Data Table. Observations may include periods of inactivity, gill movements, how the fish swims, and which fins it uses in different maneuvers. Note differences in the sexes, gill movements, and fin and tail formation.

4. After one or two days, introduce both fish into a larger breeding container. Observe your fish for 10 minutes every day, for up to two weeks. Watch for the events listed below. You may not see every event take place. Compare your observations with those of your classmates. Record all of the fish's behaviors each day and answer the questions in Observations.
   - initial reaction of the male and female bettas after being introduced into the same container
   - initial courtship behaviors
   - male building nest (between 24 hours and 5 days after introduction to female)
   - female approaching male and laying eggs
   - care of eggs
   - hatching of eggs into fry (Eggs hatch within 24 to 28 hours of being laid.) Use a hand lens to check the eggs in the water. Fry are very small and may be difficult to see without magnification.
   - care of fry by adults

© Prentice-Hall, Inc.

FAMILY LIFE OF BETTAS *(continued)*

5. When your observations are complete, plan with the teacher how to continue to care for the fish.

◆ Observations

Sketch of Male and Female Fish

Male betta	*Female betta*

1. After placing the male and female fish into the same container, what happens to the bodies of the male and female fish when they first notice each other?

_____

_____

2. What types of courtship behaviors do the fish show?

_____

_____

_____

3. While the male betta is building the nest, how do the behaviors of the two fish change?

_____

_____

_____

_____

_____

4. What behavior occurs before the eggs are laid and while the eggs are being laid?

_____

_____

_____

_____

_____

FAMILY LIFE OF BETTAS *(continued)*

5. How do the adult bettas take care of the nest, eggs, and fry?

_____

_____

_____

_____

Data Table

Day	Behavior Observations	
	Male	**Female**
1–2; fish in separate containers		
3; fish are put into one container		

5

FAMILY LIFE OF BETTAS *(continued)*

◆ Analyze and Conclude

1. Did your bettas successfully reproduce? If not, suggest some possible reasons the pair did not breed.

_____

_____

_____

2. Why are the courtship behaviors of the male and female bettas important?

_____

_____

_____

◆ Critical Thinking and Applications

1. Why are the floating plants important to the female betta?

_____

_____

_____

2. What methods could be used to prevent the male from hurting the female?

_____

_____

_____

_____

3. Based on this investigation, what other questions might you like to investigate?

_____

_____

_____

_____

5

FAMILY LIFE OF BETTAS *(continued)*

◆ More to Explore

New Problem Choose the response that interests you most from question 3 of Critical Thinking an Applications. Plan to investigate this problem.

Possible Materials Consider which materials you can use from this lab. What other materials might you need?

Safety Wash your hands after handling fish.

Procedure Make a hypothesis based on the question you want to investigate. Upon what do you base your hypothesis? Write your procedure on a separate sheet of paper. Include a control with which to compare results. Have the teacher approve your procedure before carrying out the investigation.

Observations Make a data table similar to the one for this lab.

Analyze and Conclude

1. Did your results support your hypothesis? Explain your answer.

_____

_____

_____

2. Evaluate your procedure. What worked well? If you were to repeat this experiment, what parts of the procedure would you change?

_____

_____

_____

_____

_____

C-1

Cell Membranes and Permeability

◆ Pre-Lab Discussion

Can all substances move in both directions through a cell membrane? Why do some substances enter the cell through the cell membrane, while others do not? Sometimes you can use a model to answer questions like these. Part of this investigation models a living cell, so that you can observe changes that the cell membrane controls.

The cell membrane determines what diffuses into a cell. This characteristic of a cell membrane is called permeability. Many cells are semipermeable, which means that not all substances can pass through the cell membrane. Also, the amount of a substance that diffuses through a membrane is influenced by concentration and time.

In this investigation, you will model a cell membrane, determine if the membrane is permeable to certain substances, and find out if the concentration of a substance affects its diffusion.

1. Where is the cell membrane of a cell?

_____

_____

2. What types of materials pass through the cell membrane?

_____

_____

◆ Problem

How does a cell membrane work?

CELL MEMBRANES AND PERMEABILITY (continued)

1

◆ Materials (per group)

plastic lunch bag
twist tie
100-mL graduated cylinder
starch solution
one 200-mL beaker
glass-marking pencil
water
iodine solution, three strengths
3 test tubes
test-tube rack
3 plastic cups
potato cubes
clock or watch with second hand
forceps
metric ruler

◆ Safety   *Review the safety guidelines in the front of your lab book.*

Iodine is poisonous. Keep it away from your face, and wash your hands thoroughly after using it. Iodine will stain your hands and clothing, so be careful not to spill it. Handle glass objects carefully. If they break, tell the teacher. Do not pick up broken glass.

◆ Procedure

Part A: Model of a Cell Membrane

1. Write your name on a beaker with a glass-marking pencil. Then label three test tubes as follows: (1) "Iodine BEFORE," (2) "Iodine AFTER," and (3) "Starch."

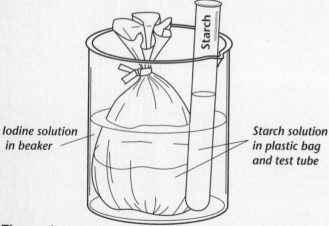

Iodine solution in beaker

Starch solution in plastic bag and test tube

Figure 1

CELL MEMBRANES AND PERMEABILITY (continued)

2. Fill the beaker with 40 mL of iodine solution. **CAUTION:** *Be careful with the iodine solution. If you spill any on yourself, immediately rinse the area with water and tell your teacher.* The iodine solution represents the environment outside the model cell.

3. Fill the test tube labeled "Iodine BEFORE" one-fourth full with iodine solution, and then set it aside in a test tube rack.

4. Fill a plastic lunch bag with 40 mL of starch solution, and seal the bag with a twist tie. Be careful not to spill starch onto the outside of the bag. Record the color of the solution in Data Table 1, and then place the bag into the solution in the beaker. The bag represents a cell.

5. Fill the "Starch" test tube about one-half full with starch solution, record the color of the solution, and then place the test tube in the beaker as shown in Figure 1. Let the beaker and its contents stand overnight.

6. The next day, remove the plastic bag and the test tube from the beaker. Record the colors of the solutions in the plastic bag and the test tube the "Color AFTER" column in Data Table 1.

7. Pour iodine solution from the beaker into the test tube labeled "Iodine AFTER" until the test tube has the same amount of solution as the test tube labeled "Iodine BEFORE."

8. Hold the two test tubes side by side, and look down through their openings. Record the colors of the solutions in the last line of Data Table 1.

Part B: Effect of Concentration on Diffusion

1. Label three plastic cups *100%*, *50%*, and *10%*.

2. Obtain about 30 mL of iodine solution at each strength, and pour that amount into the appropriate cup. Record these concentrations in Data Table 2.

3. Put a potato cube in each beaker. If necessary, add additional solution to cover the cube completely. Record the exact time the cubes were added to the solutions in Data Table 2.

4. After 30 minutes, use forceps to remove each potato cube from its solution. Keep track of which sample was in which beaker. The teacher will cut your potato cubes in half.

5. Use a metric ruler to determine the distance that the solution has diffused into each potato cube. See Figure 2. Read each distance to the closest 0.5 mm. In Data Table 2, record the distance that the solution diffused into each cube.

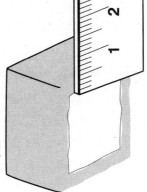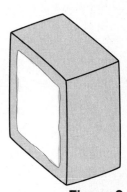

Figure 2

CELL MEMBRANES AND PERMEABILITY *(continued)*

◆ Observations

Data Table 1

Solution	Color Before	Color After
Starch in model cell		
Starch in test tube		
Iodine in test tubes		

Data Table 2

Potato Cube	Concentration of Substance	Time Cube Added to Solution	Distance of Diffusion (mm)
1			
2			
3			

◆ Analyze and Conclude

1. What part of the cell does the plastic bag represent?

_____

_____

2. What was the purpose of placing a test tube containing starch solution in the beaker of iodine?

_____

_____

_____

3. When starch mixes with iodine, the mixture turns blue. What can you infer about the contents of the plastic bag?

_____

_____

CELL MEMBRANES AND PERMEABILITY *(continued)*

4. a. Did starch move out of the bag? Give a reason for your answer.

_____

_____

b. Did iodine move into the bag? Give a reason for your answer.

_____

_____

_____

5. Based on your results, was the model cell membrane permeable or imperme-
able to iodine? To starch?

_____

_____

6. In Part B, how did the concentration of iodine influence the amount of diffusion that took place?

_____

_____

_____

◆ Critical Thinking and Applications

1. Cell membranes contain small holes, or pores. Pore size may determine why some
chemicals can or cannot pass through a cell membrane. In your model, how might the
size of the membrane pores compare to the size of the iodine molecules? Explain.

_____

_____

_____

2. In your model, how might the size of the membrane pores compare to the size
of the starch molecules? Explain.

_____

_____

_____

3. Based on what you learned from studying the diffusion of different concentrations, what might be one reason that sick or injured people wear oxygen
masks? Explain.

_____

_____

_____

© Prentice-Hall, Inc.

CELL MEMBRANES AND PERMEABILITY *(continued)*

◆ More to Explore

New Problem How does time affect the diffusion of substances across a cell membrane?

Possible Materials Consider which materials you can use from the previous part of the lab.

Safety Handle glass objects carefully. Ask your teacher to cut the potato cubes.

Procedure Develop a procedure to solve the problem. Predict what the results will show. Write your procedure on a separate sheet of paper. Have the teacher approve your procedure before you carry out the investigation.

Observations On a separate sheet of paper, make a data table like Data Table 2 in which to record your data and observations.

Analyze and Conclude Did your results support your prediction? Explain your reasoning.

_____

_____

© Prentice-Hall, Inc.

C-2   **LABORATORY INVESTIGATION**

Stomata Functions

◆ Pre-Lab Discussion

During photosynthesis, plants capture light energy and convert it into chemical energy that is stored in sugar molecules. The two raw materials needed for this process are water and carbon dioxide. Plants obtain water through their roots. They obtain carbon dioxide, a gas, through tiny openings, or pores, called stomata (singular *stoma*). Most of the stomata are located in the plant's leaves. The stomata must be open to allow carbon dioxide to pass into the leaf. The open stomata also allow water and oxygen to pass out of the leaf.

The opening and closing of the stomata is carried out by guard cells. When guard cells absorb water, they swell, and the stomata open, as shown in Figure 1. When guard cells lose water, the swelling is reduced, and the stomata close, as shown in Figure 2. Stomata are adaptations that help plants survive. When they are open, they allow carbon dioxide to enter. When they are closed, they help prevent the loss of water from the plant.

In this investigation, you will determine the number of stomata on different types of leaves.

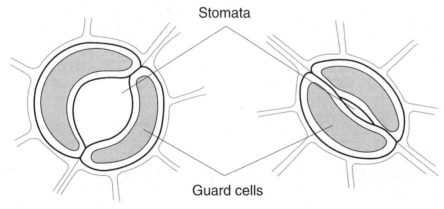

Stomata

Guard cells

Figure 1 *Stoma open*   **Figure 2** *Stoma closed*

1. Are the stomata usually open or closed during photosynthesis? Explain.

_____

_____

2. Are stomata usually open or closed during dry periods? Explain.

_____

_____

STOMATA FUNCTIONS *(continued)*

◆ Problem

Approximately how many
stomata are present on a typical leaf?

◆ Materials *(per group)*

microscope slide
coverslip
water
plastic dropper
lettuce leaf, fresh
forceps
iodine solution
compound microscope
paper towel
leaves from two different plants
metric ruler

◆ Safety   *Review the safety guidelines in the front of your lab book.*

Wipe up spills immediately. Coverslips and slides break easily, so handle them carefully. Tell the teacher if a slide breaks. If your microscope has a mirror, do not use it to reflect direct sunlight. Eye damage can occur if direct sunlight is used as a light source. Iodine solution can stain skin and clothing. If you spill any solution on your skin, rinse it off immediately with cold running water, and tell the teacher.

◆ Procedure

Part A: Identifying Guard Cells

1. Prepare to make a wet mount by placing a drop of water in the center of a microscope slide.

2. Obtain a fresh lettuce leaf, and turn it over so that it curves downward. You are now looking at the lower epidermis, or bottom, of the lettuce leaf. Locate the large central rib in the leaf.

3. Bend the leaf backward against the curve until it breaks, as shown in Figure 3. Use forceps to carefully remove a small piece of the thin epidermal layer.

4. Spread out the epidermis specimen in the water drop on the slide. Be sure that no part of the epidermis is folded over.

© Prentice-Hall, Inc.

STOMATA FUNCTIONS (continued)

Bottom side of
fresh lettuce leaf

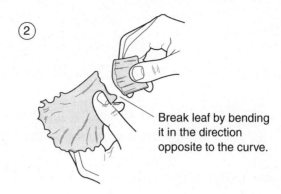

Break leaf by bending
it in the direction
opposite to the curve.

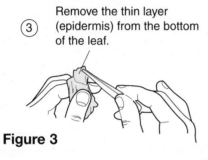

Remove the thin layer
(epidermis) from the bottom
of the leaf.

Figure 3

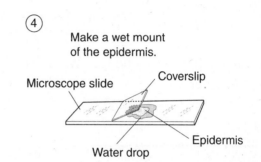

Make a wet mount
of the epidermis.

Microscope slide
Coverslip
Epidermis
Water drop

5. Add a drop of iodine to the water. **CAUTION:** *Iodine is poisonous, and it can cause stains. Handle it carefully.* Then hold a coverslip at the angle shown in Figure 3, and gently lower it over the specimen. Touch the edge of a paper towel to one side of the coverslip to remove excess water.

6. Observe the slide with a microscope under low power. **CAUTION:** *When using the microscope, follow safe procedures described on pages 1–5.* Look for different types of cells. Most of the cells you see will have an irregular shape. The rest of the cells, which are shaped like sausages, appear in pairs. The paired cells are the guard cells. Notice whether they are open or closed.

7. On the next page, make a labeled drawing of the epidermis under low power.

8. Examine a pair of guard cells under high power, and make a labeled drawing beside the one you drew in Step 7.

Part B: Comparing the Number of Stomata in Different Leaves

1. Obtain freshly cut leaves from two different kinds of plants. Record the types of plants you are using in the Data Table.

2. Use a metric ruler to determine the approximate length and width of the first leaf in millimeters. If the leaf has an irregular shape, estimate the length and width as closely as you can. Multiply the length times the width to find the area in square millimeters (mm^2). Record the area in the Data Table.

STOMATA FUNCTIONS *(continued)*

2

3. Use the procedures from Part A to examine a section of the lower epidermis of the leaf.

4. Observe the slide under low power. Count the number of stomata in your field of view. Record this number in the appropriate column in the Data Table.

5. The field of view under low power is usually about 1.33 mm^2. To determine the total number of stomata in the leaf, use the equation below. Record the results in the Data Table.

$$\frac{\text{total area of the leaf in mm}^2}{1.33 \text{ mm}^2 \text{ in field of view}} \times \text{ number of stomata in field of view} = \underline{\quad} \text{ stomata}$$

6. Repeat Steps 2 through 5 for the second leaf. Wash your hands thoroughly when you are finished handling the materials.

◆ Observations

Epidermis	Guard Cells

STOMATA FUNCTIONS *(continued)*

Data Table

Type of Leaf	Area of Leaf (mm²)	Stomata in Lower Epidermis	
		In Field of View	In Total Leaf

◆ Analyze and Conclude

1. How do the number and shape of the guard cells compare with the number and shape of the cells around them?

_____

_____

2. How do guard cells control the stomata?

_____

_____

_____

3. How do the number of stomata compare for the two leaves you examined at low power?

_____

_____

_____

4. How did the number of stomata per leaf compare?

_____

◆ Critical Thinking and Applications

1. Can photosynthesis occur if the stomata are closed? Explain.

_____

_____

_____

2. The stomata tend to be closed during dry periods. How does that pattern aid the survival of the plant?

_____

_____

STOMATA FUNCTIONS (*continued*)

◆ More to Explore

Find a way to estimate the number of stomata on a specific plant. You could start with the number of stomata on a single leaf. You may be able to count or estimate the number of leaves on a plant directly.

However, if the plant is large and has a huge number of leaves, develop a method for estimating the number of leaves. For example, estimate the number of main branches of a tree; then estimate the number of smaller branches on the main branch; then estimate the number of leaves on a smaller branch; then multiply to find the total. (*Hint:* Use round numbers and any other math strategies you know to simplify your work.)

© Prentice-Hall, Inc.

C-3   **LABORATORY INVESTIGATION**

Chromosomes and Inheritance

◆ Pre-Lab Discussion

How are traits inherited? You can investigate this question by considering an imaginary animal called the unimonster. Suppose this animal has only one pair of chromosomes. Chromosomes carry genes, which control different genetic traits, such as hair color, height, and other physical characteristics. Different forms of a gene are called alleles. The presence of different alleles on the chromosomes of unimonsters determines whether they have one horn or two horns. During reproduction, parent unimonsters pass on alleles to their offspring.

In this investigation, you will determine the different allele combinations for the offspring of two unimonsters and figure out the number of horns the young unimonsters will have.

1. What are dominant and recessive alleles?

_____

_____

2. Define *genotype* and *phenotype*.

_____

_____

3. What does it mean to say that an organism is homozygous for a trait? Heterozygous for a trait?

_____

_____

4. How do the numbers of chromosomes in cells compare with the number of chromosomes in sex cells? During reproduction, what fraction of chromosomes does each parent contribute to its offspring?

_____

_____

◆ Problem

How can you determine the traits of a unimonster's offspring?

© Prentice-Hall, Inc.

CHROMOSOMES AND INHERITANCE *(continued)*

◆ Materials *(per group)*

marker
craft sticks

◆ Procedure

Figure 1

Mother Unimonster   *Father Unimonster*

1. Figure 1 shows a mother and a father unimonster, each with different genetic traits. The allele for two horns is dominant over the allele for one horn. Look at the drawing and answer question 1 in Observations.

2. The mother unimonster is heterozygous. This means that she has one allele for two horns and one allele for one horn. Each of her sex cells will have either a chromosome with the two-horn allele or a chromosome with the one-horn allele. Follow Figure 2 and steps 3 and 4 to make a model of the mother unimonster's sex chromosomes.

Figure 2

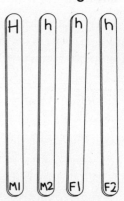

3. One of the mother unimonster's chromosomes will carry the two-horn allele. Write "M1" (for mother) at one end of a craft stick. At the other end of the stick, write *H* for the dominant two-horn allele.

4. The mother unimonster's other chromosome will carry the one-horn allele. Write "M2" at the end of a second stick. At the other end, write *h* for the recessive one-horn allele.

5. The father unimonster is homozygous (*hh*). Follow Figure 2 to make models of the father's chromosomes: F1 and F2.

6. During reproduction, the sex cells produced by the mother and father unimonsters combine to form a fertilized egg. The fertilized egg will grow into a young unimonster. Whether the young unimonster has one or two horns depends on the alleles on the chromosome contributed by each parent during reproduction. In Observations, use your chromosome models to answer questions 2–5. Remember that the allele for two horns is dominant. Anytime the dominant allele (*H*) is present, the unimonster will have two horns.

◆ Observations

1. Which unimonster parent has the dominant allele for number of horns? How do you know?

_____

_____

© Prentice-Hall, Inc.

CHROMOSOMES AND INHERITANCE *(continued)*

2. During reproduction, the sex cells containing the chromosomes M1 and F1 combine to form a fertilized egg.

   a. Which alleles are on each of the chromosomes?

   _____

   b. Will the young unimonster have one horn or two horns? Draw the appropriate number of horns on young unimonster 1 in Figure 3.

3. During reproduction, the sex cells containing the chromosomes M1 and F2 combine to form a fertilized egg.

   a. Which alleles are on each of the chromosomes?

   _____

   b. Will the young unimonster have one horn or two horns? Draw the appropriate number of horns on young unimonster 2 in Figure 3.

4. During reproduction, the sex cells containing the chromosomes M2 and F1 combine to form a fertilized egg.

   a. Which alleles are on each of the chromosomes?

   _____

   b. Will the young unimonster have one horn or two horns? Draw the appropriate number of horns on young unimonster 3 in Figure 3.

5. During reproduction, the sex cells containing the chromosomes M2 and F2 combine to form a fertilized egg.

   a. Which alleles are on each of the chromosomes?

   _____

   b. Will the young unimonster have one horn or two horns? Draw the appropriate number of horns on young unimonster 4 in Figure 3.

Young Unimonster 1	Young Unimonster 2	Young Unimonster 3	Young Unimonster 4

Figure 3

◆ Analyze and Conclude

1. Which young unimonster(s) are homozygous and have one horn?

_____

CHROMOSOMES AND INHERITANCE (continued)

2. Which young unimonster(s) are heterozygous?

_____

3. Are any young unimonster(s) homozygous with two horns? Explain.

_____

_____

◆ Critical Thinking and Applications

1. If a mother unimonster is homozygous and has two horns, and a father unimonster is homozygous and has one horn, what are the phenotypes and genotypes of the possible offspring? Remember that the two-horn allele is dominant.

_____

_____

2. Predict the phenotypes and genotypes of the offspring of a mother unimonster and a father unimonster that are both heterozygous.

_____

_____

_____

◆ More to Explore

Repeat the lab for the traits of curly hair versus straight hair. Assume that the curly-hair allele is dominant and the straight-hair allele is recessive. The mother is homozygous and has straight hair, while the father is heterozygous. Get four more craft sticks. Make all the combinations of different alleles. Determine all of the possible genotypes and the resulting phenotypes of the offspring. You may wish to use the Punnett square below to record the genotypes.

Father's Alleles for Curly Hair

	C	c
c		
c		

Mother's Alleles for Curly Hair

How Are Genes on Sex Chromosomes Inherited?

◆ Pre-Lab Discussion

Sex-linked genes are genes on the X and Y chromosomes. Traits controlled by these genes are called sex-linked traits. Two sex-linked traits include hemophilia and colorblindness. Hemophilia is a genetic disorder in which a person's blood clots slowly or not at all. If a person has the dominant allele X^H, he or she will have normal blood. If a person has only the recessive allele X^h, he or she will have hemophilia.

Red-green colorblindness is also a genetic disorder. In this disorder, the person does not see red and green properly. This person will see green as gray and red as yellow. If a person has at least one dominant allele X^C, he or she will not have colorblindness. If a person has only the recessive allele X^c, he or she will have colorblindness.

In this investigation, you will see how hemophilia and colorblindness are inherited.

1. How are the alleles for sex-linked genes passed from parent to child?

_____

_____

2. How many X and Y chromosomes do males have? How many of each do females have?

_____

_____

3. Define the carrier of a trait in terms of alleles.

_____

_____

◆ Problem

How are hemophilia and red-green colorblindness inherited?

◆ Materials (per group)

8 pennies
tape
pen
cloth to cover desktop

© Prentice-Hall, Inc.

HOW ARE GENES ON SEX CHROMOSOMES INHERITED? *(continued)*

◆ Procedure

Part A: Hemophilia

Use the following information and procedures for families 1 and 2 to model the inheritance of hemophilia. Keep in mind that only the X chromosome can carry the allele for hemophilia. A female can be $X^H X^H$, $X^H X^h$, or $X^h X^h$. A male can be $X^H Y$ or $X^h Y$.

Family 1. Parents do not have hemophilia; mother is a carrier of hemophilia ($X^H X^h$).

1. Place tape on two coins and mark them as shown in Figure 1. These coins represent the alleles of the parents. The coin with the Y chromosome on the back is the father. The coin with an X on each side is the mother.

2. Spread out a piece of cloth on your desk or tabletop. Shake the coins in your hands and drop them onto the cloth.

3. Read the combination of letters that appears. This combination represents the result that might appear in a child of these parents.

4. Use a tally mark in the correct row to record this combination of alleles in Data Table 1 in the column marked "Children Observed."

5. Repeat shaking, dropping, reading, and tallying the coins a total of 40 times. Record the totals of tally marks for each combination in Data Table 1.

Family 2. Father has hemophilia; mother is a carrier of hemophilia.

6. Place tape on two coins and mark them as shown in Figure 2.

7. Repeat steps 2–5 and tally the combinations in Data Table 2.

Part B: Colorblindness

The allele for red-green colorblindness is also located on the X chromosome. A female can be $X^C X^C$, $X^C X^c$, or $X^c X^c$. A male can be either $X^C Y$ or $X^c Y$.

Family 3. Father is colorblind; mother has two dominant alleles ($X^C X^C$).

1. Place tape on two coins and mark them as shown in Figure 3.

2. Repeat steps 2–5 of Part A and tally the combinations in Data Table 3.

Family 4. Parents are not colorblind; mother is heterozygous.

3. Place tape on two coins and mark them as shown in Figure 4.

4. Repeat steps 2–5 of Part A and tally the combinations in Data Table 4.

Figure 1

Coin 1 Male   Front   Back

Coin 2 Female   Front   Back

Figure 2

Coin 3 Male   Front   Back

Coin 4 Female   Front   Back

Figure 3

Coin 5 Male   Front   Back

Coin 6 Female   Front   Back

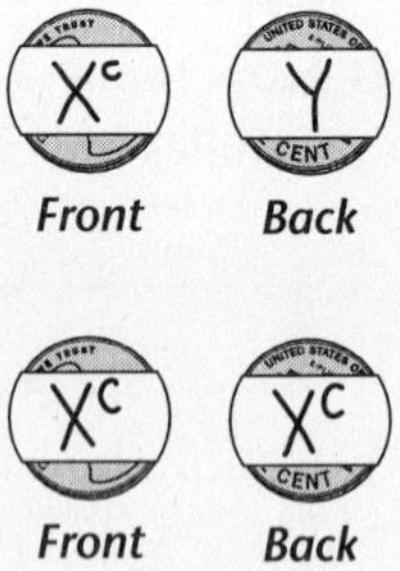

Figure 4

Coin 7 Male   Front   Back

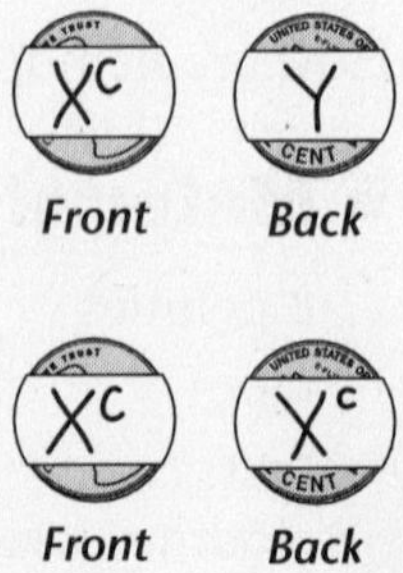

Coin 8 Female   Front   Back

HOW ARE GENES ON SEX CHROMOSOMES INHERITED? *(continued)*

◆ Observations

Data Table 1

Children of X^HY Father and X^HX^h Mother		
Allele Combination	**Children Observed**	**Total**
X^HX^H		
X^HX^h		
X^hX^h		
X^HY		
X^hY		

Data Table 2

Children of X^hY Father and X^HX^h Mother		
Allele Combination	**Children Observed**	**Total**
X^HX^H		
X^HX^h		
X^hX^h		
X^HY		
X^hY		

Data Table 3

Children of X^cY Father and X^cX^c Mother		
Allele Combination	**Children Observed**	**Total**
X^cX^c		
X^cX^c		
X^cX^c		
X^cY		
X^cY		

HOW ARE GENES ON SEX CHROMOSOMES INHERITED? *(continued)*

Data Table 4

Children of $X^c Y$ Father and $X^c X^c$ Mother		
Allele Combination	**Children Observed**	**Total**
$X^c X^c$		
$X^c X^c$		
$X^c X^c$		
$X^c Y$		
$X^c Y$		

◆ Analyze and Conclude

1. a. How many alleles for hemophilia do females have?

_____

b. How many alleles for red-green colorblindness do females have?

_____

c. How many alleles for hemophilia do males have?

_____

d. How many alleles for red-green colorblindness do males have?

_____

2. Why is there a difference in the number of alleles for hemophilia and red-green colorblindness between males and females?

_____

_____

3. Why are only females carriers for hemophilia? For red-green colorblindness?

_____

_____

_____

4. Which of the parents can pass the allele for hemophilia to a son? Explain.

_____

_____

_____

HOW ARE GENES ON SEX CHROMOSOMES INHERITED? *(continued)*

5. Which of the parents can pass the allele for hemophilia to a daughter? Explain.

_____

_____

_____

_____

6. In Family 3, why are there no colorblind children even though one of the parents is colorblind?

_____

_____

_____

_____

◆ Critical Thinking and Applications

1. The brother of a woman's father has hemophilia. Her father does not have hemophilia, but she is concerned that her son might. Could she have passed the allele for hemophilia to her son? Explain.

_____

_____

_____

_____

2. A woman's father is colorblind. She marries a colorblind man. Might their son be colorblind? Might their daughter be colorblind? Explain.

_____

_____

_____

3. What is the probability that a carrier and a person who has a sex-linked genetic disorder will have a son with the disorder? A daughter? Use your data and a Punnett square to answer these questions.

_____

4. What is the probability that a carrier and a person who does not have a sex-linked genetic disorder will have a son with the disorder? A daughter?

_____

_____

© Prentice-Hall, Inc.

HOW ARE GENES ON SEX CHROMOSOMES INHERITED? *(continued)*

◆ More to Explore

Use the Punnett squares to solve the following problems.

1. Two parents have the following alleles for hemophilia: $X^H X^h$ and $X^H Y$. What is the probability that a son will have hemophilia? That a daughter will have hemophilia?

_____

_____

2. Two parents have the following alleles for colorblindness: $X^C X^C$ and $X^c Y$. What is the probability that a son will be colorblind? A daughter?

_____

_____

3. Two parents have the following alleles for colorblindness: $X^C X^c$ and $X^C Y$. What is the probability that a son will be colorblind? A daughter?

_____

_____

4. Do your data from the lab support the results from the Punnett squares above? Explain.

_____

_____

_____

_____

C-5

Variation in a Population

◆ Pre-Lab Discussion

Are you and your friends all exactly alike? Of course not. Although you are all members of one species, you are different in many ways. These differences are called variations and exist in all species.

Some variations are inherited by the offspring of an organism. Most inherited variations are neutral, that is, they do not affect the organism's survival. Helpful inherited variations are called adaptations. Harmful inherited variations make the organism less well-suited to its environment. Better-adapted organisms are more likely to reproduce and pass beneficial traits to their offspring. This process is called natural selection.

In this investigation, you will observe variations in two types of plants and in your class population.

1. What does *variations* mean?

_____

_____

2. What variations exist among members of your class?

_____

_____

◆ Problem

How can you measure the variations in plant and animal populations?

◆ Materials *(per group)*

10 large lima beans
10 leaves of the same species
metric ruler
graph paper
3 colored pencils

◆ Safety ⬛ *Review the safety guidelines in the front of your lab book.*

Do not eat the lima beans.

VARIATION IN A POPULATION *(continued)*

◆ **Procedure**

Part A: Variation in Plant Species

1. Obtain 10 large lima beans and 10 leaves of the same species of tree.

2. Measure the length of each lima bean and leaf blade in millimeters. See Figure 1. Record your measurements, rounded to the nearest millimeter, in Data Table 1.

3. Notice in Figure 1 the petiole of the leaf. Measure the length of the petiole of each leaf. Record your measurements, rounded to the nearest millimeter, in Data Table 1.

4. Record on the chalkboard your measurements for each of the plants so that all groups' data can be seen.

5. Using data from the entire class, record the range in lengths for the lima beans, leaf blades, and petioles. Record the class findings in Data Tables 2, 3, and 4. Fill in the first row of each table with the lengths, from shortest to longest, using increments of one millimeter. Add more columns to the data tables if necessary.

6. Record the class's total number of each size of lima bean, leaf blade, and petiole in the second row of Data Tables 2, 3, and 4.

7. Using the data in Data Table 2, construct a line graph for the lima-bean lengths on a sheet of graph paper. Label the *x*-axis "Lima bean length (mm)" and the *y*-axis "Number of beans."

8. Using the data in Data Tables 3 and 4, construct line graphs for the leaf-blade lengths and the petiole lengths on your graph paper. Label the *x*-axis "Leaf blade and petiole length (mm)" and the *y*-axis "Number of leaves." Use a different colored pencil to graph each set of data and include a key for each graph.

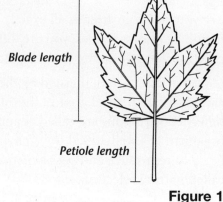

Blade length

Petiole length

Figure 1

Part B: Variation in Hand Spans

1. Measure your hand span. The measurement should be made from the top of the thumb to the tip of the little finger, as shown in Figure 2. Round off the measurement to the nearest centimeter. Record your hand span in a class chart on the chalkboard.

2. After all your classmates have recorded their hand spans in the class chart, transfer the results to Data Table 5. Your results will show the total number of hands having the same hand span.

3. Construct a line graph of the results on a sheet of graph paper. Label the *x*-axis "Hand-span length (cm)" and the *y*-axis "Number of students."

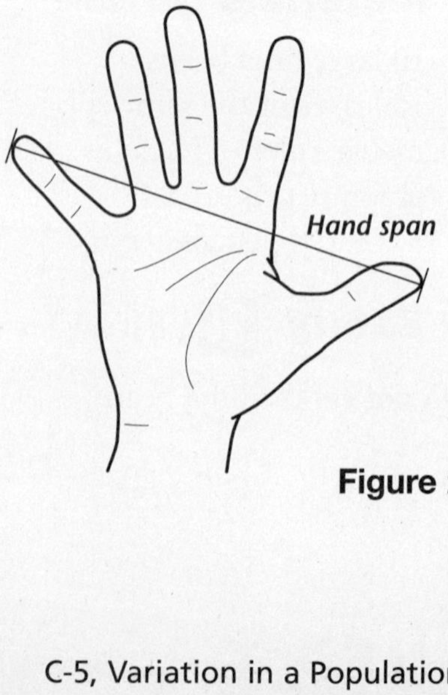

Hand span

Figure 2

VARIATION IN A POPULATION *(continued)*

◆ Observations

Data Table 1

Length (mm) (Group Data)										
	1	*2*	*3*	*4*	*5*	*6*	*7*	*8*	*9*	*10*
Lima beans										
Leaf blades										
Petioles										

Data Table 2

Class Data for Lima Bean Lengths										
Length of lima bean (mm)										
Total number of beans of this size										

Data Table 3

Class Data for Leaf Blade Lengths										
Length of leaf blade (mm)										
Total number of leaf blades of this size										

Data Table 4

Class Data for Petiole Lengths										
Length of petiole (mm)										
Total number of petioles of this size										

Data Table 5

Class Data for Hand-Span Lengths														
Length of hand span (cm)	15	16	17	18	19	20	21	22	23	24	25	26	27	28
Total number of hand spans of this size														

◆ Analyze and Conclude

1. In what length range are most of the lima beans? Most of the leaf blades? Most of the petioles?

_____

VARIATION IN A POPULATION *(continued)*

2. In what length range are the fewest beans? The fewest blades? The fewest petioles?

_____

_____

3. What is the general shape of the graphs of the lengths of the lima beans, leaf blades, and petioles? What does the shape of the graphs indicate about these lengths?

_____

_____

_____

4. Which hand-span length occurs most often? Least often?

_____

5. What is the general shape of the graph of hand spans? What does the shape of the graph indicate about the hand spans of students in your class?

_____

_____

◆ Critical Thinking and Applications

1. List two ways in which a large hand span might be a useful human adaptation.

_____

_____

2. Do you think having many seeds in a pod would be a more useful adaptation for a bean plant than having only a few seeds? Give a reason for your answer.

_____

_____

3. Why might having large leaves be a harmful characteristic for a desert plant?

_____

_____

◆ More to Explore

Investigate variations that occur in the lengths of peanut shells. Make your measurements and graph the results as you did in the previous part of this lab. Do you think that all organisms of the same species show variation in all of their traits? Give a reason for your answer. **CAUTION:** *Do not eat the peanuts.*

D-1   **LABORATORY INVESTIGATION**

Exploring Body Tissue and Body Systems

◆ Pre-Lab Discussion

Your body has four levels of organization. The smallest unit of life is the cell. Some organisms consist of only one cell, and all the organism's life activities take place in that cell. Most organisms have many cells, however, and their cells are specialized to perform specific functions. In many-celled organisms, like yourself, cells that work together to perform a function form a tissue. An organ, in turn, consists of different kinds of tissue that work together to perform a function. Your heart, lungs, and skin are organs. Groups of organs that work together to perform a specific function form an organ system.

In this investigation, you will look at several kinds of tissue. You will also explore which body systems work during a common activity.

1. What are the four basic types of human tissue?

_____

_____

2. Name the eleven organ systems in the human body.

_____

_____

_____

_____

◆ Problem

What do different human tissues look like? What organ systems work together to perform a simple activity?

◆ Possible Materials (per group)

microscope
prepared slides of skeletal muscle, surface skin cells, cartilage, and brain tissue
notebook

EXPLORING BODY TISSUE AND BODY SYSTEMS *(continued)*

◆ **Safety** *Review the safety guidelines in the front of your lab book.*

Always use both hands to pick up or carry a microscope. Hold the microscope base with one hand, and hold the microscope with your other hand. Handle glass slides carefully.

1

◆ **Procedure**

1. Using the microscope, first on low power and then on high power, observe a prepared slide of skeletal muscle.

2. Under Observations, draw the muscle tissue that you observe. Note the magnification you use to view it.

3. Using the microscope, first on low power and then on high power, observe a prepared slide of surface skin cells.

4. Under Observations, draw the skin cells that you observe. Note the magnification you use to view them.

5. Using the microscope, first on low power and then on high power, observe a prepared slide of cartilage.

6. Under Observations, draw the cartilage that you observe. Note the magnification you use to view it.

7. Using the microscope, first on low power and then on high power, observe a prepared slide of brain tissue.

8. Under Observations, draw the brain tissue that you observe. Note the magnification you use to view it.

9. Slide a notebook across the lab counter to one of your partners. What does your body have to do to move the notebook? What does your partner's body have to do to catch the notebook before it falls off the counter?

_____

_____

_____

_____

_____

_____

_____

_____

© Prentice-Hall, Inc.

EXPLORING BODY TISSUE AND BODY SYSTEMS *(continued)*

◆ Observations

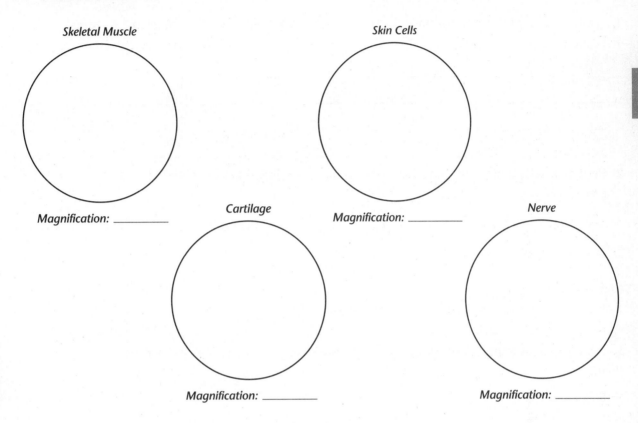

Skeletal Muscle

Magnification: _____

Cartilage

Magnification: _____

Skin Cells

Magnification: _____

Nerve

Magnification: _____

◆ Analyze and Conclude

1. What type of tissue is cartilage? Surface skin? Brain tissue?

_____

2. Choose two of the slides you observed. Compare and contrast the two tissues in the slides.

_____

_____

_____

3. What organ systems must work together for a person to successfully slide a notebook across a table? Give reasons for your answer.

_____

_____

_____

_____

_____

EXPLORING BODY TISSUE AND BODY SYSTEMS *(continued)*

◆ Critical Thinking and Applications

1. Your hand contains all four basic tissue types. Describe one function of each tissue type in your hand.

_____

_____

_____

2. Predict whether other animals have tissues that look like human tissues. Give a reason for your prediction.

_____

_____

_____

_____

3. What organ systems are working while you are sleeping? Give reasons for your answer.

_____

_____

_____

_____

_____

_____

◆ More to Explore

Design a physical activity that uses a specific organ system, such as the muscle system or the respiratory system. Write your procedure on a separate sheet of paper. Have the teacher approve your procedure before you carry out the investigation. What other systems are also involved? Can you think of specific events that could trigger other organ systems to work hard?

Examining Bones, Muscles, and Skin

◆ Pre-Lab Discussion

Have you ever seen a picture of a jellyfish? The body of the animal has no rigid shape because it has no bones. Think of what your body would be like without bones. Bones provide the structure needed for you to stand upright and to hold this paper. Bones work closely with muscles to allow your body to move. Muscles also keep important parts of your body, such as your heart, working. In Part A of the following investigation, you will examine bone and muscle cells to see how their structure relates to what they do.

Of course, you can't see your bones and muscles. They are covered by the largest organ in your body—your skin. What does skin do? One of its many purposes is to protect the inside of your body against injury and disease. It also contains sense receptors that give you your sense of touch. In Part B of this investigation, you will examine one important function of the sense of touch—the ability to distinguish different temperatures.

1. What are the three types of muscles? Explain how they differ.

_____

_____

_____

2. Name three functions of bones and three functions of skin.

_____

_____

_____

◆ Problem

How are the three types of muscle cells and bone cells alike, and how do they differ? How does your body sense differences in temperature?

◆ Materials *(per group)*

prepared slides of
    smooth muscle
    skeletal muscle
    cardiac muscle
    cross-section of compact human bone
microscope

3 transparent plastic cups
cold water
room-temperature water
paper towel
clock or watch with a second hand

© Prentice-Hall, Inc.

EXAMINING BONES, MUSCLES, AND SKIN *(continued)*

◆ **Safety** *Review the safety guidelines in the front of your lab book.*

Use caution when handling the microscope slides. If they break, tell the teacher. Do not pick up broken glass.

◆ Procedure

Part A: Observing Bone and Muscle

1. Using the microscope, first on low power and then on high power, examine a prepared slide of skeletal muscle. Look for nuclei in the cells.

2. In Part A of Observations, sketch the skeletal muscle tissue that you see. Note the magnification you use to view it. Label details of the cells such as striations (stripes) and nuclei.

3. Using the microscope, first on low power and then on high power, examine a prepared slide of cardiac muscle. Look for nuclei in the cells.

4. In Observations, sketch the cardiac muscle tissue that you see. Note the magnification you use to view it. Label details of the cells.

5. Using the microscope, first on low power and then on high power, examine a prepared slide of smooth muscle. Look for nuclei in the cells.

6. In Observations, sketch the smooth muscle tissue that you see. Note the magnification you use to view it. Label details of the cells.

7. Using the microscope, first on low power and then on high power, examine a prepared slide of compact bone. Look for cells and structural features.

8. In Observations, sketch the bone tissue that you see. Note the magnification you use to view it. Label details of the structures.

Part B: Examining the Sense of Touch

1. Place a cup of cold water and a cup of room-temperature water on two or three paper towels in front of you. Put your index finger in the cold water for about 5 seconds.

2. Remove your finger from the cold water, and put it in the room-temperature water. Immediately tell your partner how the water feels. For this step and each of the following steps, have your partner record all your observations in the Data Table.

3. Leave your finger in the room-temperature water. Describe how the water feels after a few minutes.

4. While one finger is still in the water, put your index finger from your other hand in the same cup.

5. Remove both fingers from the water. Put your original finger into the cold water and leave it there for about 20 seconds. Then move it into the room-temperature water. Leave your finger in the cup for a few minutes.

© Prentice-Hall, Inc.

EXAMINING BONES, MUSCLES, AND SKIN *(continued)*

6. Put your other index finger into the room-temperature water. Compare how the water feels now to how it felt in Step 3.

7. Remove both fingers from the water.

◆ Observations

Part A

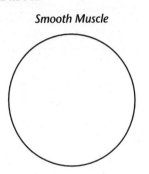

Smooth Muscle

Skeletal Muscle

Cardiac Muscle

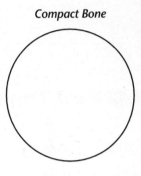

Compact Bone

Magnification: _____   Magnification: _____   Magnification: _____   Magnification: _____

Part B

Data Table

Step	What to Observe	Observations
2	How did the water feel when you first put your finger in the room-temperature water?	
3	How did the water feel when you left your finger in the room-temperature water?	
4	How did the water feel to your other finger when you put it in the room-temperature water?	
5	How did the water feel when you first put your finger in the room-temperature water this second time?	
6	How did the water feel when you left your finger in the room-temperature water this second time?	
7	How does the water feel now compared to how it felt in Step 5?	

◆ Analyze and Conclude

1. What structure can you clearly see in the muscle cells that you cannot see in the bone? Describe this structure.

_____

_____

EXAMINING BONES, MUSCLES, AND SKIN (continued)

2. What is the main structural difference between cardiac and skeletal muscle?

_____

_____

3. Did the sensors in your fingers respond in the same manner to the room-temperature water? Explain your answer.

_____

_____

_____

◆ **Critical Thinking and Applications**

1. Can you infer that striations, or stripes, have anything to do with whether a muscle is voluntary or involuntary? Explain.

_____

_____

_____

2. You looked at a cross-section of a bone. Describe how you could model the interior structure of an entire bone.

_____

_____

_____

3. Suppose one person has been outdoors on a hot day and another person has been in an air-conditioned room. They both go into a room of average temperature. Use your results from Part B to explain the temperature sensed by both people in the room of average temperature.

_____

_____

_____

◆ **More to Explore**

Repeat Part B of this experiment, using warm water in place of cold water.
CAUTION: *Do not use water that is hot enough to burn you or cause discomfort.*
Record all of your observations in a table similar to the one used in Part B.

D-3　　　　　　　　　　　　　　　　　　　**LABORATORY INVESTIGATION**

Nutrient Identification

◆ Pre-Lab Discussion

Do you know what foods have a lot of protein? Plenty of carbohydrates? Carbohydrates, fats, proteins, vitamins, minerals, and water are all nutrients in your food. You can detect the presence of some of these nutrients by taste. For example, all foods that taste sweet contain some form of sugar unless they are artificially sweetened. On the other hand, some foods, such as milk and onions, contain sugar but do not taste sweet. Therefore, scientists do not rely on taste or appearance to determine what nutrients a food contains. They use other tests to identify nutrients.

In this investigation, you will perform tests to detect starches, sugars, and proteins in foods.

1. What are the two groups of carbohydrates? What are their common names?

_____

_____

2. What functions do proteins perform in your body?

_____

_____

◆ Problem

How can you determine what nutrients are in various kinds of food?

◆ Materials *(per group)*

samples of various foods, including flour, honey, and gelatin
paper towels
3 medicine droppers
iodine solution
hot plate
beaker, 400-mL
water
2 test tubes
Benedict's solution
test-tube holder
Biuret solution

© Prentice-Hall, Inc.

NUTRIENT IDENTIFICATION (continued)

◆ **Safety**   *Review the safety guidelines in the front of your lab book.*

Iodine solution and Biuret solution can stain skin and clothing. Benedict's solution can burn skin. If you spill any of these solutions on your skin, rinse it off immediately with cold running water and tell the teacher. Use a test-tube holder when handling hot test tubes.

◆ Procedure

Part A: Test for Starches

1. Place a small amount of flour on a paper towel.

2. Use a medicine dropper to put 1 or 2 drops of iodine solution on the flour. **CAUTION:** *Keep iodine solution off your skin because it will leave a stain.*

3. Notice that the iodine solution turns purplish blue or blue-black. This color change indicates that flour contains starch. If the iodine remains yellow-brown, starch is not present.

4. Choose two to five other foods to test. Predict whether each food contains starch. Give a reason for your prediction.

_____

_____

_____

5. Test these additional foods for the presence of starch and record your results in Data Table 1.

Part B: Test for Sugars

1. Set up a hot-water bath by placing a beaker half full of water on a hot plate and starting to heat the water.

2. Use a medicine dropper to put 30 drops of honey-and-water solution in a test tube.

3. Use another medicine dropper to add Benedict's solution until the test tube is about one-third full. **CAUTION:** *Keep Benedict's solution away from your skin because it can burn you. If you spill some on you, rinse it off immediately with cold running water and inform the teacher.*

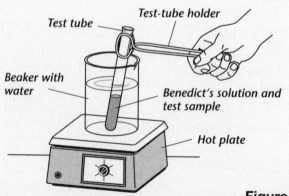

Test tube

Test-tube holder

Beaker with water

Benedict's solution and test sample

Hot plate

Figure 1

© Prentice-Hall, Inc.

NUTRIENT IDENTIFICATION *(continued)*

4. Wait until the water in the water bath is boiling. **CAUTION:** *Be careful when using the water bath. Adjust the heat so that the water does not boil too vigorously. Take care not to point the opening of the test tube toward anyone. Remember to wear your safety goggles.* Use a test-tube holder to hold the test tube upright in the water bath. See Figure 1. Gently boil the mixture for 2 to 5 minutes.

5. Remove the test tube from the water bath. The solution should have turned green, yellow, orange, or orange-red. Any of these colors indicates that sugar is present. If the Benedict's solution remains blue, sugar is not present. Note: Benedict's solution indicates the presence of simple sugars such as glucose and fructose, which are found in most fruits. It does not detect the presence of complex sugars such as lactose (milk sugar).

6. Choose two to five additional foods to test. If you use solid foods, crush the material to be tested, put it in a test tube, and add 30 drops of water. If you use liquids, test 30 drops.

7. Predict whether each of these foods contains sugar. Give a reason for your prediction.

_____

_____

_____

8. Test these additional foods for sugar and record your results in Data Table 2.

Test C: Test for Proteins

1. Use a medicine dropper to fill a test tube about one-third full of gelatin solution.

2. Add 10 drops of Biuret solution. **CAUTION:** *Biuret solution will burn skin and clothing. If you spill any solution on yourself, rinse it off immediately with cold running water and inform your teacher.*

3. Hold the tube against a white background. Notice that the mixture has turned violet. This color change indicates the presence of protein. If there is no color change, protein is not present.

4. Choose two to five other foods to test. Predict whether each contains protein. Give a reason for your prediction.

_____

_____

_____

5. Test these additional foods for protein and record your results in Data Table 3.

© Prentice-Hall, Inc.

NUTRIENT IDENTIFICATION *(continued)*

◆ Observations

Data Table 1

Food Tested	Color with Iodine Solution	Is Starch Present?
Flour	Purplish-black or blue-black	Yes

Data Table 2

Food Tested	Color with Benedict's Solution	Is Simple Sugar Present?
Honey and water	Green, yellow, orange, or orange-red	Yes

Data Table 3

Food Tested	Color with Biuret Solution	Is Protein Present?
Gelatin solution	Violet	Yes

NUTRIENT IDENTIFICATION (*continued*)

◆ Analyze and Conclude

1. Of the foods you tested, which contain starch? How do you know? Were your predictions correct?

_____

_____

_____

2. Of the foods you tested, which contain sugar? How do you know? Were your predictions correct?

_____

_____

_____

3. Of the foods you tested, which contain protein? How do you know? Were your predictions correct?

_____

_____

_____

◆ Critical Thinking and Applications

1. If a food does not turn Biuret solution violet, do you know what nutrients the food contains? Give a reason for your answer.

_____

_____

_____

2. Why is it important to include starches, sugars, and proteins in your diet?

_____

_____

_____

3. Write at least two new questions about other nutrients (such as minerals, vitamins, and so forth) that might be in the foods you tested.

_____

_____

_____

4. Briefly, how would you go about answering your questions above? (**CAUTION:** *Do not perform any experiment unless the teacher approves your written plan.*)

_____

_____

_____

_____

_____

◆ More to Explore

Chemical tests can detect different vitamins in foods. Indophenol is a chemical that tests for vitamin C. To conduct this test, wear safety goggles and a lab apron. Pour indophenol into a test tube to a depth of 2 cm. Add the substance to be tested, one drop at a time. Keep track of the number of drops added and shake the test tube after each drop is added. Continue until the blue color disappears. The more drops of test substance required to eliminate the blue color, the less vitamin C the substance contains. Compare the vitamin C content of various fruit juices, such as orange, apple, grapefruit, or lemon, or various brands of one kind of juice.

Direction of Blood Flow

◆ Pre-Lab Discussion

If you're healthy, you probably don't think much about your circulatory system. It just pumps along, keeping you alive. But think about this: liquids flow downhill. How can blood travel up to your heart, against the flow of gravity, as well as down? Somehow the muscle that is your heart and the arteries, veins, and capillaries work together to keep blood flowing to every part of your body.

In this investigation, you will demonstrate a feature of your veins that helps keep blood flowing throughout your body.

1. Compare and contrast the structures of arteries and veins.

_____

_____

_____

2. Why is it essential that blood flow upward in the body?

_____

_____

_____

◆ Problem

What prevents blood from flowing backward toward the lower part of the body?

◆ Materials *(per group)*

◆ Safety ⚠ *Review the safety guidelines in the front of your lab book.*

Be gentle when exerting pressure on veins.

DIRECTION OF BLOOD FLOW *(continued)*

◆ Procedure

1. Work with two partners. Decide which partner will observe, which one will be the subject, and which one will record observations.

2. Have the subject stand with both arms down at his or her sides until the veins on the back of the hands stand out.

3. The subject should keep both arms down. The observer should put one finger from each hand next to each other on one of the subject's raised veins. See Figure 1.

4. The observer leaves the finger closest to the ground where it is. He or she slides the other finger upward along the vein for about 4 cm, pressing firmly but gently.

5. The observer tells the recorder what happens to the vein. The recorder writes the observations in the Data Table.

6. The observer keeps the finger closest to the ground in place, then releases the upper finger. The observer tells the recorder what happens to the vein, and the recorder writes the observations in the Data Table.

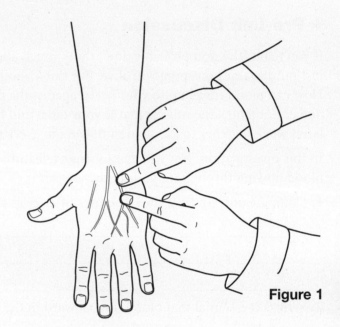

Figure 1

7. The observer releases the finger that is still in place and tells the recorder what happens to the vein. The recorder writes the observations in the Data Table.

8. Everyone switches roles and repeats steps 2–7.

◆ Observations

Data Table

Step	Effect on Vein	
	Subject 1	**Subject 2**
Observer moves fingers apart.		
Observer releases upper finger.		
Observer releases both fingers.		

DIRECTION OF BLOOD FLOW *(continued)*

◆ Analyze and Conclude

1. How do veins and valves contribute to the effect you saw when the observer's fingers moved apart?

_____

_____

_____

2. How do veins and valves contribute to the effect you saw when the observer released the upper finger?

_____

_____

3. How do veins and valves contribute to the effect you saw when the observer released both fingers?

_____

_____

4. Use your observations to summarize why blood doesn't flow backward in your body.

_____

_____

_____

◆ Critical Thinking and Applications

1. What would have happened if you had used an artery instead of a vein in this experiment?

_____

_____

_____

2. In terms of circulation, why is it important to wear clothes that are not too tight? Include evidence from the lab in your answer.

_____

_____

_____

DIRECTION OF BLOOD FLOW *(continued)*

3. Many buildings have plumbing in rooms that are below ground level, so the plumbing is lower than the building's drain pipe. Use what you learned in the investigation to explain how someone could design a bathtub drain in such a room. The drain water must not flow back into the bathtub.

_____

_____

_____

◆ More to Explore

New Problem When you exercise for cardiorespiratory fitness, you want your heart to beat at a target heart rate. What kind of exercise takes you closer to your target heart rate in 1 minute?

Possible Materials Use a stopwatch or other timer with a second hand.

Safety Do not exercise if you have health conditions, such as asthma, that might make exercise harmful.

Procedure Take your pulse while resting, and calculate the low end of the range of your target heart rate. See pages 112 and 259 in your textbook.

Develop a procedure to determine whether 1 minute of jumping rope or 1 minute of running in place gets you closer to your target heart rate. On a separate sheet of paper, list the steps of your procedure. Have the teacher approve your procedure before you carry out the investigation.

Observations On a separate sheet of paper, create a data table to record the resting heart rate, calculated target heart rate, and actual heart rate for both types of exercise.

Analyze and Conclude

1. Why do different exercises affect how long it takes you to reach your target heart rate?

_____

_____

2. Why do you think it is important for the heart rate to stay in the target range?

_____

_____

_____

D-5   LABORATORY INVESTIGATION

Measuring the Volume of Exhaled Air

◆ Pre-Lab Discussion

If you have healthy lungs, you usually are not conscious of breathing. But have you ever felt like you were "out of breath"? Maybe you had to run to answer the phone or catch the school bus. Maybe you were ill, and your lungs were congested. Whatever the reason, you felt that the volume of air your lungs could hold was not enough for the amount of air you needed.

The amount of air that lungs can hold varies from person to person. It also varies in any one person from time to time. In this investigation, you will design and use a plan to measure and compare the volume of air you exhale when you exercise and the volume of air you exhale when you are not exercising.

1. How does the respiratory system work?

_____

_____

_____

2. Explain the difference between *breathing* and *respiration*.

_____

_____

◆ Problem

How can you measure the volume of exhaled air?

◆ Possible Materials *(per group)*

2-hole rubber stopper
2-L plastic bottle
glass tubing, long and short
rubber or flexible plastic tubing, 2 pieces
100-mL graduated cylinder
paper towels
cloth towel
glycerin
timer

MEASURING THE VOLUME OF EXHALED AIR *(continued)*

◆ Safety   *Review the safety guidelines in the front of your lab book.*

When you blow through the tubing, first place a paper towel over the end of it and blow through the towel. Do not put your mouth directly on any of the tubing. If you insert glass tubing into the rubber stopper, use extreme caution and follow the teacher's instructions. Inform the teacher of any physical reasons you should not exercise. Your teacher must approve your plan before you can perform the experiment.

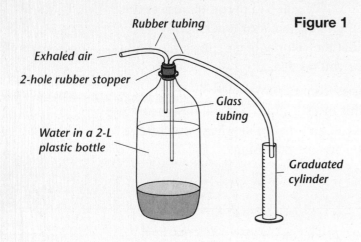

Figure 1

◆ Procedure

5

1. Read through this entire lab before you perform any part of it.

2. Use the materials listed here or other materials to assemble a spirometer—an instrument that can be used to measure the volume of air that your lungs can exhale. A spirometer is shown in Figure 1.

3. Plan how you will use your instrument to measure your lung volume. Consider what unit you will use for this measurement. On another sheet of paper, write a step-by-step plan for using your spirometer to measure the volume of your exhaled air.

4. Use Data Table 1 in Observations to record your data. You will need to record data for at least three trials; you may want to do more. You will then calculate the average volume of water displaced for all of your trials.

5. After the teacher has approved your plan, carry out your investigation. Then answer questions 1 and 2 in Observations.

© Prentice-Hall, Inc.

MEASURING THE VOLUME OF EXHALED AIR *(continued)*

6. After you have completed Data Table 1, run in place for two minutes.
CAUTION: *Do not perform this part of the activity if you have any medical condition that makes the activity unsafe.* Repeat your experiment, using Data Table 2. Perform the same number of trials as before and average the trials. Then answer question 3 in Observations.

7. Rest for a few minutes until your breathing returns to normal. Then repeat the experiment using Data Table 3.

◆ Observations

1. How is the volume of water that is forced out of the bottle related to the volume of air you exhale?

_____

2. In the spirometer in Figure 1, why is it important that one glass tube is above the surface of the water and one glass tube is beneath it?

_____

_____

_____

_____

3. How does your average volume of exhaled air when you have not been exercising compare to your average volume of exhaled air right after you exercise?

_____

_____

Data Table 1
(before exercising)

Trial	Volume of Water (mL)
1	
2	
3	
Average	

Data Table 2
(after exercising)

Trial	Volume of Water (mL)
1	
2	
3	
Average	

Data Table 3 (when breathing returns to normal)

Trial	Volume of Water (mL)
1	
2	
3	
Average	

MEASURING THE VOLUME OF EXHALED AIR (continued)

◆ Analyze and Conclude

1. Why is it important to perform several trials for each part of the investigation?

_____

_____

2. Choose one of your data tables. Were the volumes the same for each trial? What could you change about your plan to assure that your data are more consistent?

_____

_____

_____

3. Infer why the volume of air you exhaled after exercise differed from the volume you exhaled before exercising.

_____

_____

_____

◆ Critical Thinking and Applications

1. What might cause differences in lung volume among students in the class?

_____

_____

2. Denver, Colorado, is located at a high altitude. Miami, Florida, is located at sea level. Predict how the average Data Table 1 results for students who live in Denver compare to those of students who live in Miami. Explain your reasoning.

_____

_____

_____

◆ More to Explore

How could you determine the total volume of air someone can exhale in one minute? Write a procedure that you would follow to answer this question. Have the teacher approve your procedure before you carry out the investigation.

D-6   **LABORATORY INVESTIGATION**

Do Mouthwashes Work?

◆ Pre-Lab Discussion

What do you use to take care of your teeth: toothbrush, toothpaste, dental floss, mouthwash? Mouthwashes are supposed to kill microorganisms that contribute to tooth decay, gum disease, and bad breath. They contain antiseptics, chemicals that kill or prevent growth of disease organisms on living tissues. How well do these mouthwashes work? Do they really kill microorganisms?

In this investigation, you will compare the effects of two mouthwashes.

1. Name four groups of organisms that cause diseases.

_____

_____

2. From where do disease-causing microorganisms come?

_____

_____

◆ Problem

How well do mouthwashes control the growth of bacteria?

◆ Materials *(per group)*

3 petri dishes with sterile nutrient agar
pen
masking tape
2 types of mouthwash
2 small jars
filter paper
scissors
metric ruler
forceps
transparent tape

◆ Safety   *Review the safety guidelines in the front of your lab book.*

Do not drink the mouthwashes. Have the teacher dispose of the sealed petri dishes at the end of the activity.

DO MOUTHWASHES WORK? *(continued)*

◆ Procedure

1. Obtain three petri dishes containing sterile agar. Do *not* open the dishes. Using a pen and pieces of masking tape, label the bottoms of the petri dishes *A*, *B*, and *C*. Also put your initials on each dish.

2. Wash your hands thoroughly with soap, then run a fingertip across the surface of your worktable. Your partner should hold open the cover of petri dish A, while you run your fingertip gently across the agar in a zigzag motion. Close the dish immediately.

3. Repeat Step 2 for dishes B and C.

4. Obtain a small sample of each mouthwash in separate containers. Use a pen and masking tape to label the containers.

5. Cut two 2-cm squares of filter paper. Soak a square in each mouthwash.

6. Using forceps, remove one square from a container. Open the cover of dish A just long enough to put the filter paper in the center of the agar. Close the cover immediately. Record the name of the mouthwash in the Data Table.

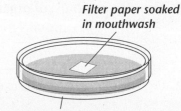

Filter paper soaked in mouthwash

Petri dish with sterile agar

Figure 1

7. Repeat Step 6 for dish B, using the filter paper soaked in the second mouthwash.

8. Do not add anything to dish C.

9. Tape the covers of all three petri dishes so that they will remain tightly closed. Let the three dishes sit upright on your work surface for at least 5 minutes before moving them. **CAUTION:** *Do not open the petri dishes again.* Wash your hands with soap and water.

10. As directed by the teacher, store the petri dishes in a warm, dark place where they can remain for at least three days. You will remove them only for a brief examination each day.

11. Predict what you will observe over the next three days in the three petri dishes.

_____

_____

_____

12. After one day, observe the contents of each dish without removing the cover. Estimate the percentage of the agar surface that shows any changes. Record your observations in the Data Table. Return the dishes to their storage place and wash your hands with soap and water.

13. Repeat Step 12 after a second day and after a third day.

14. After you and your partner have made your last observations, give the unopened petri dishes to the teacher.

DO MOUTHWASHES WORK? *(continued)*

◆ Observations

Data Table

Petri Dish	Mouthwash	Day 1	Day 2	Day 3
A				
B				
C				

◆ Analyze and Conclude

1. How did the appearance of dish C change during three days?

_____

2. How did the appearance of dishes A and B compare with dish C? Explain any similarities or differences.

_____

_____

_____

3. How did the appearance of dishes A and B compare with each other? How can you account for any differences?

_____

_____

_____

4. Explain why it is important to set aside one petri dish that does not contain any mouthwash.

_____

_____

_____

© Prentice-Hall, Inc.

DO MOUTHWASHES WORK? *(continued)*

◆ Critical Thinking and Applications

1. Based on the results of this lab, what recommendation would you make to your family about mouthwashes?

_____

_____

_____

2. What other products could you test using a procedure similar to this lab?

_____

_____

◆ More to Explore

Test one of the products in your answer to question 2 above. For example, visit a store and look at antibacterial soaps. How do their ingredients differ from other soaps? How do their prices compare to regular soap?

_____

_____

New Problem How well do antibacterial soaps control the growth of bacteria?

Possible Materials Consider which materials you can use from the previous part of this lab. What else will you need?

Procedure Develop a procedure to solve the problem. Write your procedure on a separate sheet of paper. Have the teacher approve your procedure before you carry out the investigation.

Observations On a separate sheet of paper, make a data table like the one in the previous part of this lab in which to record your data.

Analyze and Conclude

What effects of antibacterial soap do your results show?

_____

_____

_____

6

D-7

Locating Touch Receptors

◆ Pre-Lab Discussion

Have you ever wondered why your hand instantly pulls back when it touches a hot pan on the stove? Have you noticed that smooth fabrics feel better to your skin than rough fabrics do? Both of these reactions involve your sense of touch.

Touch receptors in your skin help you respond to your environment. Your body responds to different stimuli, including pain, temperature, and pressure. Not all parts of your body respond equally to these stimuli. Different parts of the body contain different numbers of receptors for a given amount of skin area.

In this investigation, you will test several areas of your skin and compare their sensitivity to touch.

1. How does the location of the sense of touch differ from the location of other senses?

_____

_____

2. Where in the skin are the receptors that would sense a light touch?

_____

◆ Problem

Where are the touch receptors located on the body?

◆ Materials *(per group)*

scissors
metric ruler
piece of cardboard, 6 cm × 10 cm
marker
9 toothpicks
blindfold

◆ Safety   *Review the safety guidelines in the front of your lab book.*

Use caution in handling sharp scissors. Tie the blindfold loosely, using special care if the blindfolded student is wearing contact lenses. Students who wear eyeglasses should remove them before wearing a blindfold.

LOCATING TOUCH RECEPTORS *(continued)*

◆ Procedure

1. Using scissors, cut the piece of cardboard into five rectangles, each measuring 6 cm × 2 cm. Label the pieces A–E.

2. As shown in Figure 1, insert two toothpicks 5 mm apart into rectangle A. Insert two toothpicks 1 cm apart into rectangle B, two toothpicks 2 cm apart into rectangle C, and two toothpicks 3 cm apart into rectangle D. In the center of rectangle E, insert one toothpick.

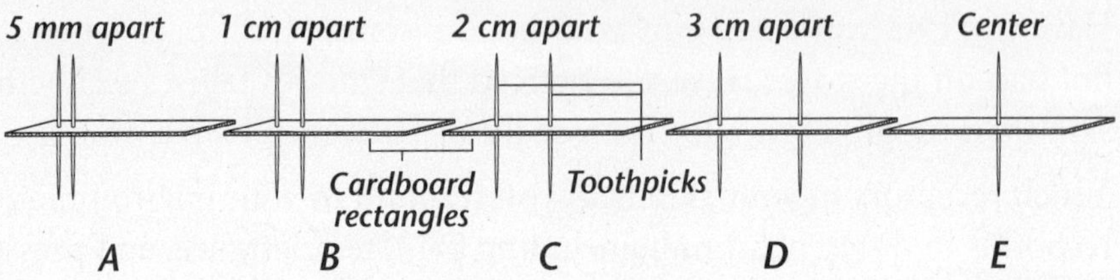

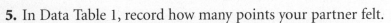

5 mm apart   1 cm apart   2 cm apart   3 cm apart   Center

Cardboard rectangles   Toothpicks

A   B   C   D   E

Figure 1

3. Carefully blindfold your partner.

4. Using one of the rectangles, carefully touch the palm side of your partner's fingertip with the ends of the toothpicks. **CAUTION:** *Only* touch *the toothpicks to the skin; do not press them against the skin.* Ask your partner how many points he or she feels.

5. In Data Table 1, record how many points your partner felt.

6. Repeat steps 4 and 5, touching the palm of the hand, back of the neck, back of the hand, and inside the lower arm.

7. Repeat steps 4–6 with the other cardboard rectangles. Select each rectangle randomly, not in alphabetical order.

8. Reverse roles with your partner and repeat the investigation using Data Table 2.

9. Answer question 1 in Observations.

◆ Observations

Data Table 1

Body Part	Number of Points Felt				
	A 5 mm apart	**B** 1 cm apart	**C** 2 cm apart	**D** 3 cm apart	**E** 1 point
Subject 1					
Fingertip					
Palm of hand					
Back of hand					
Back of neck					
Inside lower arm					

7

LOCATING TOUCH RECEPTORS *(continued)*

Data Table 2

Body Part	Number of Points Felt				
	A 5 mm apart	B 1 cm apart	C 2 cm apart	D 3 cm apart	E 1 point
Subject 2					
Fingertip					
Palm of hand					
Back of hand					
Back of neck					
Inside lower arm					

1. On which area of the skin were you best able to feel two separate points?

_____

◆ Analyze and Conclude

1. Which area of the skin that you tested probably had the most touch receptors? The fewest? On what observations do you base this conclusion?

_____
_____
_____

2. Rank the tested skin areas in order from the most to the least sensitive.

_____
_____
_____

3. In Step 7, why was it important to select each rectangle randomly instead of in alphabetical order?

_____
_____
_____

© Prentice-Hall, Inc.

7

LOCATING TOUCH RECEPTORS *(continued)*

4. Did you and your partner sense the same number of points in each test? If not, why do you think your results were different?

_____

_____

_____

◆ Critical Thinking and Applications

1. Think about the test area that had the most touch receptors. How does having a lot of receptors in this area benefit you?

_____

_____

_____

2. Explain how a lack of touch receptors in the bottom of your feet would affect your ability to walk.

_____

_____

_____

3. Why is it important to you that your body respond to pain?

_____

_____

_____

◆ More to Explore

New Problem Can you identify similar objects by touch alone?

Possible Materials Consider which materials you can use from the previous part of the lab. What else will you need?

Procedure Develop a procedure to solve the problem. Write your procedure on a separate sheet of paper. Have the teacher approve your procedure before you carry out the investigation.

Observations On a separate sheet of paper, create a table to organize data for two subjects trying to identify three coins each.

Analyze and Conclude Do different people have different touch sensitivity? Support your answer with data from your experiment.

_____

_____

© Prentice-Hall, Inc.

7

Model of a Negative Feedback Mechanism

◆ Pre-Lab Discussion

The endocrine system, along with the nervous system, controls your body's daily activities. It also controls how your body develops. Endocrine glands produce chemicals called hormones, which move directly into the bloodstream. Hormones affect specific cells called target cells. These target cells are often in another part of the body. To control the amount of hormone an endocrine gland produces, the endocrine system sends chemical information back and forth in a negative feedback system. Negative feedback is an important way that the body maintains homeostasis. In this investigation, you will model how a negative feedback system works.

1. How does the pancreas act as an endocrine gland?

_____

_____

2. Your blood carries hormones to every part of your body. Why doesn't a hormone affect all your cells the same way?

_____

_____

_____

◆ Problem

How does the pancreas use negative feedback to help maintain glucose at a certain level in the blood?

◆ Materials *(per group)*

2-liter plastic soft-drink bottle
scissors
rubber ball, solid, 2.5–4.0 cm in diameter
2 screw eyes
string
fishing float
dowel, about 6 cm long
sink or bucket
water
large pitcher
marker

8

MODEL OF A NEGATIVE FEEDBACK MECHANISM *(continued)*

◆ Safety *Review the safety guidelines in the front of your lab book.*

Take care when cutting off the bottom of the soft-drink bottle. To prevent slips or falls, immediately wipe up any water spilled on the floor.

◆ Procedure

1. Carefully cut off the bottom half of the plastic bottle.

2. Insert a screw eye into a rubber ball. Cut a piece of string 20 cm long. Tie one end of the string to the screw eye and the other end to a fishing float.

3. Insert a second screw eye into the other side of the rubber ball, directly opposite the first screw eye. Cut a piece of string 10 cm long. Tie one end of the string to the screw eye and the other end to the middle of the dowel.

4. Hold the bottle upside down. Lower the float, the rubber ball, and the attached rod into the bottle. Carefully pass the rod through the neck of the bottle so that the rod hangs below the mouth, as shown in Figure 1.

Figure 1

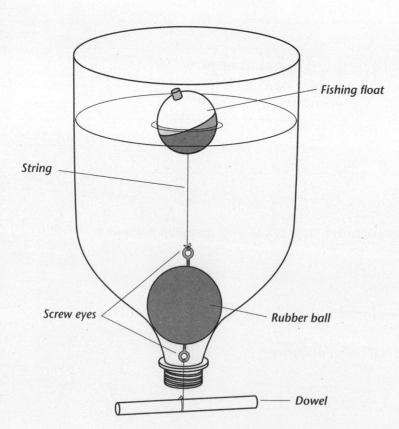

8

© Prentice-Hall, Inc.

MODEL OF A NEGATIVE FEEDBACK MECHANISM *(continued)*

5. One of you should hold the bottle over a sink or bucket, while the other slowly pours water into the bottle until the string stretches to its full length. Do not lift the ball out of the bottle opening. Mark the level of the water on the outside of the bottle.

6. Slowly add more water to the bottle and observe what happens. Answer questions 1 and 2 in Observations.

7. Add about 100 mL of water rapidly to the model. Be careful not to overfill the bottle. Observe what happens and answer question 3 in Observations.

◆ Observations

1. What happens to the water level when you add more water after the string has stretched to its full length?

_____

_____

_____

_____

_____

2. What happens to the float and ball whenever you add water slowly?

_____

_____

_____

_____

_____

3. How does the model act when you pour the water quickly, compared to when you pour it slowly?

_____

_____

_____

_____

_____

8

MODEL OF A NEGATIVE FEEDBACK MECHANISM *(continued)*

◆ Analyze and Conclude

Figure 2 shows the role of the pancreas in a negative feedback loop that controls the amount of glucose in the blood. The pancreas makes the hormone insulin. Insulin enables body cells to take in glucose from the bloodstream. When the glucose level in the blood is high, the pancreas releases insulin, which enables body cells to take glucose from the blood. When the glucose level in the blood drops, the pancreas stops releasing insulin. Body cells stop removing glucose from the bloodstream. When blood glucose increases, the cycle starts again.

Figure 2

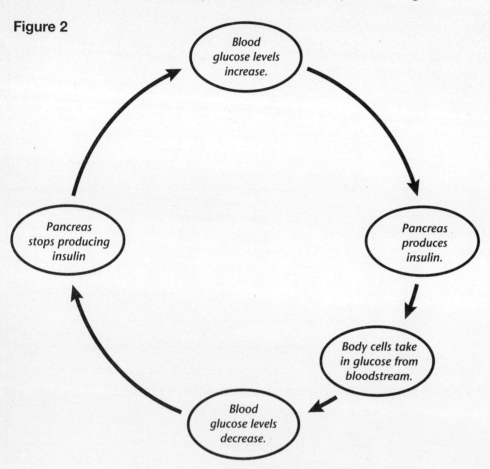

1. The water in the model represents blood glucose. Which part of your model represents the pancreas? (Drawing a cycle like the one in Figure 2 might help you find an answer.) Give a reason for your answer.

_____

_____

_____

MODEL OF A NEGATIVE FEEDBACK MECHANISM *(continued)*

2. Which part of your model represents the body cells? Give a reason for your answer.

_____

_____

_____

3. Which part of your model represents insulin? Give a reason for your answer.

_____

_____

_____

4. Explain how your model demonstrates the negative feedback mechanism used by the pancreas to control glucose levels in the blood.

_____

_____

_____

_____

_____

◆ Critical Thinking and Applications

1. How would lengthening the string between the float and the ball affect the water level? How would shortening this string affect the water level?

_____

_____

_____

2. Based on this model, explain how negative feedback works.

_____

_____

_____

_____

_____

8

MODEL OF A NEGATIVE FEEDBACK MECHANISM *(continued)*

3. What part of the negative feedback mechanism that keeps blood glucose at one level is not represented in the model? How could you improve the design of the model to make it more accurate?

_____

_____

_____

_____

_____

_____

◆ More to Explore

The body's regulation of glucose levels is more complicated than the model you made of it. Use the library to find out more about glucose regulation. Which part of the regulation process is missing from your model?

8

© Prentice-Hall, Inc.

LABORATORY INVESTIGATION

Weather and Whooping Cranes

◆ Pre-Lab Discussion

The whooping crane is a tall white bird with red markings on its forehead and face. It is native to certain North American wetlands. In the twentieth century, the population of this magnificent bird has decreased almost to the point of disappearing. In 1941, only 14 cranes were living. Although about ten times as many cranes are now living, they are still at risk. About half of the cranes live in the wild. They breed in Wood Buffalo National Park in Canada and winter in Aransas National Wildlife Refuge in Texas.

Scientists, working to save the whooping cranes, investigated what abiotic factors affect the birds. In this investigation, you will analyze the data from one such study.

1. What do whooping cranes need to obtain from their habitat?

_____

_____

2. What abiotic factors might limit the population of whooping cranes?

_____

_____

◆ Problem

How does precipitation affect the population of whooping cranes?

◆ Materials *(per group)*

ruler
calculator
pencil

◆ Procedure

1. Using Figure 1 and the data in Data Table 1, plot a graph showing how the crane population changed from year 1 to year 16 of the study. The crane population in any given year is the total number of migrating adults and hatched eggs. Answer questions 1–3 in Observations.

2. Study the data in Data Table 1. Answer questions 4–6 in Observations.

© Prentice-Hall, Inc.

WEATHER AND WHOOPING CRANES *(continued)*

3. Using a calculator, determine the hatching success rate for each year.

$$\text{Hatching success rate} = \frac{\text{Number of eggs hatched}}{\text{Number of eggs laid}} \times 100\%$$

Write these values in the corresponding boxes in Data Table 2. Answer question 7 in Observations.

Data Table 1

One Study Relating Weather and Reproductive Rate of Whooping Cranes

Year	Migrating Adults	Number of Nests	Eggs Laid	Hatched Eggs	Rainfall (cm)	Snowfall (cm)
1	21	6	6	4	8.9	3.6
2	20	3	2	0	15.0	0.5
3	20	4	4	3	11.7	2.0
4	22	5	5	4	6.1	2.8
5	23	4	6	2	6.4	14.2
6	23	8	8	4	8.1	4.6
7	30	6	6	5	7.4	0.0
8	32	0	0	0	19.3	7.6
9	28	4	6	2	15.0	1.3
10	26	10	10	7	8.1	2.0
11	32	10	10	6	7.4	2.5
12	36	2	2	0	13.7	7.4
13	30	4	4	3	8.9	1.0
14	32	3	4	3	7.1	1.8
15	33	3	3	1	14.7	6.1
16	32	5	5	4	5.3	1.5

© Prentice-Hall, Inc.

WEATHER AND WHOOPING CRANES *(continued)*

◆ Observations

Figure 1

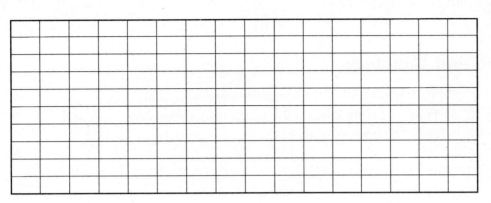

1. When was the crane population at its highest level? When was it at its lowest level?

   _____

   _____

2. During which year did the population increase the most?

   _____

3. In which year did the most adult cranes die?

   _____

4. Which four years were the poorest breeding years for the cranes? In which year were the most eggs laid and hatched successfully?

   _____

   _____

5. During which five summers was rainfall greatest?

   _____

6. Was snowfall ever high the same year that rainfall was high? If so, in which year or years?

   _____

Data Table 2

Year	1	2	3	4	5	6	7	8	9	10	11	12	13	14	15	16
Hatching success rate (%)																

© Prentice-Hall, Inc.

WEATHER AND WHOOPING CRANES (continued)

7. In which year was total precipitation (rainfall plus snowfall) lowest? What was the hatching success rate that year?

_____

◆ Analyze and Conclude

1. Using data from data tables 1 and 2, plot the points that relate hatching success rate to rainfall on Figure 2 below. What is the relationship between rainfall and hatching success rate? Why do you think this relationship exists?

_____

_____

_____

Figure 2

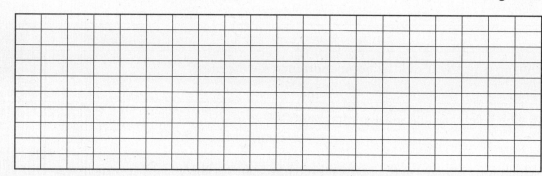

Rainfall (cm)

2. Suppose you want to find out how rainfall affects the whooping-crane population. Why would you use daily or weekly amounts of rainfall rather than seasonal amounts?

_____

_____

_____

3. Suppose that years 10 and 11 had high levels of precipitation. How would this have affected the population? Give a reason for your answer.

_____

_____

_____

_____

WEATHER AND WHOOPING CRANES *(continued)*

◆ Critical Thinking and Applications

1. What other factors besides weather might influence the population growth of whooping cranes? What do you think lowered the whooping-crane population to the endangered level?

_____

_____

_____

_____

2. Once laws protecting the American alligator went into effect, the alligator population recovered quite rapidly. In contrast, the whooping-crane population has remained low in spite of protection. What factors might prevent a rapid increase in the number of cranes?

_____

_____

_____

_____

_____

3. Why is international cooperation necessary to protect species that migrate, such as the whooping crane?

_____

_____

_____

_____

4. Whooping cranes often lay two eggs. However, a pair can rarely raise two chicks. Therefore, wildlife biologists sometimes "steal" one of the two eggs in the nest and replace it with a fake one of plastic. What do you think the biologists do with the stolen eggs? Why?

_____

_____

_____

_____

_____

© Prentice-Hall, Inc.

WEATHER AND WHOOPING CRANES *(continued)*

◆ More to Explore

Find out the difference between an endangered species and a threatened species. Is the whooping crane endangered or threatened? List three species that are endangered and three species that are threatened. What is being done to protect each species?

1

E-2   LABORATORY INVESTIGATION

Ecosystem Food Chains

◆ Pre-Lab Discussion

Ecosystems are made up of both living (biotic) and nonliving (abiotic) things. Energy moves through ecosystems in the form of food. When an organism eats another organism, it obtains energy from the food. A food chain is a series of events in which one organism eats another and thereby obtains energy.

Do you know what makes up the ecosystems in your area? In this investigation, you will become an ecologist studying a local ecosystem. You will observe and collect data about the biotic and abiotic factors found at your site. You will also study the relationships among the different biotic and abiotic features you observe.

1. What is a consumer? What are the four classifications of consumers?

_____

_____

2. What is the source of all the food in an ecosystem? What process is generally used to make this food?

_____

_____

◆ Problem

What food chains can you observe in a local ecosystem?

◆ Possible Materials (per group)

meterstick   colored pencils
4 stakes   hand lens
string
notebook
pen

◆ Safety   *Review the safety guidelines in the front of your lab book.*

Use care when working with stakes. Be careful when working around land and water sites so that you do not fall and injure yourself or others. Review the safety rules on pages v–vi in the front of this book for handling plants and animals.

© Prentice-Hall, Inc.

ECOSYSTEM FOOD CHAINS (continued)

◆ Procedure

Part A: Class Preparation

1. As a class, discuss the different types of ecosystems found around your home and school. Determine which ecosystem you will examine. Be aware that the type of ecosystem you choose will influence the types of food chains you will find.

2. Use different colored pencils to represent the different types of organisms you expect to find within your chosen ecosystem. Make a key representing the different organisms in the Data Table under Observations. Types of organisms might include trees, bushes, flowers, grasses, mosses, fungi, insects, and other animals. You might also include evidence of animals, such as burrows, nests, and egg cases. Finally, consider including dead organic materials such as logs, dead trees, fallen leaves, and animal remains.

3. Make a list of the materials that you need to conduct your field study of the ecosystem. Develop a plan for gathering these materials. Decide who will gather what materials.

Part B: Field Study

1. At your study site, measure a 25-square-meter site with a meterstick (5 m × 5 m). Place one stake at each corner of the site. Loop string around one stake and continue to the next stake until you have formed the boundaries for the site. See Figure 1.

2. On a separate sheet of paper, draw a map of your site. Draw the abiotic features on your map, such as streams, sidewalks, trails, or boulders.

Figure 1

3. Draw colored circles on the map to represent the different organisms you find. Some of your circles will likely overlap. For example, if your site is mostly grass, you may have a colored circle around the entire map. Within this circle might be other colored circles representing trees.

4. Observe your site quietly for 30 minutes. On a separate sheet of paper, record any interactions between organisms that you observe. Such interactions may include getting food or just moving across the site.

5. When you have finished your observations, remove the string and stakes. Leave the site as you found it; do not take anything from it or damage it in any way.

ECOSYSTEM FOOD CHAINS *(continued)*

◆ Observations

Data Table

Color Key for Organisms			
Color	*Type of Organism*	*Color*	*Type of Organism*

◆ Analyze and Conclude

1. What producers did you observe at your site? What characteristics do these organisms have in common?

_____

_____

_____

_____

2. Think about the consumers you observed at your site. Categorize them according to the four main types of consumers that you listed in Pre-Lab question 1.

_____

_____

_____

3. What are the most important abiotic features of your site? Explain your answer.

_____

_____

_____

_____

ECOSYSTEM FOOD CHAINS *(continued)*

◆ Critical Thinking and Applications

1. Draw two food chains you observed in your site that contain a producer, a primary consumer, and a secondary consumer. Include appropriate organisms in your drawings even if you did not observe the actual consumption of food.

2. How do the abiotic factors in your ecosystem affect how the living things in the ecosystem are distributed?

_____

_____

_____

3. What would happen to the producers and consumers at your site if there were no decomposers?

_____

_____

_____

4. Predict how the biotic and abiotic features might change at your site during different seasons.

_____

_____

_____

◆ More to Explore

Compare your site to other sites nearby. Consider both biotic and abiotic features. Also describe any evidence of human influence on your site.

© Prentice-Hall, Inc.

E-3 **LABORATORY INVESTIGATION**

Managing Fisheries

◆ Pre-Lab Discussion

When explorers first came to the shores of North America, they were amazed at the abundance of resources—towering forests, clear streams, vast grasslands, and a large variety of wildlife. As they began to use these resources, they also began to affect them. Throughout the years, populations of plants and animals have increased and decreased as a result of both natural events and human actions.

One example of a population that has changed over the years is fish. The waters off the shores of North America have supplied large quantities and varieties of fish. Overfishing and other abuses of the fishing areas have caused the populations to greatly decrease. But people are also taking action to protect the fish. In this investigation, you will model a population of cod fish off the Grand Banks— a famous fishing area off the coast of Newfoundland, Canada. You will determine the effect of different events on that fish population.

1. Is a fishery a renewable resource or a nonrenewable resource? Explain your answer.

_____

_____

_____

2. Aquaculture is the farming of water organisms. How might increased aquaculture of fish in an area help the local fisheries? How might it harm them?

_____

_____

_____

◆ Problem

How does a fish population change over time?

◆ Materials *(per group)*

notebook paper, 1 sheet
colored construction paper, 8 sheets of one color
scissors
pencil or pen
set of event cards

MANAGING FISHERIES *(continued)*

◆ Safety *Review the safety guidelines in the front of your lab book.*

Use caution when cutting with scissors.

◆ Procedure

1. As a group, make 8 "fish cards" from each sheet of colored paper, for a total of 64 cards. Write "Fish" on one side of each card. These fish cards represent the population of cod in fisheries off the Grand Banks. Each card represents many fish.

2. Divide a sheet of notebook paper in half. Label one half "Live Fish" and the other half "Dead Fish."

3. Obtain a set of event cards from your teacher. These cards represent events that can affect a fish population.

4. Shuffle and spread out the event cards, facedown. Count off 25 fish cards and place them by the notebook paper, as shown in Figure 1. Set the remaining 39 fish cards aside.

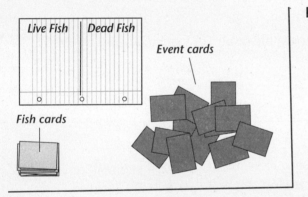

Figure 1

5. Pick up an event card. As a group, discuss and decide if the event you have chosen will likely increase or decrease the fish population.

6. If the event will increase the population, place a fish card from the stack of 25 on the Live Fish area of the notebook paper. If it will decrease the population, place a fish card on the Dead Fish area of the paper.

7. Replace the event card and mix up the event cards again.

8. Repeat this procedure until all 25 of the fish cards have been placed on either live or dead fish piles on the paper.

9. Count the number of live fish cards on the paper. Add half that number of fish cards from the remaining 39 cards to the live fish stack to represent additional fish added by reproduction. Remove the dead fish cards and set them aside with the remaining fish cards. Complete the Data Table in the Observations section for Generation 1.

MANAGING FISHERIES *(continued)*

10. The stack of live fish cards now represents the beginning of the second generation of fish. Repeat steps 5–9 to find out what happens to the second generation of fish.

11. Repeat steps 5–9 to find out what happens to the third generation of fish.

◆ Observations

Data Table

Starting number of fish cards: 25		
Generation	**Number of Live Fish Cards at End of Generation Before Reproduction**	**Number of Fish Cards After Reproduction**
1		
2		
3		

◆ Analyze and Conclude

1. How did your fish population change over time?

_____

_____

_____

2. Compare the number of fish at the end of each generation. Explain your results.

_____

_____

_____

3. What are some ways this investigation models natural selection?

_____

_____

_____

4. What are some ways in which natural selection differs from this model?

_____

_____

_____

MANAGING FISHERIES *(continued)*

◆ Critical Thinking and Applications

1. How would fishing crews using a net with a large mesh affect the fish population compared to fishing crews using a net with a small mesh?

_____

_____

_____

_____

2. List two other factors not listed in the questions or on the event cards that
would affect the fish population.

_____

3. Think about the effect that an increase in the predator population has on the fish
population. Does this effect apply to all animal populations? Explain your answer.

_____

_____

_____

◆ More to Explore

Choose a different species to investigate. Make your own set of event cards and a
data table. Be sure some events will likely increase the population and some will
likely decrease it. Repeat the activity, using your event cards and data table. Write
a paragraph explaining your results.

E-4

Choosing Packing Materials

◆ Pre-Lab Discussion

You've just opened a box containing the new CD player you bought. You pull out packing material, more packing material, and more packing material. It's obvious why the shippers used all that packing material—dropping the box could damage your CD player. It has to be cushioned against a jolt.

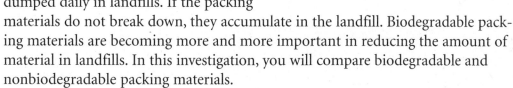

Packing materials are certainly helpful, but there are some problems with them, too. They are among the many materials dumped daily in landfills. If the packing materials do not break down, they accumulate in the landfill. Biodegradable packing materials are becoming more and more important in reducing the amount of material in landfills. In this investigation, you will compare biodegradable and nonbiodegradable packing materials.

1. What makes a material biodegradable?

_____

_____

2. How do biodegradable materials break down in a landfill?

_____

_____

◆ Problem

How do biodegradable packing materials compare to nonbiodegradable packing materials?

CHOOSING PACKING MATERIALS *(continued)*

◆ **Possible Materials** *(per group)*

biodegradable packing material,
    about 1 L
nonbiodegradable packing material,
    about 1 L
2 hard-boiled eggs
2 reclosable plastic bags, 1-L size
2 transparent plastic cups
water
hand lens
metric ruler
several heavy books
balance
graduated cylinder
2 stirring rods

◆ **Safety**   *Review the safety guidelines in the front of your lab book.*

Do not eat or taste any materials in the lab. Wash your hands after the lab.

◆ **Procedure**

Part A: Appearance

1. Do biodegradable and nonbiodegradable packing materials differ in what they look like when viewed through a hand lens? Predict whether their structures will look the same or different. Explain your prediction.

_____

_____

2. Look at both types of packing materials through a hand lens. Record what you observe in the Data Table in the row for Part A.

Part B: Change in Shape

1. To be effective, a packing material must not change much in size or shape while it is being used. Predict which material, if either, will change less in size or shape. Explain your prediction.

_____

_____

2. Design an experiment that compares how well the packing materials withstand forces of compression. Write your procedure on a separate sheet of paper.

3. Have the teacher approve your procedure before you carry out the experiment. Record your results in the Data Table in the row for Part B.

© Prentice-Hall, Inc.

CHOOSING PACKING MATERIALS *(continued)*

Part C: Effectiveness

1. Is one type of packing material more effective than the other type? Predict which type will better protect a fragile object. Explain your prediction.

_____

_____

2. On a separate sheet of paper, design an experiment that compares how well both types of packing materials protect a fragile object such as an egg.

3. Have the teacher approve your procedure before you carry out the experiment. Record your results in the Data Table in the row for Part C.

Part D: Biodegradability

1. What do you think will happen to each type of packing material when you put it into water? Explain your prediction.

_____

_____

2. Design an experiment that compares what happens to each type of packing material in water. Write your procedure on a separate sheet of paper.

3. Have the teacher approve your procedure before you carry out the experiment. Record your results in the Data Table in the row for Part D.

◆ Observations

Data Table

Part	Observations
A	
B	
C	
D	

◆ Analyze and Conclude

1. How do your predictions compare with your observations? For each prediction that differs from the observations, explain why it differs.

_____

_____

_____

CHOOSING PACKING MATERIALS *(continued)*

2. How do air pockets make a packing material useful?

_____

_____

_____

3. What factors did you keep constant in Part B?

_____

_____

◆ Critical Thinking and Applications

1. Do you think that breaking apart in water is a good way for a packing material to degrade? Give a reason for your answer.

_____

_____

_____

2. What other uses can you think of for a material that breaks down in water?

_____

_____

3. What are some disadvantages of using biodegradable materials as packing materials?

_____

_____

4. If you were shipping a fragile gift to a friend, which of the two packing materials from this lab would you use? Why?

_____

_____

_____

◆ More to Explore

Think about other materials that would make good packing materials and are biodegradable. Examine several of these materials. For each, explain why it would or would not be a practical packing material. Predict its effectiveness at protecting a package's contents. On a separate sheet of paper, write a procedure you could use to test your predictions. Have the teacher approve your procedure before you carry out your investigation.

E-5

Pollution Prevention With Rocks

◆ Pre-Lab Discussion

Pollution that increases the acidity of lakes and streams is not a new problem. For millions of years, natural sources of air pollution, such as volcanoes, have released materials that react with rainwater to produce acids. However, the problem has increased as more pollutants enter the air from industry and motor vehicles. Acid rain pollutes land and water, harming the life found there. Because wind can carry these pollutants a long way, the problem is not limited to areas with extensive industry and lots of traffic.

Another source of acid pollution is water that drains from coal-mining sites. Acids form when water flows through the coal layers and rocks. The polluted water then flows into nearby streams.

To monitor acid content in a stream or lake, scientists test the pH of water. pH indicates how acidic or basic the water is. The pH scale ranges from 0 to 14. Pure water is neutral and has a pH of 7. A solution with a pH less than 7 is an acid, and one with a pH greater than 7 is a base.

In this investigation, you will see how rocks can be used naturally to help solve the problem of acidic lakes and streams.

1. What are two sources of acid pollution?

_____

_____

2. If acid pollution killed most of the plants in a pond, what would happen to the fish population? Give a reason for your answer.

_____

_____

_____

◆ Problem

How can acid pollution from mines be prevented?

POLLUTION PREVENTION WITH ROCKS *(continued)*

◆ Materials *(per group)*

granite chips
limestone chips
vinyl rain gutter, 30–40 cm long
block of wood, about 7 cm high
block of wood, about 10 cm high
plastic bowl or cup
white vinegar, 100 mL
beaker, 250-mL
pH test paper and chart

◆ Safety   *Review the safety guidelines in the front of your lab book. Be careful not to spill any of the materials.*

◆ Procedure

1. Use granite chips to line the bottom of a piece of rain gutter.

2. Set each end of the gutter on a block of wood so that the gutter has a gentle slope. The slope should be gentle enough so that the rocks do not slide.

3. Place a plastic bowl under the lower end of the gutter to catch any liquid that drains through.

4. Pour about 50 mL of vinegar into the beaker.

5. Dip the end of a strip of pH test paper into the vinegar. Match the color of the pH paper to the number on the pH indicator chart. Record the pH in the Data Table.

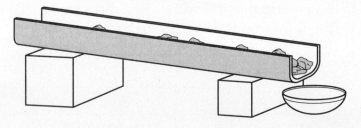

Figure 1

6. Slowly pour the vinegar into the upper end of the gutter, allowing it to flow through the granite to the lower end. Observe what, if anything, happens as the vinegar touches the rocks.

7. Dip the end of a strip of pH test paper into the vinegar that has flowed through the granite and collected in the bowl. Match the color to the chart and record the pH in the Data Table.

8. Remove the rocks from the gutter. Rinse the rocks and the gutter with water.

9. Repeat the experiment, using limestone chips instead of granite.

10. Answer question 1 in Observations.

© Prentice-Hall, Inc.

POLLUTION PREVENTION WITH ROCKS *(continued)*

◆ Observations

Data Table

Type of Rock	pH of Vinegar Before Flowing Through Rocks	pH of Vinegar After Flowing Through Rocks
Granite		
Limestone		

1. What did you observe as you watched the vinegar flow through the rocks in the two trials?

_____

_____

◆ Analyze and Conclude

1. Is vinegar an acid, a base, or neither? Give a reason for your answer.

_____

_____

2. Compare the acidity of vinegar before and after it flowed through the granite and before and after it flowed through the limestone.

_____

_____

_____

3. Use your observations and data to state which rock could be used to help prevent pollution from acid mine drainage. Explain your answer.

_____

_____

◆ Critical Thinking and Applications

1. Some streams flow over limestone. How do you think the limestone affects the pH of the stream?

_____

_____

© Prentice-Hall, Inc.

5

POLLUTION PREVENTION WITH ROCKS (continued)

2. Ditches that are lined with limestone are often seen in coal-mining areas. Would these ditches help prevent pollution of groundwater? Give a reason for your answer.

_____

_____

_____

3. Farmers often spread lime, made from powdered limestone, on their fields. Why do you think they use lime?

_____

_____

_____

4. Powdered limestone is often dumped into lakes that have become highly acidic. Why do you think powdered limestone is used instead of limestone chips?

_____

_____

_____

_____

5. Why wouldn't powered limestone be used in a stream or drainage ditch?

_____

_____

_____

More to Explore

New Problem What other materials could help prevent acid pollution from mines?

Possible Materials Consider which materials you can use from the previous part of this lab. Consider what materials you would like to test.

Safety Wear lab aprons and safety goggles.

Procedure Develop a procedure to solve the problem. Write your procedure on a separate sheet of paper. Have the teacher approve your procedure before you carry out the investigation.

Observations On a separate sheet of paper, make a data table in which to record your data.

© Prentice-Hall, Inc.

Solar Heating

◆ Pre-Lab Discussion

It has been estimated that 1,000 times more energy reaches Earth's surface from the sun each year than could be produced by burning all the fossil fuels mined and extracted during that year. Imagine if people could use even a small fraction of that solar energy; many of our resource and pollution problems would be solved!

The idea of using the sun's energy is not new. Many ancient peoples used solar energy for heating their homes, including the Egyptians, the Greeks, the Romans, and Native Americans. These peoples built their homes facing the south or south-west, where the sun is located in the sky most often in the Northern Hemisphere. This passive solar-heating system, in which sunlight heats an area, is used today to provide renewable, nonpolluting energy. But the sun is not always shining, so the sun's heat must be collected and stored for later use during the night and on cloudy days. This task is usually part of an active solar-heating system, in which solar energy is collected and distributed throughout a building using fans and pumps.

Solar collectors are used to absorb and collect solar energy. A solar collector is basically a box mounted on a roof. The box is covered with a material that absorbs the sun's energy. This energy transfers to air or water in the box and moves into the building where it can be used. In this investigation, you will discover how the color of an object affects the amount of solar energy it absorbs.

1. What forms of energy are constantly given off from the sun?

_____

2. What is the difference between a passive solar-heating system and an active solar-heating system?

_____

_____

_____

◆ Problem

How does the color of an object affect the amount of solar energy it absorbs?

© Prentice-Hall, Inc.

SOLAR HEATING *(continued)*

◆ **Materials** *(per group)*

black and white construction paper
tape
scissors
2 metal or plastic containers with plastic lids
2 thermometers
tongs or gloves
clock or watch
colored pens or pencils

◆ **Safety**   *Review the safety guidelines in the front of your lab book.*

Be careful when using scissors.

◆ **Procedure**

1. Tape two layers of black paper completely around one container. Also tape two layers of black paper over one of the lids. Keep the edge of the lid paper-free so that it will fit on the can. Tape two layers of white paper completely around the other container. Cover its lid with two layers of white paper.

2. Using scissors, carefully punch a small hole through the center of each lid. Each hole should be just large enough to hold a thermometer.

3. Cover each container with its plastic lid of the same color. Place the containers on a sunny windowsill.

4. Carefully insert a thermometer through the hole in each lid as shown in Figure 1. Make sure the bulb of the thermometer is near but not touching the bottom of the container.

5. Record the temperature of the air in each container every 3 minutes for 30 minutes. Record your data in the Data Table. Then answer the questions in Observations.

6. Use the graph paper on page 151 to make a graph of your data. Plot temperature on the vertical axis and time on the horizontal axis.

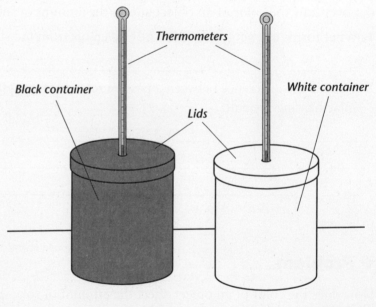

Figure 1

© Prentice-Hall, Inc.

SOLAR HEATING *(continued)*

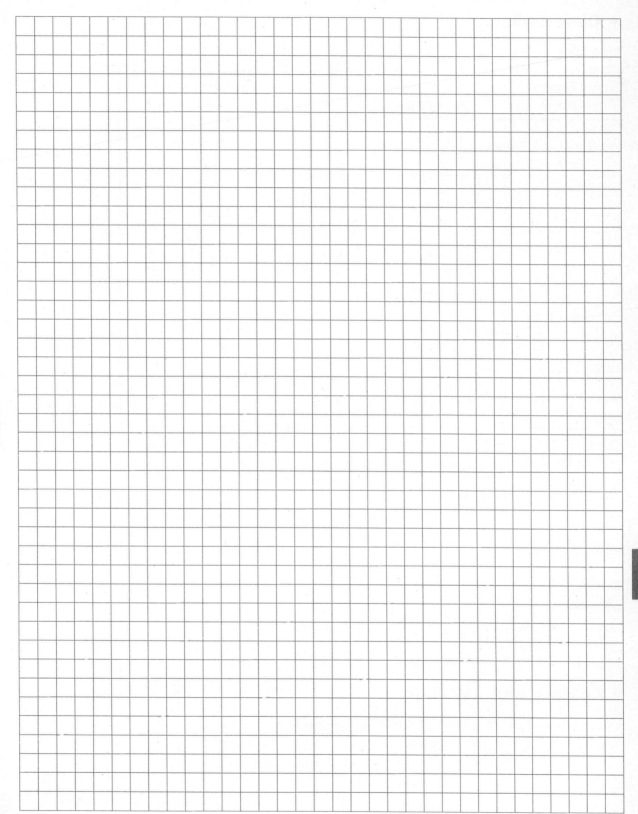

Temperature (°C)

Time (min)

SOLAR HEATING *(continued)*

◆ Observations

Data Table

Time (min)	Temperature in Black Container (°C)	Temperature in White Container (°C)
0		
3		
6		
9		
12		
15		
18		
21		
24		
27		
30		

1. During which time interval did the temperature in the black container begin to rise? During which time interval did the temperature in the white container begin to rise?

_____

_____

2. What was the final temperature of the air in the black container? In the white container?

_____

_____

◆ Analyze and Conclude

1. Did the color of the containers affect the amount of solar energy they absorbed? Explain your answer.

_____

_____

_____

© Prentice-Hall, Inc.

SOLAR HEATING *(continued)*

2. Did your experiment represent a passive or an active solar-heating system? Explain.

_____

_____

3. What additional variables might have affected your results?

_____

_____

_____

◆ Critical Thinking and Applications

1. Why was it important that both containers be the same size?

_____

_____

_____

2. How would this system need to be modified if it were to be used to heat a home?

_____

_____

3. Based on the results of this experiment, what color clothing would best help you stay warm in the winter? Cool in the summer? Explain.

_____

_____

_____

4. In what other situations would you be able to apply the knowledge you gained in this investigation? Consider surfaces used both indoors and outdoors, in which heat absorption or reflection is important.

_____

_____

_____

5. What are some advantages of solar energy compared with fossil fuels?

_____

_____

_____

6

SOLAR HEATING *(continued)*

◆ More to Explore

New Problem What effect do different colors (other than black and white) have on the absorption of solar energy?

Possible Materials Consider which materials you can use from the lab. What other materials might you need?

Safety Be careful when using sharp scissors.

Procedure Make a hypothesis based on the question you want to investigate. Upon what do you base your hypothesis? Make sure to include a control for analyzing and comparing results. Write your procedure on a separate sheet of paper. Have the teacher approve your procedure before you carry out your investigation.

Observations Keep records of your observations on a separate sheet of paper.

Analyze and Conclude

How effective are the different colors at absorbing heat from the sun?

_____

_____

6

© Prentice-Hall, Inc.

F-1   **LABORATORY INVESTIGATION**

Mapping a Future World

1

◆ Pre-Lab Discussion

You can't feel the land underneath you moving every day, but it is! The surface of Earth is divided into continents and oceans. These landmasses and water bodies are slowly but surely changing their positions and shapes. Scientists have measured these movements of a few centimeters a year.

What will Earth look like in the future? No one can be sure where the continents will end up. In this investigation, you will predict what Earth will look like as you map the movement of the continents.

1. What are plates in the Earth's crust?

_____

_____

2. What does plate tectonics mean?

_____

_____

◆ Problem

Where will the continents be in the distant future, and how will their position affect mountains and oceans around the world?

◆ Materials *(per group)*

2 outline maps of the world showing
   latitude and longitude lines
scissors
colored pencils or markers
envelope
pencil or pen
clear tape
world map or globe

◆ Safety *Review the safety guidelines in the front of your lab book.*

Use caution in handling sharp scissors.

MAPPING A FUTURE WORLD (continued)

◆ Procedure

1. You will ignore the movement of Antarctica in this activity. Label the other continents and the oceans on the two outline maps.

2. You will need reference points when you start moving continents. Use a world map or globe to locate and label one city on each continent on both of the maps. In Data Table 2 in Observations, record the current latitude and longitude of each reference-point city.

3. From one map, carefully cut out the continents. Keep these pieces in an envelope when you are not using them.

4. Assemble a complete world map—the base map—by cutting out the map on one page and overlapping it with the map on the other page. The 20°W longitude lines (also called meridians) should overlay each other. Carefully tape the map together along the 20°W longitude line.

5. Lay the cutout continents on the base map in their current positions. You should be able to slide your cutouts easily over your base map.

6. Predict where the continents will be in 100 million years. Slowly move the continents to where you predict they will be. Trace their outlines lightly in pencil. Assume that the Indo-Australian Plate splits in a few million years, and India and Australia continue to move at the same rate.

7. Now, check your predictions. Use the plate speeds in Data Table 1 and the map in your textbook (p. 43) to find the direction and rate of movement for each plate that carries a continent. Calculate how far each continent will drift in 100 million years. Record these figures in Data Table 2 in Observations.

Data Table 1

Plate	Speed (cm/yr)
African	0.66
Eurasian	0.95
Indo-Australian	8.50
North American	2.31
South American	3.55

8. Use the scale on the base map to help you decide where the continents will be in 100 million years. Slowly move the cutout continents to their new locations. Trace their outlines on your base map, using a different color for each continent. Some continents may overlap in their new positions. Trace the outlines overlapping.

9. Mark and record the new location of each reference point.

10. Compare your completed map to your predictions. Then compare it to those of your classmates and discuss any differences.

MAPPING A FUTURE WORLD *(continued)*

◆ Observations

Data Table 2

Continent	Reference Point	Location Now (Latitude and Longitude)	Distance Traveled in 100 Million Years	Location in 100 Million Years (Latitude and Longitude)
Africa				
Asia				
Australia				
Europe				
North America				
South America				

◆ Analyze and Conclude

1. How did your predicted locations of continents compare with the locations in Step 8?

_____

2. What will happen to the location of North and South America as sea-floor spreading widens the Atlantic Ocean?

_____

3. What will happen to the size of the Pacific Ocean as North America moves west?

_____

4. How did the latitude and longitude of your reference point in South America change?

_____

_____

5. What might happen to the Himalayas over the next several million years? Give a reason for your answer.

_____

_____

MAPPING A FUTURE WORLD *(continued)*

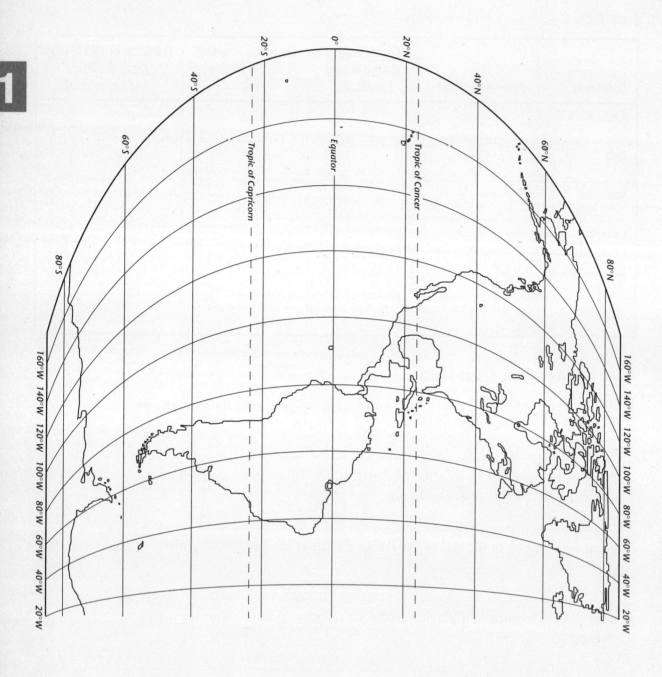

MAPPING A FUTURE WORLD *(continued)*

Scale

0 1000 2000 3000 4000 km

MAPPING A FUTURE WORLD *(continued)*

◆ Critical Thinking and Applications

1. Why did many scientists not accept the early theories of continental drift?

_____

_____

2. Based on your movements of the continents, where do you predict new mountain ranges will be forming in 100 million years? Explain your reasoning.

_____

_____

_____

3. Why do continents move at different rates?

_____

_____

4. Which is more important in determining the future location of a city—what continent it is on or what plate it is on? Give a reason for your answer.

_____

_____

◆ More to Explore

New Problem Near what city's location will Los Angeles, California, be in about 17 million years? (Hint: The rate of plate movement along the San Andreas Fault is about 3.4 cm/yr.)

Possible Materials Use the same map and continent shapes as before. You may also need scissors again.

Safety Use caution in handling sharp scissors.

Procedure Predict where Los Angeles will be. Then develop a procedure to test your prediction. Get the teacher's approval before carrying out your investigation.

Observations Record your prediction. Also record any appropriate observations on your base map.

Analyze and Conclude Where do you think Los Angeles will be located in about 17 million years?

F-2   LABORATORY INVESTIGATION

Investigating the Speed of Earthquake Waves

◆ Pre-Lab Discussion

An earthquake produces waves that travel away from the earthquake's epicenter, like ripples on a pond when you throw in a pebble. An earthquake produces three types of waves, primary (P waves), secondary (S waves), and surface waves. Seismologists track how far and how fast P and S waves travel to find the epicenter of the quake.

In this investigation, you will construct a travel-time graph for P and S waves. You will use the graph to answer some questions about earthquakes.

1. What causes an earthquake?

_____

_____

2. What is the epicenter of an earthquake?

_____

_____

◆ Problem

How can you use a graph of earthquake waves' travel distance and time to find an epicenter?

◆ Materials *(per group)*

pen or pencil

◆ Procedure

1. An earthquake produced P and S waves that were recorded by instruments at 20 stations. These waves are listed in the Data Table on the next page. The table shows the distance traveled and the travel time for each wave. Using these data, construct a graph showing the relationship between the distance traveled by P and S waves and their travel times. Label the curves *P wave* or *S wave*.

2. Use your graph to answer the questions.

INVESTIGATING THE SPEED OF EARTHQUAKE WAVES *(continued)*

Data Table

Wave Type	Distance Traveled From Epicenter (km)	Travel Time (min)	(s)
P	1600	3	20
P	6500	9	50
P	5400	8	40
P	2000	4	00
P	9600	12	40
P	700	1	30
P	7000	10	20
P	3400	6	10
P	8800	12	00
P	4000	7	00
S	2200	8	00
S	4000	12	40
S	5200	15	20
S	1700	6	30
S	6000	17	00
S	1100	4	20
S	7400	19	40
S	8200	21	00
S	500	2	10
S	9000	22	10

2

INVESTIGATING THE SPEED OF EARTHQUAKE WAVES *(continued)*

◆ Observations

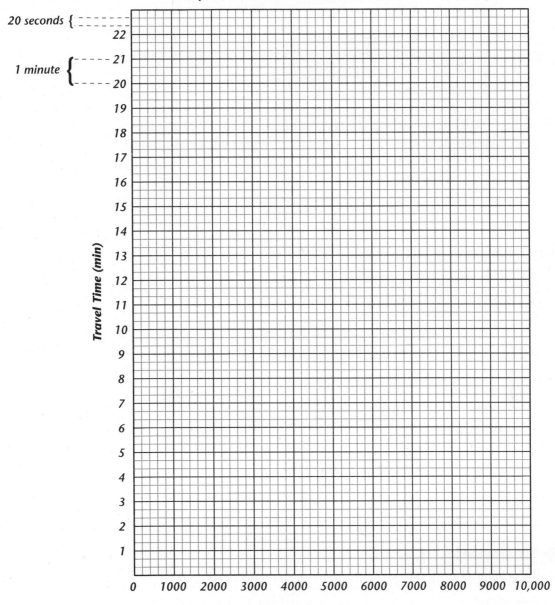

Earthquake S Wave and P Wave Travel-Time Graph

◆ Analyze and Conclude

1. If an earthquake occurred near you, would P waves or S waves reach you first? Give a reason for your answer.

_____

_____

INVESTIGATING THE SPEED OF EARTHQUAKE WAVES *(continued)*

2. How long would a P wave take to travel 8000 km from an earthquake epicenter? How long would an S wave take to travel the same distance?

_____

_____

3. Approximately how far is an observer from an earthquake epicenter if he or she observed a P wave 8 min after the earthquake?

_____

4. How could you tell which of two observers was farther from an earthquake epicenter by comparing the arrival times of P and S waves for the two locations?

_____

_____

◆ Critical Thinking and Applications

1. How far from an earthquake epicenter is an observer who measured a difference of 8 min 40 s in the arrival times of P and S waves?

_____

2. If a curve for surface waves was added to the graph, where would it appear? Explain.

_____

3. States along the West Coast, such as California and Washington, have much earthquake and volcanic activity. What does this activity indicate about the underlying rock structure of this part of the country?

_____

_____

◆ More to Explore

Tie a piece of colorful yarn to a coil near the middle of a spring toy. Move the spring to create a P wave. Then move the spring to create an S wave. Which wave travels faster? Which kind of wave produces the most overall motion of the yarn? Which wave would cause more damage as a seismic wave?

F - 3 · **LABORATORY INVESTIGATION**

Predicting Lava Flows

◆ Pre-Lab Discussion

You know that a liquid becomes a solid if its temperature is lowered enough that the substance freezes. If you freeze a mixture of cream, eggs, and flavoring in an ice-cream maker, the result is ice cream. When the molten wax on a candle cools, it turns into a solid. The type of material that results depends on the liquid you started out with.

Volcanic rocks form on Earth's surface when lava cools and "freezes." But are all rocks formed from lava the same?

Because different types of lava are made from different materials, they also behave differently when they flow on Earth's surface and harden into rock. Two main types of lava differ in how easily they flow because of their silica content. In this investigation, you will relate the ease of flow of different types of lava to the shapes of the volcanoes they form.

1. In addition to silica content, what are two other differences between different types of lava?

_____

2. If you are comparing how easily different types of lava flow, why do you have to make sure that the temperature of each is the same?

_____

_____

◆ Problem

How do the temperature and composition of lava affect the way it flows?

◆ Possible Materials *(per group)*

molasses, about 20 mL	graduated cylinder, 100 mL
cornstarch, about 25 mL	water
spoon	paper towels
watch or clock with second hand	newspaper
	meterstick
cookie sheet or food tray	3 paper cups or beakers, at least 100 mL each

PREDICTING LAVA FLOWS *(continued)*

◆ **Safety** 🧍 🥽 🗑 🧹 *Review the safety guidelines in the front of your lab book.*

Wear a lab apron and safety goggles while doing this activity.

◆ Procedure

Part A: Modeling Types of Lava

1. Add about 25 mL of cornstarch to a cup or beaker. Add about 25 mL of water, a small amount at a time, to the cornstarch while mixing. A runny mixture, about the thickness of milk, should result. This mixture is a model of low-silica lava.

2. To model high-silica lava, use a spoon to place about 5 mL of molasses into a different cup or beaker.

3. Compare and contrast the thickness of the two types of "lava." Predict which type will move faster down a slope. Explain your reasoning.

_____

_____

   Design an experiment to test your prediction. Write your procedure on another sheet of paper.

4. Decide what types of data you will need to collect. Add columns, rows, and headings to the Data Table in Observations as appropriate.

5. After the teacher has approved your procedure and Data Table, conduct your investigation.

Part B: Modeling Lava at Different Temperatures

1. Use molasses to investigate the effect of temperature on lava flow.

2. Predict whether a hot sample or a room-temperature sample of molasses will move faster down a slope. Explain your reasoning.

_____

_____

3. Design an experiment to test your prediction. Write down your precedure on a separate sheet of paper. Repeat Steps 4 and 5 from Part A. Obtain a hot sample of molasses from your teacher.

4. Follow any special instructions the teacher gives you about cleaning up your work area. Throw any "lava" materials, paper towels, and newspaper in the trash can. Do not wash any materials down the drain. Wash your hands after everything else is cleaned up.

© Prentice-Hall, Inc.

PREDICTING LAVA FLOWS *(continued)*

◆ Observations

Data Table

◆ Analyze and Conclude

1. In Part A, which type of "lava" flowed slower, high-silica or low-silica "lava"? In Part B, which type of "lava" flowed slower, hot "lava" or room-temperature "lava"?

_____

2. Compare two types of lava: pahoehoe and aa. How are they similar? How are they different? How were these two types of lava represented in this experiment?

_____

_____

_____

3. On the left below, sketch and name the type of volcano that would be formed from low-silica lava. On the right below, sketch and name the type of volcano that would be formed from high-silica lava.

4. Describe the kind of eruptions you would expect as a volcano forms from low-silica lava.

_____

PREDICTING LAVA FLOWS *(continued)*

5. Describe the kind of eruptions you would expect as a volcano forms from high-silica lava.

_____

◆ Critical Thinking and Applications

1. How does the shape of a volcano help you draw conclusions about the type of magma near the surface beneath the volcano?

_____

_____

_____

2. What type of magma occurs near the surface beneath a composite volcano? Give a reason for your answer.

_____

_____

_____

◆ More to Explore

New Problem How does the gas content in magma affect the shape of a volcano?

Possible Materials
   modeling clay
   vinegar
   baking soda
   paper towels

Safety Wear safety goggles and laboratory aprons.

Procedure Develop a plan to determine how volcano shape depends on the gas content of the magma. Write the steps of your plan on another sheet of paper. Have the teacher approve your plan before you carry out your investigation. (*Hint:* Vinegar and baking soda will react to form a gas.)

Observations Record your observations in a data table on a separate sheet of paper.

Analyze and Conclude Based on your observations, write a statement of how the gas content of magma is related to the shape of the volcano.

_____

_____

_____

F-4   LABORATORY INVESTIGATION

How Tessellating!

◆ Pre-Lab Discussion

A floor covered with tiles may be made of repeated squares. A honeycomb is made of repeated hexagons. Crystal shapes within a mineral have definite repeating patterns, too. A pattern tessellates if it repeats and covers a plane (such as a sheet of paper, a floor, or a wall) with no gaps or overlaps. See Figure 1. In this investigation, you will model crystal shapes by creating patterns that tessellate.

Figure 1

Sample Tessellation

1. Think about what makes up a mineral. Why isn't coal a mineral?

_____

_____

_____

2. How many sides does a hexagonal figure have?

_____

◆ Problem

What patterns tessellate?

◆ Materials *(per group)*

    index cards
    tape
    scissors
    plain white paper
    colored pencils
    ruler

HOW TESSELLATING! *(continued)*

◆ **Safety** ✂ *Review the safety guidelines in the front of your lab book.*

Use caution in handling sharp scissors.

◆ **Procedure**

1. Use a ruler and scissors to carefully cut simple geometric shapes with straight edges from an index card. Begin with squares, rectangles, or hexagons. The simpler the shape, the easier it will be to get it to tessellate.

2. Tape the pieces of the card together to form an interesting new shape that you think will tessellate. Remember, if you make your shape very complicated, you will have trouble getting it to repeat.

3. Trace your new shape repeatedly onto a piece of paper. Does the shape tessellate? Sketch it in the appropriate space in the Observations section below. If it doesn't tessellate, try taping the pieces in a different arrangement or make a different pattern. Sketch shapes that do not tessellate in the appropriate space below.

4. Once you get a shape to tessellate, cover the entire area in the Observations section on the next page with your design.

5. Look for other patterns that tessellate in your design. Can you find any? Use colored pencils to outline several different shapes that tessellate.

◆ **Observations**

Patterns That Tessellate	*Patterns That Don't Tessellate*

HOW TESSELLATING! *(continued)*

Tessellation

◆ Analyze and Conclude

1. Did your first pattern tessellate? With what basic geometric shape did you begin?

_____

2. Could you use a circle or an oval to tessellate? Give a reason for your answer.

_____

_____

3. A mineral has a definite crystal shape, as shown in your textbook (p. 124). Which crystal shapes tessellate? Are any of the shapes the same as the ones that tessellated for you?

_____

_____

HOW TESSELLATING! *(continued)*

◆ Critical Thinking and Applications

1. How is your tessellating pattern like a crystal's shape?

_____

_____

_____

2. List examples of tessellating patterns in your everyday life.

_____

_____

3. How does your model of tessellating patterns differ from actual crystal shapes?

_____

_____

◆ More to Explore

The crystals found within all minerals form tessellating patterns. Almost all of these patterns have another interesting property—symmetry. A pattern has symmetry if it looks exactly the same on either side of a center line through the pattern.

New Problem How can you determine whether your pattern has symmetry?

Possible Materials Use your tessellating pattern from the previous activity. Think of how you could use a mirror to find out if your pattern tessellates.

Safety Use caution in handling any sharp items or items that could break.

Procedure Write a procedure you would follow to answer the question. Have the teacher approve your procedure before you carry out the investigation.

Observations Make a drawing of your shape that shows how the pattern does or does not have symmetry.

Analyze and Conclude

1. Does your shape have symmetry? How do you know?

_____

2. What are some examples of symmetry in nature?

_____

F-5   LABORATORY INVESTIGATION

Making Models of Sedimentary Rocks

◆ Pre-Lab Discussion

Layers of rock that formed at the bottom of ancient seas in some cases now lie exposed, thousands of meters above sea level. The processes that formed this rock lasted millions of years. So did the Earth movements that exposed the rock, pushing and tilting it into high mountains. To study such slow natural processes, scientists and engineers use models in their laboratories to imitate, or simulate, the real thing. They try to give their models the look and feel of actual rock.

The three types of rocks—igneous, metamorphic, and sedimentary—are all formed in different ways. In this investigation, you will create models of sedimentary rocks and explore their properties.

1. How do sedimentary rocks differ from other rocks?

_____

_____

2. What four steps occur during the formation of a clastic sedimentary rock?

_____

◆ Problem

How is sedimentary rock formed, and what are its properties?

◆ Possible Materials *(per group)*

sand	pans
soil	spoons
gravel	water
fossils	paper towels
plaster of paris	streak plate
powdered chalk	materials of known hardness
salt	newspapers

MAKING MODELS OF SEDIMENTARY ROCKS *(continued)*

◆ **Safety**   *Review the safety guidelines in the front of your lab book.*

Wear safety goggles and lab aprons. Wash hands frequently during this activity.

◆ **Procedure**

1. Starting with the list of materials, brainstorm with other students how to create models of sedimentary rocks. You may also be able to collect natural materials outside of your school or near your home. You do not have to use all of the listed the materials. You may want to use other materials as well.

2. **CAUTION:** *Put on your safety goggles and lab apron.* Start to experiment with materials to create your model rocks. How will you form layers? How could your model imitate the pressures that cement particles and fragments into rock? Will the rock layers have fossils?

3. Start to record your rock-making procedures on a separate sheet of paper. Your plans should include all classes of sedimentary rock: clastic, organic, and chemical. What materials can you use to model clastic rock? How will you model layered formations? How can you simulate different-size particles for a conglomerate? How might you model an organic rock? A chemical rock?

4. After the teacher approves your procedure, create your rock models. If your models are not coming out the way you want, modify your procedures. Sketch your rock models in Observations. Set the models aside to dry. Wash your hands when you're finished.

5. When your model rocks are completely dry, explore their properties. Observe and record in the Data Table color, texture, overall hardness, pattern, and resistance to weathering. Resistance to weathering is determined by whether the rock remains intact or crumbles when tested. What type of test could show whether your rock is weak or strong? What other properties should you evaluate? Have the teacher approve any test before you conduct it.

6. Compare models with several classmates. For each model rock, state what type of sedimentary rock it represents, how it was made, and its properties.

◆ **Observations**

Sketches of Sedimentary Rock Models		
Clastic	*Organic*	*Chemical*

© Prentice-Hall, Inc.

MAKING MODELS OF SEDIMENTARY ROCKS *(continued)*

Data Table

Properties of Model Rocks			
	Type of Sedimentary Rock		
Property	**Clastic**	**Organic**	**Chemical**
Color			
Texture			
Hardness			
Pattern			
Resistance to Weathering			

◆ Analyze and Conclude

1. What determines the properties of your model rocks?

_____

_____

2. Why might you choose to have fossils in your rock models?

_____

_____

3. How does compaction during the model-making process change the strength of the model rock?

_____

_____

© Prentice-Hall, Inc.

MAKING MODELS OF SEDIMENTARY ROCKS *(continued)*

◆ Critical Thinking and Applications

1. Compare and contrast the different types of sedimentary rocks.

_____

_____

_____

_____

2. Would the actual rocks that your models represent be a good material to use to build bridges or buildings? Why or why not?

_____

_____

_____

3. What properties of your rocks make them useful or limit their usefulness?

_____

_____

◆ More to Explore

You have seen how sedimentary rocks differ in their resistance to physical weathering. How resistant are they to chemical weathering? Write a procedure you would follow to answer this question. Use actual sedimentary rocks and vinegar. Have the teacher approve your procedure before you carry out the investigation. Wear safety goggles and laboratory aprons while carrying out your procedure.

5

G-1   **LABORATORY INVESTIGATION**

Using a Topographic Map

◆ Pre-Lab Discussion

When was the last time you used a map? Perhaps you used a road map to help plan a trip. You may have looked at a world map to locate a country for a school assignment. Did you ever use a map mounted in a mall to find a certain store? Maps provide a variety of information. They can show not only where something is but what it looks like. That's what topographic maps do. They show the shape of the land by providing a three-dimensional view of Earth's surface. With a little practice, you can read a topographic map and picture the landscape as if you were flying over it in a plane.

Imagine that your class is completing a three-day outdoor education program. You've learned about the plants and animals that live near your town of Mountain View. You've learned about the landforms in the area and how to read them on a topographic map. As a final exercise, the program leader has arranged a treasure hunt. She will fly a plane over the area and drop a bright red canister attached to a bright red parachute. Inside the canister are all kinds of gift certificates for the class. In this investigation, you will use clues and interpret a topographic map to find the canister. To do so, you need to know that each degree of latitude and longitude is divided into units called minutes. One degree is 60 minutes. The number of minutes for a given latitude is listed right after the number of degrees. The symbol for minutes is an apostrophe. The map in Observations shows examples of latitude and longitude using minutes.

1. Explain what a contour line is.

_____

2. What kind of information do contour lines provide?

_____

_____

3. How would you write the latitude of a point that is half way between 35° N and 36°N? Use degrees and minutes.

_____

◆ Problem

How can you use a topographic map to pinpoint a location?

◆ Materials *(per group)*

metric ruler
pencil

USING A TOPOGRAPHIC MAP *(continued)*

◆ Procedure

The Program Leader has sent the following radio message from her plane: "Attention outdoor ed. students . . . heading northwest . . . over crossroads and school . . . marsh on my left . . . following river . . . over woods now . . . cliff approaching . . . turning northeast . . . crossing river . . . winds are calm . . . tree-tops . . . CANISTER AWAY!"

1. Use the message and the topographic map in Observations to determine where the pilot started sending the message.

2. Trace on the map the probable path taken by the pilot.

3. On the map, shade in an area where you would concentrate your search for the canister.

◆ Observations

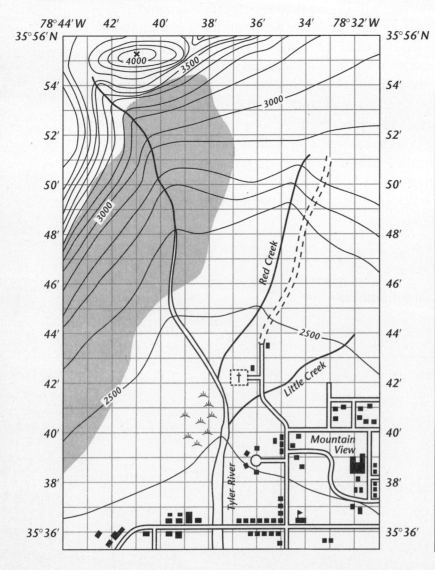

KEY
- ■ Building
- ⚑ School
- [†] Cemetery
- ═ Road
- ╌ Unimproved road
- Marsh
- Woods

0 ½ 1 Mile

0 ½ 1 Kilometer

Contour Interval 100 ft

N
W — E
S

© Prentice-Hall, Inc.

USING A TOPOGRAPHIC MAP *(continued)*

◆ Analyze and Conclude

1. What are the latitude and longitude of the highest elevation on the map?

_____

2. In which direction does the Tyler River flow? How do you know?

_____

_____

_____

_____

3. What clues in the pilot's radio message tell you where to start looking for the canister? What other clues might the pilot have given?

_____

_____

_____

_____

_____

4. What are the latitude and longitude of the most likely place to find the canister? Give a reason for your answer.

_____

_____

_____

_____

_____

5. How far will you have to travel to reach the drop site? Assume that you will travel in a straight line.

_____

◆ Critical Thinking and Applications

1. Look at the area where the canister probably came down. What problems might you have retrieving the canister?

_____

_____

_____

_____

USING A TOPOGRAPHIC MAP (continued)

2. Your class has decided to divide into teams to see which team could find the canister first. What suggestions would you make to your team for getting to the site quickly? Give reasons for your suggestions.

_____

_____

_____

_____

3. Suppose a steady wind is blowing from the west at 18 km/hr. How might this affect your search for the canister?

_____

_____

_____

◆ More to Explore

In the space below, draw a topographic map of a small island. Use the following description. Show direction on the map and state the contour interval.

- The highest point of the island is 172 feet. The island is steeper on the east side than it is on the west side.
- A stream flows from the center of the island northwest to the coast.
- A marsh exists at the shoreline of the west side of the island.

LABORATORY INVESTIGATION

Investigating Soils and Drainage

◆ Pre-Lab Discussion

Suppose that your community has a new soccer field, but it is hard to find a place to park. Many people park on the grass, which is now a muddy mess. Why didn't the water that created the mud just run off the land or soak into the soil? You think the answer to this problem lies in the soil. Different types of soil allow water to drain differently. Sandy soil drains differently than soil containing a lot of clay or soil that doesn't have much sand or clay. In this investigation, you will test how fast water drains through different types of soil.

1. What is soil made of?

_____

_____

2. The size of soil particles gives soil its texture. List the four major types of soil particles in order from largest to smallest.

_____

_____

◆ Problem

How fast does water drain through different types of soil?

◆ Possible Materials *(per group)*

4 plastic 2-L soft-drink bottles with bottoms removed
4 plastic 2-L soft-drink bottles with tops cut off and a hole punched high in the side
4 pieces of gauze or cheesecloth, about 8 cm × 8 cm
4 rubber bands
potting soil
sand
clay mixed with soil
gravel mixed with soil
plastic container, at least 1-L
timer or watch
permanent marker or wax pencil
graduated cylinder or metric measuring cup, 100-mL

© Prentice-Hall, Inc.

INVESTIGATING SOILS AND DRAINAGE *(continued)*

◆ Safety   *Review the safety guidelines in the front of your lab book.*

Wear safety goggles and lab aprons throughout the activity. To prevent slips or falls, wipe up spills immediately.

◆ Procedure

2

1. Read through the entire lab before carrying out your investigation.

2. Design a way to compare how quickly water flows through different soils. Figure 1 shows one possible setup. Write your procedure on a separate sheet of paper. Your procedure should address the following questions:

- What types of soil will you test?

- How much soil and water will you use?

- How will you pour the water: quickly and all at once, or more slowly and continuously?

- When will you start and stop timing?

- What variables will you control?

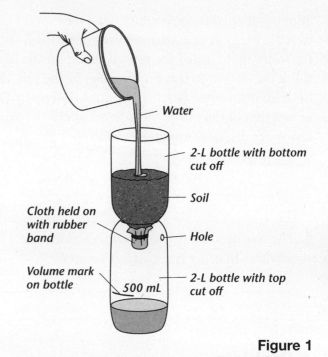

Water

2-L bottle with bottom cut off

Soil

Cloth held on with rubber band

Hole

Volume mark on bottle

500 mL

2-L bottle with top cut off

Figure 1

3. Predict which soil will drain most slowly and which soil will drain most quickly. Give reasons for your predictions.

_____

_____

_____

_____

4. Have the teacher approve your procedure before you carry out the investigation.

5. Fill in the first column of the Data Table in Observations. Record your data in the second column.

INVESTIGATING SOILS AND DRAINAGE *(continued)*

◆ Observations

Data Table

Soil Type	Draining Time

◆ Analyze and Conclude

1. Describe what happens to the water from the time you pour it into the soil until the time it drains into the plastic bottle.

_____

_____

2. Through which soil did water drain the fastest? Why do you think this happened?

_____

_____

_____

3. Do your results agree with your predictions? If they do not, explain why you think they don't agree.

_____

_____

_____

_____

4. What was most surprising about your results?

_____

_____

_____

INVESTIGATING SOILS AND DRAINAGE *(continued)*

◆ Critical Thinking and Applications

1. Why did water drain through the soils at different rates?

_____

_____

2. If you wanted to test other soils, what might you change in your experimental procedure?

_____

_____

3. Why do you think people put gravel on parking lots?

_____

_____

_____

4. Think of what happens to rain that lands on a paved parking lot. What would be an advantage of paving a lot? What would be a disadvantage?

_____

_____

_____

5. Suppose another sports field is being built. What kind of soil should be used for the best drainage? Give a reason for your answer.

_____

_____

_____

_____

◆ More to Explore

Drainage is only one of many considerations when building a sports field. Another concern is how well grass will grow on the field. Is the soil that drains the best able to support a healthy crop of grass? What soil would be best to use for a new field? On a separate sheet of paper, write a procedure to answer these questions. Have the teacher approve your procedure before you carry out your investigation. Be sure to wear safety goggles and a lab apron.

The Daily Grind

◆ Pre-Lab Discussion

A river or stream is more than just water in motion. Such moving bodies of water also carry along rocks and other materials, which change as they move. One kind of change is called mechanical weathering. As the water moves, it repeatedly tosses the rocks against each other and against the sides of the streambed. Each day, little by little, the rocks are ground into smaller and smaller pieces in a process called abrasion. Abrasion is one cause of the mechanical weathering of rocks.

In this investigation, you will model one way that abrasion causes the erosion of rocks. You will also find out how different kinds of rocks are affected by this process.

1. What provides the energy for the abrasion of rocks by rivers and streams?

_____

_____

_____

◆ Problem

How do time and the properties of specific rocks affect the way abrasion weathers rocks?

◆ Materials (per group)

balance
large plastic spoon
100-mL graduated cylinder
plastic jar, approximately 500 mL,
    with screw-on lid
limestone chips, pre-soaked
granite chips, pre-soaked
rock salt, coarse (dry)
fine wire screen
paper towels
water
watch or clock with second hand
graph paper
wide-mouthed plastic jar,
    approximately 1 L
newspapers
paper cups

THE DAILY GRIND *(continued)*

◆ Safety   *Review the safety guidelines in the front of your lab book.*

Use caution in handling any glass equipment. Do not touch broken glass. Report any breakage to your teacher.

◆ Procedure

Part A: Modeling Rock Erosion Over Time

1. Cover your work area with newspaper in case of spills. Obtain two large spoonfuls of pre-soaked limestone chips. Dab them briefly with a paper towel to remove any dripping water. Then use the balance to find the initial mass of the rocks, and record it in Data Table 1. (*Hint:* Find the mass of a dry container such as a paper cup, find the mass of the container plus the rocks, and then subtract to find the mass of the rocks.)

2. Observe the appearance of the rock chips, and record your observations on a separate sheet of paper. Read over the rest of the procedure for Part A. Then, on the same sheet of paper, write a prediction for the way the rocks will change as they are weathered mechanically.

3. Place the rock chips in a plastic jar with a screw-on lid. Add 250 mL of water. Cover the jar, and seal it tightly.

4. Decide on the motion with which you will shake the jar, for example, up and down. You must use that same shaking motion throughout this lab. Shake the jar for exactly 3 minutes.

5. Place a fine wire screen over a second, wide-mouthed jar. Pour the rocks and water onto the screen, letting the water flow into the wide-mouthed discard jar. Be careful not to lose any chips. Briefly dab the wet chips with a paper towel to remove any dripping water. Then measure and record the mass of the rock chips.

6. Return the rocks to the first jar, and repeat Steps 4 and 5 three times. You should have a total of five mass readings in Data Table 1.

7. Observe the appearance of a few of the rocks. Record your observations on a separate sheet of paper.

Part B: Comparing the Erosion of Different Kinds of Rocks

1. In Part B, you will follow the overall procedures from Part A, but you will shake each type of rock for one 3-minute period only. Use Data Table 2 to record the results for Part B.

2. For limestone, find the initial mass of the chips you used in Part A by reading the mass at time 0 in Data Table 1. Record that mass as the original mass of the limestone chips in Data Table 2.

THE DAILY GRIND *(continued)*

3. Find the mass of the limestone chips after 3 minutes in Data Table 1, and record this in Data Table 2 as the Final Mass of the limestone chips.

4. Obtain two spoonfuls of pre-soaked granite chips, dab them briefly with a paper towel to remove excess water, and then find their initial mass. "Weather" the rocks by shaking them for 3 minutes, dab them briefly with a paper towel, and then find their final mass. Record your data in Data Table 2.

5. Obtain two spoonfuls of dry rock salt chips, and find their initial mass. "Weather" them by shaking for 3 minutes. Dab them dry with a paper towel, and then find their final mass. Record your data in Data Table 2.

6. For each type of rock in Data Table 2, find the mass of the rocks lost to weathering by subtracting the final mass from the original mass. Record the results in the fourth column of the data table.

7. For each type of rock in Data Table 2, determine the percent of change in mass using the equation below. Enter the results in the last column of your data table.

$$\frac{\text{mass lost to weathering}}{\text{original mass}} \times 100\% = ?\%$$

◆ Observations

Data Table 1

Weathering Time (min)	Mass of Rocks (g)
0	
3	
6	
9	
12	

Data Table 2

Type of Rock	Original Mass of Rocks (g)	Final Mass of Rocks (g)	Mass of Rocks Lost to Weathering (g)	Percent of Change
limestone				
granite				
rock salt				

THE DAILY GRIND *(continued)*

◆ Analyze and Conclude

1. Graph the results from Part A. Place time on the horizontal axis and mass on the vertical axis. How did the mass of the limestone chips change over time?

_____

_____

2. In Part A, how did the appearance of the limestone chips change over time?

_____

_____

3. In Parts A and B, what happened to the rock that was "lost" to mechanical weathering? In your model, where did that lost rock go?

_____

_____

◆ Critical Thinking and Applications

1. Based on your results from Part A, what can you conclude about the mechanical weathering of rocks carried along by the water in rivers and streams?

_____

_____

_____

2. Based on your results from Part B, what can you conclude about the mechanical weathering of rocks carried by moving water? How might those results be explained?

_____

_____

◆ More to Explore

How does the amount of rock "lost" during abrasion by water compare with the amount of sediment produced? Use ideas from the lab just completed to design an experiment to investigate that question. Your teacher must approve your procedure before you begin. Remember to wear your safety goggles and lab apron while carrying out your procedure.

_____

_____

_____

_____

Exploring Geologic Time Through Core Samples

◆ Pre-Lab Discussion

One way in which scientists study past geologic events is to examine rock layers that are buried beneath Earth's surface. Over a long period of time, sediment and the remains of organisms have been deposited, layer upon layer, and have hardened into rock. Scientists collect rock samples by driving hollow tubes into the rock and withdrawing the tubes with the rock and their fossils inside. This process is called coring. Scientists examine and interpret the core samples, which show the various layers of rock and fossils they contain. In this investigation, you will create sediment deposits to represent rock layers and fossils. You will then take core samples of such deposits and interpret them—just as scientists do.

1. Define the law of superposition.

_____

_____

2. Define index fossils and tell how they help scientists date rocks.

_____

_____

◆ Problem

How are core samples collected and interpreted?

◆ Possible Materials *(per group)*

1-L milk carton, clean and empty
sediments:
    loose clay or red-colored sand
    white-colored sand
    potting soil or mud
    ground-up leaves or grass
fossils (variety of small grains and seeds
    such as rice, barley, millet, lentils,
    and split peas)
mixing bowl
thick plastic drinking straws
wooden or plastic rod that fits into the straw
several sheets of paper
metric ruler

EXPLORING GEOLOGIC TIME THROUGH CORE SAMPLES *(continued)*

◆ **Safety**   *Review the safety guidelines in the front of your lab book.*
Immediately sweep up or wipe up any materials that spill.

◆ **Procedure**

1. Decide on the type and order of the sediments that will be placed in your milk carton. Use at least two different types of sediments. Also decide how you will use fossils in your model. Include at least one type of index fossil.

2. Build your model of sediment layers with fossils. For your bottom layer, take two or three handfuls of the chosen sediment. Mix in a few pinches of "fossils." Place the mixture in the bottom of the milk carton. Add a small amount of water so that the sediments become slightly damp.

3. Continue this process, following your sediment order, until the carton is almost full. You can make the sediment layers of different thicknesses but keep them horizontal. As you build your model, record the sediment order and width, and the type and placement of fossils in the first milk carton in Observations.

4. Exchange your milk carton for a milk carton prepared by another group.

5. Collect a core sample from this container by holding a straw with your fingers near the soil surface and slowly pushing the straw "corer" straight down into the sediments. Push until your straw is close to the bottom of the milk carton.

6. Fold a sheet of paper in half lengthwise. Write *Top* at the top and *Bottom* at the bottom of the paper. You will use the crease to hold the core sample after you have removed the sample from the straw.

7. Gently remove the straw with the sample from the sediment container. Using the rod, carefully push the sediment out of the bottom of the straw into the crease of the folded paper so that the core sample rests in the crease. The top of the sample should be near the top of the paper. See Figure 1.

8. Record the sediments in their correct order by drawing them in the second milk carton in Observations. Measure the height of each layer in centimeters and write the measurements next to the recorded layers.

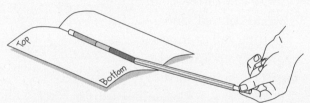

Figure 1

9. Look through the sediment layers one at a time for fossils. Since the fossils are small, you may need to take several core samples to find any fossils. Record the type of fossil (type of bean, seed, and so on) you found and the sediment layer you found it in.

10. Check your results with the group that set up the sediment carton.

EXPLORING GEOLOGIC TIME THROUGH CORE SAMPLES *(continued)*

◆ **Observations**

Your group's layers

Layers from other group

◆ **Analyze and Conclude**

1. In the carton you examined, which layer is the oldest? How do you know?

_____

_____

2. Which layer is the youngest? How do you know?

_____

3. What conclusions can you make from studying the "fossils" in your core samples?

_____

_____

_____

◆ **Critical Thinking and Applications**

1. Why should a geologist exercise great care and patience when taking and preparing a core sample?

_____

_____

_____

EXPLORING GEOLOGIC TIME THROUGH CORE SAMPLES *(continued)*

2. If an earthquake causes a fault to form in these sediments, how could the fault affect the core sample?

_____

_____

3. How could index fossils help a geologist figure out the relative ages of sediment layers after an earthquake?

_____

_____

_____

4. How could a core sample be useful in choosing a site to build a large building?

_____

_____

◆ More to Explore

New Problem How can you make a model of a fossil?

Possible Materials empty quart or half-gallon milk carton, modeling clay, petroleum jelly, plaster of paris, water, bowl, spoon

Safety Wear safety goggles and lab aprons during the activity. Wash your hands when you are finished.

Procedure

1. Choose an extinct animal or plant to represent in a fossil exhibit. Research this organism in the library.

2. Design a procedure for making a fossil by creating a mold of the organism or traces of the organism, such as a footprint. Write the steps for your procedure on a separate sheet of paper.

3. Design a procedure for making a fossil by creating a cast of the organism or traces of the organism from the mold. How will you keep your mold and your cast from sticking together? Write the steps for your procedure on a separate sheet of paper.

4. When the teacher has approved your procedures, carry out the lab.

5. Prepare an information card that includes the name of the organism and the geologic era in which the organism lived. Use your card, your mold, and your cast in a classroom display of fossils.

Analyze and Conclude In terms of fossils, compare and contrast molding and casting.

_____

_____

© Prentice-Hall, Inc.

Properties of Water

◆ Pre-Lab Discussion

Water is the only substance on Earth that commonly exists in all three states—solid, liquid, and gas. Water also has some other unusual properties. In this investigation, you will examine some properties of the substance that covers most of Earth's surface.

1. What are three properties of water that are caused by the attractions among water molecules?

_____

_____

2. Why can water dissolve so many other substances?

_____

_____

◆ Problem

What are some of the unique properties of water?

◆ Materials *(per group)*

plastic cup	distilled water
tap water	hot plate
3-cm square of metal	thermometer, metal
window screening	spoon
dark food coloring	salt
paper towel	hot pad
scissors	wax pencil
250-mL beaker	

◆ Safety 🥽 🧤 👕 🧥 ⚗️ *Review the safety guidelines in your lab book.*

Handle the thermometer carefully. If it breaks, do not touch it and immediately tell your teacher. Use tongs or a hot pad when handling hot objects. Always wear safety goggles when heating objects.

PROPERTIES OF WATER *(continued)*

◆ Procedure

Part A: Surface Tension

1. Fill a plastic cup three-fourths full with tap water.

2. Bend up the sides of the window screening to form the shape shown in Figure 1. Be careful of any sharp edges on the screen.

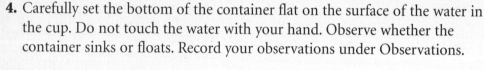

Figure 1

3. Predict what will happen if you place the screening on the water's surface. Explain your reasoning.

_____

_____

4. Carefully set the bottom of the container flat on the surface of the water in the cup. Do not touch the water with your hand. Observe whether the container sinks or floats. Record your observations under Observations.

Part B: Capillary Action

1. Put about 2 cm of tap water in the plastic cup. Add 2 or 3 drops of food coloring to the water.

2. Cut a strip of paper towel about 1 cm wide. Drape it over the lip of the glass so that one end is in the water. See Figure 2.

Figure 2

3. Predict what will happen to the paper strip. Explain your reasoning.

_____

_____

4. Set the cup aside. After about 20 minutes, observe the strip of paper towel. Record your observations under Observations.

Part C: Changing States

1. **CAUTION:** *Put on your safety goggles and apron.* Fill a 250-mL beaker two-thirds full of distilled water. Place the beaker on a hot plate.

2. Heat the water until it boils. Measure the temperature of the boiling water. **CAUTION:** *Handle the thermometer carefully; it is breakable.*

3. Let the water cool slightly. Add a spoonful of salt to the water. Predict how you think adding salt will affect the water's boiling point. Explain your reasoning.

_____

_____

4. Heat the water until it boils and record the temperature of the boiling water in the Data Table under Observations.

5. Repeat Steps 3 and 4 three more times. **CAUTION:** *Use a hot pad or beaker tongs to handle the beaker.*

PROPERTIES OF WATER *(continued)*

◆ Observations

Part A

1. What happened when you placed the screening on the water's surface?

_____

_____

Part B

1. What did you observe about the end of the paper towel that was outside the glass?

_____

Part C

Data Table

	Boiling-Point Temperature
Distilled water	
Distilled water + 1 spoon of salt	
Distilled water + 2 spoons of salt	
Distilled water + 3 spoons of salt	
Distilled water + 4 spoons of salt	

◆ Analyze and Conclude

1. Explain your observations in Part A based on what you know about the surface tension of water.

_____

_____

2. Explain your observations in Part B based on what you know about capillary action.

_____

_____

3. How does dissolving salt in water affect the temperature at which the water boils?

_____

_____

_____

PROPERTIES OF WATER *(continued)*

◆ Critical Thinking and Applications

1. What do you think would happen if you put a penny on the screening? Give a reason for your answer.

_____

_____

2. If you cut off a centimeter from the bottom of a celery stalk and put the cut end into water colored with blue food coloring, in about an hour the stem would be streaked with blue. Explain what happens in terms of capillary action.

_____

_____

_____

3. When some people cook vegetables, they add salt to the cooking water. They say this makes the vegetables cook faster. Are they correct? Give a reason for your answer.

_____

_____

◆ More to Explore

New Problem Does dissolving salt in water change the freezing point of the water?

Possible Materials Consider what materials you will need to use. Write a list of your materials.

Safety Handle thermometers carefully. Wear your safety goggles and apron.

Procedure Write a procedure you could follow to find the answer to the problem. Have the teacher approve your procedure before you carry out the investigation. (Hint: You do not necessarily need to make salt water freeze to answer this question.)

Observations Make a data table and record your observations.

Analyze and Conclude

1. How does dissolving salt in water affect its freezing point?

_____

_____

2. Why do some communities spread salt on icy roads in winter?

_____

_____

© Prentice-Hall, Inc.

H-2

Field Testing a Body of Fresh Water

◆ Pre-Lab Discussion

Fresh water in streams, ponds, rivers, and lakes is far from pure. Fresh water usually contains dissolved substances and a range of sediments suspended in the water. Some suspended substances can make fresh water look dirty and murky. The amount of acid in a substance is measured by pH values. Dissolved substances can sometimes change the pH of water.

Oxygen dissolved in water is necessary for fish to live. Around 4 to 5 mg/L of dissolved oxygen is the lowest amount that will support fish. The presence of nitrogen in the form of nitrate indicates pollution. Nitrates cause the growth of plankton and water weeds that provide food for fish. However, if algae grow too much, oxygen levels will be reduced and fish will die. Nitrate levels below 90 mg/L have little effect on warm-water fish, but cold-water fish are more sensitive to nitrate levels.

Phosphorus can come from phosphate-containing rocks or from fertilizers, detergents, and pesticides. Too much phosphorus causes overgrowth of algae and reduces dissolved oxygen. The recommended maximum for phosphorus is 0.1 mg/L. Most freshwater organisms can live only in water between 0°C and 35°C.

When determining water quality in a body of fresh water, the factors described above are only some of those that must be considered. In this investigation, you will examine a body of fresh water near your school.

1. How do sediments get into fresh water?

_____

_____

2. How is the amount of oxygen in a body of water affected by a large amount of algae in the water? Explain how this might occur.

_____

_____

_____

◆ Problem

What is the quality of a nearby body of fresh water?

FIELD TESTING A BODY OF FRESH WATER *(continued)*

◆ Possible Materials

(per group)

water samples of a stream,
    pond, river, or lake
thermometer
pH paper
graduated cylinders
large test tubes with stoppers
beakers
large jars
hand lens
petri dishes with agar
plankton net
water quality test kits
waterproof boots

◆ Safety   *Review the safety guidelines in the front of your lab book.*

Use caution when near a body of water. Wear waterproof boots. Wash all equipment thoroughly before taking water samples and doing tests. Wash your hands thoroughly after completing this investigation.

◆ Procedure

1. As a class, discuss the bodies of fresh water in your community. Determine which body of water you will examine. The type of water body chosen may influence some of the tests you want to do. For example, if you are investigating a stream or river, you may want to measure water velocity.

2. Some of the tests you may want to perform include the following: temperature, pH, dissolved oxygen, nitrate, phosphorus, suspended solids, dissolved solids, bacteria content, salinity, and types of microorganisms present in the water.

3. With your group, decide what tests you will perform. List the different tests you plan to do in the Planning Table on the next page. Research the methods of doing these tests and read the instructions in the water-testing kits to determine how much water you need to test and what materials you will need.

4. Decide how you are going to gather your water samples. What observations can you make at the water site? You may also want to examine the soil at the water's edge and complete a plant and animal survey in the immediate area around the water.

© Prentice-Hall, Inc.

FIELD TESTING A BODY OF FRESH WATER *(continued)*

Planning Table

Water Test	Amount of Water Needed	Materials Needed to Complete Test

5. Predict whether the water site is polluted. What were the reasons behind your prediction?

_____

_____

_____

6. On a separate sheet of paper, write a procedure to follow to complete your water quality investigation. After the teacher approves your investigation plan, gather your material for the field study. Be sure all of your water-sampling equipment is clean before you use it. You do not want to contaminate your samples.

7. Complete the tests you have decided to do. Use the Data Table provided on the next page to record your observations and the data you gather. If you are doing a plant and animal survey, record your results on a separate sheet. Compare your data with that of other groups in your class.

FIELD TESTING A BODY OF FRESH WATER *(continued)*

◆ Observations

1. What observations can you make at the water site? Is the water clean or dirty? What plants and animals are in the immediate area around the water?

_____

_____

_____

_____

_____

_____

2

Data Table

Water Test	Observations	Test Results

FIELD TESTING A BODY OF FRESH WATER (continued)

◆ Analyze and Conclude

1. The pH of most rivers, lakes, and streams in the United States falls within the range of 6.0 to 8.0. Many species of fish can live in water with this pH range. Would the water in your sample support fish life? Explain.

_____

_____

_____

_____

_____

2. Which of your tests indicates a problem with the body of water you tested? Which did not?

_____

_____

_____

_____

_____

3. How did the plants and animals found in and around the body of water give an indication of water quality?

_____

_____

_____

_____

_____

◆ Critical Thinking and Applications

1. How might the amount of suspended solids in a stream or pond differ if you measured them right after a heavy rainstorm?

_____

_____

_____

_____

_____

© Prentice-Hall, Inc.

FIELD TESTING A BODY OF FRESH WATER *(continued)*

2. Different fish have different temperature requirements. The following list contains the maximum water temperature in which each species of fish can survive.

brook trout	25.5°C
carp	41.0°C
bluegill sunfish	34.3°C
yellow perch	30.8°C
fathead minnow	33.7°C
brown bullhead	34.8°C

Would any of these fish be able to survive in the water you tested? If so, which ones?

_____

_____

_____

_____

_____

3. Water in a swampy or boggy area is usually very acidic, or has a low pH. Imagine that water from a swamp flows into a stream at point A. How do you think the pH of water samples taken upstream and downstream from point A would compare?

_____

_____

_____

_____

◆ More to Explore

If the conditions you found in the fresh water you investigated need improvement, write a plan for steps that should be followed to improve the water quality. Share your plan with the class and mail it along with a cover letter to an appropriate local official or environmental agency.

H-3

Pollution of a Water Supply

◆ Pre-Lab Discussion

Many communities get their water from sources deep in the ground. This groundwater seeps slowly through the pores of sediment and rock layers. The rate of movement depends largely on the slope of the rock layers and the permeability of the rock.

People bring groundwater to the surface in wells. If water is pumped out too fast, a well can go dry. Besides the quantity of groundwater, its quality is also a concern. Many pollutants that contaminate surface water also contaminate groundwater.

In this investigation, you will create a model of a well system and add pollutants. You will study the spread of the pollutants and their effect on the water supply.

1. What are three sources of groundwater pollution?

_____

_____

_____

2. What is the difference between point sources and nonpoint sources of water pollution? Give an example of each.

_____

_____

_____

_____

◆ Problem

How does groundwater pollution affect a community's water supply?

◆ Materials *(per group)*

plastic or transparent glass loaf pan, approximately 10 cm × 20 cm	blue food coloring
2 blocks of modeling clay	paper towels
2 cups of coarse sand	medicine dropper
14 heavy plastic drinking straws	watering can
red food coloring	metric ruler

POLLUTION OF A WATER SUPPLY (continued)

◆ Safety   🔥 *Review the safety guidelines in the front of your lab book.*

To prevent slips or falls, immediately wipe up any water spilled on the floor. Handle glass objects carefully. If they break, tell the teacher. Do not pick up broken glass. Wear safety goggles and an apron at all times.

◆ Procedure

1. Cover the bottom of the pan with a layer of modeling clay to a depth of 1–2 cm. Build it up at one end to create a slope. See Figure 1. Press the clay tightly against the bottom and sides of the pan.

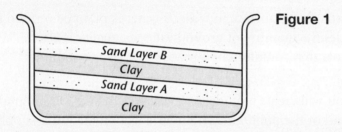

Figure 1

2. Cover the clay with sand. The sand layer should be about 1–2 cm thick and follow the slope of the clay. Lightly sprinkle the sand with water, using the watering can. This is sand layer A.

3. Place a thin layer of modeling clay (about 1 cm thick) on top of the sand, following the slope of the layers below. Press the clay tightly against the sides of the pan.

4. Finally, cover the clay with about 1 cm of sand, following the slope of the layers below. Lightly sprinkle the sand with water. This is sand layer B. Your final model should resemble Figure 1.

5. Hold your finger over the top of a drinking straw. Insert the straw on one side of the model about 5 cm from the highest spot. See Figure 2. The end of the straw should just go into the bottom layer of clay. Withdraw the straw. A slight twist will help to remove it. The clay and sand should come out with the straw, leaving a hole.

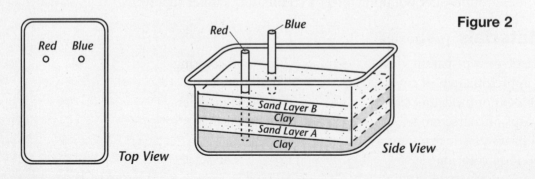

Figure 2

© Prentice-Hall, Inc.

POLLUTION OF A WATER SUPPLY *(continued)*

6. Carefully insert another straw in the same hole to about the same depth. Put five or six drops of red food coloring in the straw. Do not drip the food coloring on the surface of the sand. Remove the straw. Rinse the plastic dropper.

7. Using the same method as in Step 5, insert a third straw in the other side of the pan, but this time just until it touches the **top** layer of clay. Withdraw the straw. Again, the clay and sand should come out with the straw.

8. Carefully insert another straw in the same hole. Put five or six drops of blue food coloring in this straw. Remove the straw carefully.

9. The food coloring represents pollutants that have been introduced into a shallow well (blue) and a deep well (red).

10. Lightly, but thoroughly, sprinkle the surface of the sand with water. This process simulates rainfall. Wait a few minutes for the water to soak into the layers.

11. Insert another straw to the bottom of the pan, uphill or downhill from a well. See Figure 3. Remove it and lay it on a paper towel. Record the sample distance from the original well in the Data Table, and label it *uphill* or *downhill.*

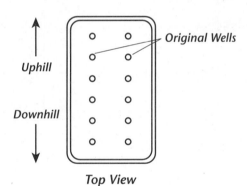

Figure 3

Top View

12. Predict the color of the sand from each sand layer the straw passed through. Record your predictions in the table. Ask your teacher to cut the side of the straw. **CAUTION:** *Do not cut the straw yourself.* Examine the contents of the core, and record your observations in the table. Note any color, how strong the color is, and in which sand layer the color appears.

13. Using the method in steps 11 and 12, take ten core samples uphill and downhill in a straight line from both wells. See Figure 3. Record your predictions and your observations.

POLLUTION OF A WATER SUPPLY *(continued)*

◆ Observations

Data Table

Core Sample	Distance From Well (Indicate Uphill or Downhill)		Color			
			Sand Layer A		Sand Layer B	
	Red Well	Blue Well	Prediction	Actual	Prediction	Actual
1						
2						
3						
4						
5						
6						
7						
8						
9						
10						

1. In which direction do the pollutants travel faster? Why?

_____

_____

_____

_____

POLLUTION OF A WATER SUPPLY (continued)

2. In which sand layer do the pollutants travel faster? Why?

_____

_____

_____

_____

◆ Analyze and Conclude

1. What does the modeling clay represent?

_____

2. Did you find any red coloring in sand layer B? Why or why not?

_____

_____

3. Did you find any blue coloring in sand layer A? Why or why not?

_____

_____

4. Which sand layer is harder to pollute from the surface? Why?

_____

5. Which sand layer is harder to purify if it does become contaminated? Why?

_____

◆ Critical Thinking and Applications

1. How could wastes buried in soil eventually pollute the groundwater?

_____

_____

_____

2. How does the pollution of groundwater differ from the pollution of surface water?

_____

_____

_____

_____

POLLUTION OF A WATER SUPPLY (continued)

3. Do you agree that water in deep wells is less likely to be polluted than water in more shallow wells? Give a reason for your answer.

_____

_____

_____

_____

◆ More to Explore

New Problem How do different kinds of sediments affect the movement of pollutants?

Possible Materials Consider which materials you can use from the previous part of this lab. Choose additional materials to represent different sediments.

Safety Wipe up spills immediately. Handle glass objects carefully. Be sure to wear your safety goggles and apron.

Procedure Develop a procedure to solve the problem. Write your procedure in your notebook. Have the teacher approve your procedure before you carry out the investigation.

Observations In your notebook, make a data table similar to the one in the previous part of this lab in which to record your data and observations.

Analyze and Conclude Do certain types of materials act as filters for pollutants? Describe the evidence for your answer.

_____

_____

_____

_____

_____

© Prentice-Hall, Inc.

H-4 **LABORATORY INVESTIGATION**

Density and Salinity

◆ Pre-Lab Discussion

The average salinity of ocean water is 35 parts of salt per thousand parts of water. Ocean salt comes from minerals on land, which dissolve into water that flows over them. Dissolved salts affect water density, and density affects the way ocean waters move and form layers. By studying the salinity of water, oceanographers learn about ocean layers and currents.

In this investigation, you will model ocean water of different salinity and use the models to determine how ocean waters form layers.

1. Define salinity.

_____

_____

2. What causes differences in the salinity of ocean water in different areas?

_____

_____

_____

◆ Problem

How do differences in salinity create layers in ocean water?

◆ Materials *(per group)*

salt	red food coloring
spoon	blue food coloring
balance	3 small plastic foam cups
4 1000-mL beakers	metric ruler
graduated cylinder	tape
water at room temperature	toothpick
250-mL beaker	

◆ Safety *Review the safety guidelines in the front of your lab book.*

To prevent slips and falls, immediately wipe up any water spilled on the floor. Handle glass objects carefully. If they break, tell your teacher. Do not pick up broken glass.

DENSITY AND SALINITY *(continued)*

◆ Procedure

1. Make a 5% salt solution: Measure 50 g of salt and pour it into a 1000-mL beaker. Add 950 mL of water to the beaker. Stir until all the salt dissolves.

2. Make a 10% salt solution: Measure 10 g of salt and pour it into the 250-mL beaker. Add 90 mL of water to the beaker. Stir until all the salt dissolves. Add enough blue food coloring to make the water deep blue.

3. Fill a second 1000-mL beaker with 400 mL of water.

4. Pour 10 mL of the 5% salt solution into a plastic foam cup. Add enough red food coloring to make the water deep red. Tape the cup inside the beaker of water, so that the bottom of the cup is just below the water level. See Figure 1.

Figure 1

5. Holding the plastic foam cup steady, use a toothpick to poke a small hole near the bottom of the cup.

6. Be careful not to bump the beaker. Observe what happens to the colored water. Record your observations in the Data Table. Sketch and color what you observe.

7. Fill the third 1000-mL beaker with 5% salt solution to within 10 cm of the top.

8. Pour 10 mL of the blue 10% salt solution into the second plastic foam cup. As before, tape the cup inside the beaker so that the bottom of the cup is just below the water level.

9. Repeat Steps 5 and 6.

10. As a control, fill the fourth 1000-mL beaker with 5% salt solution to within 10 cm of the top. Pour 10 mL of tap water into the third plastic foam cup. Add blue food coloring to the tap water until the tap water is the same color as the 10% salt solution in Step 2. Tape the cup to the inside of the beaker as before. Repeat steps 5 and 6.

© Prentice-Hall, Inc.

DENSITY AND SALINITY *(continued)*

◆ Observations

Data Table

	Observations	Sketch
5% red salt solution in tap water		
10% blue salt solution in 5% salt solution		
Blue tap water in 5% salt solution		

◆ Analyze and Conclude

1. Which water was the least dense? The most dense? Explain your reasoning.

_____

_____

_____

2. How does the amount of salt dissolved in water affect its density? Give the evidence that supports your answer.

_____

_____

_____

DENSITY AND SALINITY *(continued)*

3. In the ocean, where would you expect to find water with the greatest salinity? Give a reason for your answer.

_____

_____

_____

◆ Critical Thinking and Applications

1. Predict how the following kinds of water would form layers: (1) warm, slightly salty water; (2) cold, slightly salty water; (3) cold, very salty water; (4) warm rainwater. List them in order, starting with the deepest layer. Give a reason for your answer.

_____

_____

_____

_____

_____

2. Why was it important that all the water in the experiment was the same temperature?

_____

_____

_____

3. Would you expect the salinity to be high or low in the ocean off the coast of a hot, dry area? Give a reason for your answer.

_____

_____

_____

◆ More to Explore

What would happen if you added red 5% salt solution and blue 10% salt solution from two cups at the same time to a container of tap water? Develop a hypothesis for this problem. Then write a procedure you would follow to test your hypothesis. Have the teacher approve your procedure before you carry it out. Remember to wear your safety goggles and apron.

Microscopic Marine Life

◆ Pre-Lab Discussion

Much marine life is too small to see without a microscope. But these tiny organisms play an important role in marine habitats. They serve as food for larger organisms. At the base of all food webs are algae plankton that use sunlight to produce their own food. Their cells contain chlorophyll, a green pigment. In turn, these plankton become food for other organisms.

In this investigation, you will examine and compare microscopic organisms that live in the ocean.

1. What are plankton?

_____

_____

2. Describe the two major groups of plankton.

_____

_____

_____

◆ Problem

What can you learn about plankton by observing them?

◆ Materials *(per group)*

prepared slides of
    marine plankton
compound microscope
colored pencils

◆ Safety   *Review the safety guidelines in the front of your lab book.*

Always use both hands to pick up or carry a microscope. Hold the microscope base with one hand and the microscope arm with your other hand. Handle glass slides carefully.

◆ Procedure

1. Place a slide under the clips on the microscope stage. Adjust the mirror or lamp to shine light through the slide. **CAUTION:** *If the microscope has a mirror, do not use direct sunlight as a light source. Direct sunlight can damage your eyes.*

MICROSCOPIC MARINE LIFE *(continued)*

2. Watching the microscope from the side, use the coarse-adjustment knob to lower the low-power objective slowly until it is close to the slide. Do not let the objective touch the slide. Look into the eyepiece and raise the tube until you can see the organism. You may need to move the slide slightly to center the organism. Use the fine-adjustment knob to focus the image.

3. In Observations, record the name of the organism. Then draw and color what you see under the low-power lens. Record the magnification of the low-power lens.

4. Turn the revolving nosepiece to move the high-power objective into place. Carefully focus the image with the fine-adjustment knob. **CAUTION:** *Never focus the high-power objective with the coarse-adjustment knob. The objective could break the slide.*

5. Draw and color what you see under the high-power lens. Record the magnification of the high-power lens.

6. Repeat steps 1–5 with each slide.

◆ Observations

Name of Organism	View Under Low Power Magnification: _____	View Under High Power Magnification: _____
_____ _____		
_____ _____		

5

Name _____ Date _____ Class _____

MICROSCOPIC MARINE LIFE *(continued)*

Name of Organism	View Under Low Power Magnification: _____	View Under High Power Magnification: _____
_____ _____		
_____ _____		
_____ _____		
_____ _____		

MICROSCOPIC MARINE LIFE *(continued)*

◆ Analyze and Conclude

1. Were all the organisms you observed single-celled? If not, which ones were not?

_____

2. What similarities did you observe in the organisms?

_____

_____

_____

3. What differences did you observe in the organisms?

_____

_____

_____

◆ Critical Thinking and Applications

1. Which of the organisms you observed produced their own food through photosynthesis? Give a reason for your answer.

_____

_____

2. Which of the organisms you observed relied on other plankton as a food source? Give a reason for your answer.

_____

_____

3. Explain how an organism can be part of the plankton at one stage of its life and part of the nekton at another stage.

_____

_____

_____

◆ More to Explore

What do snails in an aquarium eat? Observe the activity of snails in an aquarium. Using toothpicks, scrape some green film from an aquarium glass and other surfaces. Make slides of your samples and examine them using a microscope. Wear your safety goggles. Wash up after completing the activity.

© Prentice-Hall, Inc.

I-1   LABORATORY INVESTIGATION

Examining Acid Rain

◆ Pre-Lab Discussion

Moisture in the air dissolves many pollutants. When the moisture falls as rain or snow, it removes the pollutants from the air. In many cases, this process is beneficial because it cleans the air. When the pollutants in the moisture are nitrogen oxides and sulfur oxides, however, the result is acid rain.

How can you tell whether rain is acidic? The process is simple. You dip specially treated paper in rainwater and compare the color of the paper to a pH color scale. The pH scale ranges from 0 to 14 and is a measure of how acidic or basic a substance is. Pure water is neutral and has a pH of 7. Solutions with a pH greater than 7 are basic, and those with a pH less than 7 are acidic. The lower the number, the more acidic the solution is. Grapefruits, lemons, vinegar, and other sour foods are acidic.

In this investigation, you will use pH indicator paper to determine the pH of some common substances. You will examine how acids affect materials used for buildings, statues, and other structures.

1. What acids are likely to be in acid rain?

_____

2. What is the main source of the pollutants that cause acid rain?

_____

_____

◆ Problem

How can acid rain affect building materials?

◆ Possible Materials *(per group)*

distilled water   pH indicator paper
lemon juice   8 beakers, 100 mL
white vinegar   glass marker
carbonated water   2 small samples each of limestone,
pH scale   sandstone, marble, and granite
balance

◆ Safety   *Review the safety guidelines in this lab book.*

To prevent slips or falls, immediately wipe up any water spilled on the floor. Notify the teacher immediately if any glass breaks.

© Prentice-Hall, Inc.

EXAMINING ACID RAIN *(continued)*

◆ Procedure

Part A: Modeling Acid Rain

1. Read the entire lab before continuing your investigation.

2. You will design an experiment to test the effects of acid rain on building materials. First, you need to decide what you will use for acid rain. Experiment with different solutions. Use the indicator paper to determine the pH of each solution to find out if it is a good model of acid rain. Record your data in Data Table 1.

3. Decide what you will use as a control. Your control should be a solution that has a pH of typical rainwater (5–5.6). Add this information to Data Table 1.

4. Get the teacher's approval of your models before going on to Part B.

Part B: Testing Acid Rain on Materials

1. Brainstorm some materials that buildings, monuments, and other structures are made of. Then decide what building materials you will test and how you will test them. Write your procedure on a separate sheet of paper.

2. Use Data Table 2 to record your observations and other data. Add headings to the data table. Plan to make observations today and tomorrow. You may need to make another data table on a separate sheet of paper for tomorrow's observations.

3. Have the teacher approve your procedure before carrying out your experiment.

4. Predict which building material will be the most affected by acid rain. Which material will be least affected? Give reasons for your predictions.

_____

_____

_____

_____

◆ Observations

Data Table 1

Acid Rain Model (description)	Acid Rain Model (pH)	Control (description)	Control (pH)

EXAMINING ACID RAIN *(continued)*

Data Table 2

Day: _____	Building Material			
Acid Rain Model				
Control				

◆ Analyze and Conclude

1. Did any building material have an immediate reaction that you could see? If so, which one(s), and what was the reaction?

_____

2. Which building material changed the most in a day? How did you measure the change?

_____

_____

3. Which building material changed the least? How did you measure the change?

_____

_____

4. How can acid rain affect buildings, statues, and other structures made of the materials you tested?

_____

_____

_____

◆ Critical Thinking and Applications

1. How would your results have been affected if your acid rain had been more acidic? Less acidic?

_____

_____

_____

© Prentice-Hall, Inc.

EXAMINING ACID RAIN (*continued*)

2. Cleopatra's Needles are large obelisks, each weighing about 200 tons. They are made of red granite and carved with hieroglyphics. Figure 1 shows an obelisk. One of the Needles was shipped from Egypt to New York City in 1880. The New York monument's hieroglyphics have almost disappeared, while a similar monument in the Egyptian desert has changed little over the past 3,000 years. Explain one of the probable reasons this difference exists.

 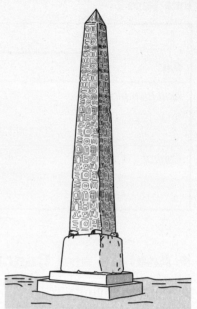

_____

_____

_____

_____

_____

Figure 1

◆ More to Explore

New Problem   How is *Elodea*, a freshwater plant, affected by acid rain falling into a pond where it grows?

Possible Materials   Consider which materials you can use from this lab. What other materials will you need?

Safety   To prevent slips or falls, immediately wipe up any liquid spilled on the floor. Handle glass objects carefully. If they break, tell the teacher. Do not pick up broken glass. Be sure to wear safety goggles and an apron and wash up after you're done.

Procedure   Write a hypothesis about the effects that acid rain has upon *Elodea* plants. Then write a procedure you could follow to test your hypothesis. Have the teacher approve your procedure before you carry out the investigation.

Observations   Keep careful records of your observations on a separate sheet of paper.

Analyze and Conclude

1. Does acid rain affect *Elodea*? Support your conclusions with data collected during the investigation.

_____

_____

2. How might acid rain affect other plants and animals that live in fresh water?

_____

_____

I-2

Using a Psychrometer to Determine Relative Humidity

◆ Pre-Lab Discussion

Even without rain, the air can be very wet because it contains invisible water vapor. The amount of water vapor in the air is known as humidity. As air gets warmer, it can hold more moisture. Meteorologists usually speak of relative humidity—the amount of water vapor in the air compared to the maximum amount that air can hold at a particular temperature.

You can measure relative humidity with a psychrometer, which consists of two thermometers. One thermometer has a dry bulb, and one has a wet bulb. A piece of wet cloth surrounds the bulb of the wet-bulb thermometer. When the wet bulb is exposed to air, water in the cloth evaporates, just as it does from wet clothing. Water evaporation requires heat energy, so it cools the wet bulb.

In this investigation, you will construct a sling psychrometer and use it to measure the relative humidity of the classroom.

1. What is the difference between humidity and relative humidity?

_____

_____

_____

2. Would you expect the temperature of the wet-bulb thermometer to be higher on a humid day or on a dry day? Give a reason for your answer.

_____

_____

_____

◆ Problem

How can you use a psychrometer to find the relative humidity of the classroom?

USING A PSYCHROMETER TO DETERMINE RELATIVE HUMIDITY *(continued)*

◆ Materials *(per group)*

2 identical thermometers
strip of gauze, 10 cm
piece of thread, 20 cm
piece of cardboard, approximately
    20 cm × 30 cm
water at room temperature
transparent tape
bucket
small plastic cup
plastic dropper
large index card

◆ Safety *Review the safety guidelines in the front of your lab book.*

Handle the thermometer carefully. If it breaks, tell your teacher. Do not pick up broken glass.

◆ Procedure

1. **CAUTION:** *Handle the thermometer carefully; it's breakable.* Wrap the gauze around the bulb of one thermometer and tie it in place with the thread.

2. Tape the thermometers side by side with the two bulbs extending over the edge of the cardboard. See Figure 1.

Figure 1

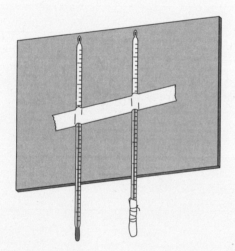

3. Scoop some water from the bucket into a small plastic cup. Use this water and the plastic dropper to thoroughly wet the gauze.

USING A PSYCHROMETER TO DETERMINE RELATIVE HUMIDITY (continued)

4. Hold the cardboard up in the air. Carefully fan the thermometer bulbs with the index card until the temperature of the wet-bulb thermometer stops dropping. Predict the difference in temperatures between the two thermometers. Explain your reasoning.

_____

_____

Read the temperatures on both thermometers. Record these numbers in the data table next to the sample data. Calculate the difference between the two readings.

5. Find the relative humidity in Data Table 1 below, using the temperature difference between the dry bulb and the wet bulb. Express relative humidity as a percentage. For example, suppose the dry-bulb reading is 21°C and the wet-bulb reading is 15°C. The difference is 6°C. The number on the table where the row of the dry-bulb reading (21) and the column of the difference (6) intersect shows the relative humidity (53%). These numbers are included in Data Table 2 as sample data. Record your own data next to them.

Data Table 1: Relative Humidity (%)

Dry-Bulb Reading (°C)	Difference Between Dry-Bulb and Wet-Bulb Readings (°C)									
	1	2	3	4	5	6	7	8	9	10
10	88	76	65	54	43	34	24	15	6	
11	89	78	67	56	46	36	27	18	9	
12	88	78	67	57	48	39	29	21	12	
13	89	79	69	59	50	41	32	23	15	7
14	89	79	69	60	50	42	34	26	18	10
15	90	80	71	61	53	44	36	27	20	13
16	90	80	71	62	54	46	38	30	23	15
17	90	81	72	64	55	47	40	32	25	18
18	91	81	72	64	56	49	41	34	27	20
19	91	82	74	65	58	50	43	36	29	22
20	91	82	74	66	58	53	46	39	32	26
21	91	83	75	67	60	53	46	39	32	26
22	92	83	75	68	60	54	47	40	34	28
23	92	84	76	69	62	55	48	42	36	30
24	92	84	76	69	62	56	49	43	37	31
25	92	84	77	70	63	57	50	44	39	33
26	92	85	77	70	64					

USING A PSYCHROMETER TO DETERMINE RELATIVE HUMIDITY *(continued)*

◆ Observations

Data Table 2

	Sample Data	Your Data
Dry-bulb reading	21°C	
Wet-bulb reading	15°C	
Difference	6°C	
Relative humidity	53%	

2

1. Which of the two thermometers measures the air temperature?

_____

2. What is the relative humidity in your classroom?

_____

_____

◆ Analyze and Conclude

1. What is the relationship between evaporation and the wet-bulb temperature?

_____

_____

2. Explain your answer to question 1 in terms of energy.

_____

_____

_____

3. What is the relationship between evaporation and relative humidity?

_____

_____

4. Predict the difference between the dry-bulb and wet-bulb readings when the relative humidity is 100%. Give a reason for your answer.

_____

_____

_____

_____

© Prentice-Hall, Inc.

USING A PSYCHROMETER TO DETERMINE RELATIVE HUMIDITY *(continued)*

5. Predict how the relative humidity inside your classroom compares with the relative humidity outdoors. How could you test your prediction?

_____

_____

_____

_____

◆ Critical Thinking and Applications

1. Does the air in your classroom tend to be moist, dry, or somewhere in between? Give a reason for your answer.

_____

_____

_____

2. Would you feel more comfortable in a desert where the temperature is 35°C or in a rain forest where the temperature is 35°C? Give a reason for your answer.

_____

_____

_____

_____

_____

3. How can you tell, without using a psychrometer, whether the air is moist or dry?

_____

_____

_____

_____

4. Why does running a dehumidifier in your home during the summer help make you feel more comfortable?

_____

_____

_____

_____

© Prentice-Hall, Inc.

USING A PSYCHROMETER TO DETERMINE RELATIVE HUMIDITY *(continued)*

5. Antarctica is the coldest place on Earth. Explain why the parts of Antarctica not covered by glaciers are a frigid desert.

_____

_____

_____

◆ More to Explore

In Analyze and Conclude question 5, you predicted how the relative humidity in the classroom compares with the relative humidity outdoors. Now test your prediction. Write a procedure you can follow. You may wish to include other areas in your school in your investigation, for example, the cafeteria or gym. Be sure to make predictions for these places before testing them. Have the teacher approve your procedure before you carry out the investigation. Be sure to wear your safety goggles.

Investigating Weather Maps

◆ Pre-Lab Discussion

Accurate weather forecasting requires analysis of detailed information about atmospheric conditions in many locations. In the United States, weather data from more than 300 local weather stations are used to prepare daily maps of the weather throughout the country. A detailed map may contain more than 10,000 data points. Such detailed maps are useful for making weather predictions.

Every minute of the day, weather stations, weather ships, satellites, balloons, and radar are recording temperature, pressure, wind direction, and other data and feeding them into the Global Telecommunications System (GTS). From this information, powerful supercomputers develop an image of conditions in the entire atmosphere and make forecasts for up to one week.

In this investigation, you will study how weather is presented, then prepare a simplified weather map and analyze it to discover relationships between weather and certain variables such as temperature and pressure.

1. What are three kinds of information that you could get from a newspaper weather map?

_____

_____

_____

2. What kind of weather is associated with a low?

_____

3. What kind of weather is associated with a high?

_____

◆ Problem

How can you make a weather map and use it to understand relationships between weather and certain atmospheric variables?

◆ Materials *(per group)*

pencil
colored pencil

© Prentice-Hall, Inc.

INVESTIGATING WEATHER MAPS *(continued)*

◆ Procedure

Part A

Read the following steps and study the diagrams to learn how weather data are presented on station circles.

1. Figure 1 shows the correct notation of some weather data recorded at an observation station. The circle represents the observation station. The data have specific positions inside and outside the station circle.

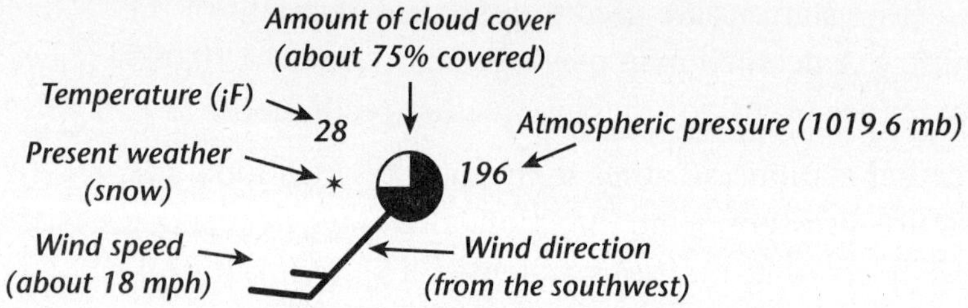

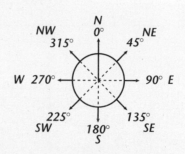

Amount of cloud cover
(about 75% covered)

Temperature (¡F) → 28

Present weather (snow) → *

Wind speed (about 18 mph) →

Atmospheric pressure (1019.6 mb)

196

Wind direction (from the southwest)

Figure 1
Station Circle

2. Isobars are lines on a weather map that connect stations that report the same atmospheric pressure. These pressures are measured in millibars (mb), so isobars are labeled in millibars. To record the pressure on the station circle, use only the last three digits of the pressure and omit the decimal point. Look at the atmospheric pressure shown on the station circle in Figure 1. The atmospheric pressure is 1019.6 mb, which is recorded on the station circle as 196.

3. Think of the station circle as the point of an arrow. Attached to the station circle is a line, which is the arrow's shaft. The wind direction is represented as moving along the arrow's shaft *toward* the center of the station circle. Wind directions are given in degrees and represent the direction *from which* the wind is blowing. Figure 2 will help you determine wind direction. In Figure 1, the wind is blowing from the southwest toward the northeast.

4. Look at Figure 19 on page 103 of your textbook. It shows the data from station circles placed on a map. Compare the symbols discussed above with the symbols in Figure 19. Notice that the temperature is in degrees Fahrenheit.

N
0°
NW   NE
315°   45°

W 270° ——————— 90° E

225°   135°
SW   SE
180°
S

Figure 2

Part B

1. The Data Table on the next page lists data collected at various weather stations on a particular day. Starting with Seattle, transfer all the data provided on the table to the appropriate observation stations on the map. Use the station circles and weather symbols discussed above. The station circle for San Francisco is done for you.

INVESTIGATING WEATHER MAPS *(continued)*

Data Table: Observation Stations

Weather Station	Wind Speed (mph	Wind Direction	Atmospheric Pressure (mb)	Temperature (°F)	Type of Precipitation	Cloud Cover (%)
Seattle	7	260°	1020.8	42		0
Bend	10	200°	1023.5	40		0
San Francisco	8	135°	1020.0	48	fog	25
Los Angeles	12	150°	1021.1	41	fog	25
Phoenix	11	50°	1021.1	45		0
Ely	2	15°	1025.1	37		0
Dubois	18	225°	1024.0	38		0
Helena	15	315°	1020.0	41		0
Medicine Hat	20	345°	1020.1	40		0
Bismarck	18	0°	1014.3	48		0
Casper	12	350°	1016.0	50		0
Pueblo	8	315°	1015.3	50		0
Roswell	22	350°	1016.0	48		0
Del Rio	38	315°	1012.0	50	thunderstorms	100
Galveston	5	225°	1016.0	72		25
Dallas	29	315°	1007.9	60	hail	100
Oklahoma City	45	315°	1007.7	57	thunderstorms	100
Kansas City	2	215°	1002.3	58	rain	100
Burwell	22	325°	1009.3	52	rain	100
Minneapolis	15	45°	1008.2	51	drizzle	100
Sioux Lookout	20	50°	1016.8	46		25
Chicago	10	45°	1005.2	58	drizzle	100
Little Rock	8	225°	1009.3	67		25
New Orleans	5	225°	1017.9	73		0
Nashville	5	220°	1011.1	68		25
Cincinnati	7	90°	1009.8	57	rain	100
Detroit	10	75°	1011.9	54	drizzle	100
Sault Ste. Marie	15	45°	1013.1	50	drizzle	100
Quebec	8	100°	1017.0	50		25
Boston	12	100°	1018.1	52	fog	25
Buffalo	7	75°	1016.0	52	drizzle	100
New York	10	80°	1017.6	56	fog	50
Hatteras	14	90°	1019.1	60		50
Charleston	15	225°	1017.8	70		25
Atlanta	3	225°	1014.6	70		0
Jacksonville	2	200°	1018.1	73		0
Tampa	2	230°	1018.0	74		25
Miami	8	180°	1019.8	78		0

INVESTIGATING WEATHER MAPS *(continued)*

2. On your map, find the observation station with the highest atmospheric pressure. Just above it, write *H* (for high). Find the observation station with the lowest atmospheric pressure. Just above it, write *L* (for low). Starting at this point, which is the center of a low-pressure area, sketch a cold front and a warm front. Refer to page 103 in your textbook for the way fronts should look. The cold front will be between stations where winds change from southwest to northwest and temperatures decrease suddenly. The warm front will be between stations where winds change from east to southwest and temperatures rise suddenly.

3. Draw the following isobars on your map: 1008 mb, 1012 mb, 1016 mb, 1020 mb, and 1024 mb. Label each isobar.

4. Draw a line around all the locations where precipitation has fallen. Shade the precipitation area with a colored pencil.

◆ Observations

3

Weather Map

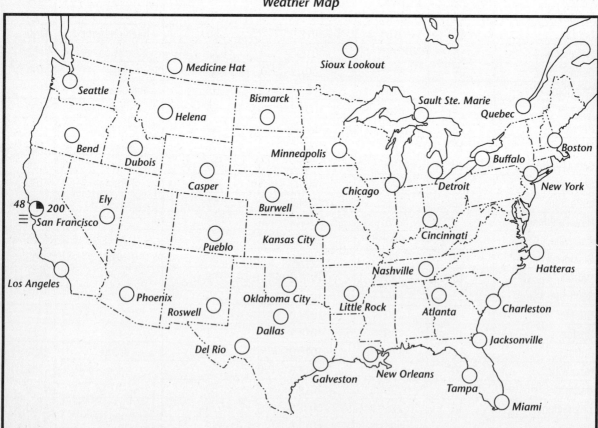

1. Which observation station reported the highest atmospheric pressure? The lowest atmospheric pressure?

_____

INVESTIGATING WEATHER MAPS *(continued)*

◆ Analyze and Conclude

1. According to your map, is precipitation usually associated with an area of low pressure or an area of high pressure?

_____

2. Compare wind direction around the low-pressure center with wind direction around the high-pressure center. Use clock directions in your answer.

_____

_____

3. Compare the type and location of precipitation associated with the cold front to those associated with the warm front.

_____

_____

_____

4. Describe changes in temperature and wind direction associated with the passage of the warm front.

_____

_____

_____

5. Describe changes in temperature, wind direction, and atmospheric pressure associated with the passage of the cold front.

_____

_____

_____

◆ Critical Thinking and Applications

1. Look at your weather map. Assume that the storm center is moving in a north-easterly direction. Describe at least three changes in the weather in Cincinnati, Ohio, if the low-pressure center moves to Sault Ste. Marie.

_____

_____

_____

2. Can yesterday's weather map help you predict tomorrow's weather? Give a reason for your answer.

_____

_____

INVESTIGATING WEATHER MAPS (continued)

3. Before weather satellites existed, weather forecasts for cities on the West Coast were not as reliable as those for cities in the Midwest. Explain this difference.

_____

_____

_____

_____

◆ More to Explore

Refer to the two maps below to answer the questions.

March 27

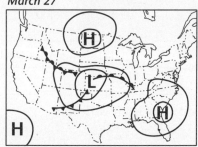

March 28

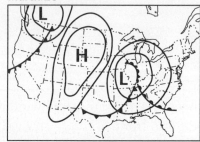

1. If the low-pressure area in the middle of the country on March 27 continues at its present speed and direction, where will it be centered on March 29?

_____

2. Predict the weather conditions in Mississippi as the cold front moves through on March 29.

_____

_____

3. Draw a weather map that predicts the locations of the fronts, highs, and lows for March 29.

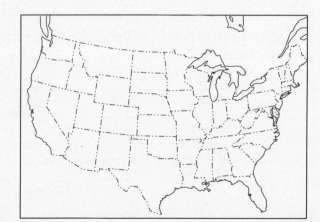

Investigating Differences in Climate

◆ Pre-Lab Discussion

Many factors are responsible for the different types of climates. However, each factor falls into one of two major categories: those that affect the average yearly temperature of an area and those that affect the average yearly precipitation. The amount of available energy helps to determine the temperature of a region.

One measure of energy is evapotranspiration—the total water loss from the land through evaporation and transpiration. In transpiration, the surface of leaves and other plant parts gives off moisture. In this investigation, you will use the ratio of average yearly precipitation (P) to average yearly potential evapotranspiration (E_p). This climate ratio, written as P/E_p, represents the average yearly moisture supply divided by the moisture demand, or need, at a certain location. Four different climates, based on P/E_p, are arid, semiarid, subhumid, and humid. The table below lists each climate and its ratio.

Climate Ratios

P/E_p	Climate
less than 0.4	arid
0.4–0.8	semiarid
0.8–1.2	subhumid
greater than 1.2	humid

In this investigation, you will study how the relationship between available energy and moisture affects climate.

1. What conditions produce a "dry" climate?

_____

2. Why might a cool place with low rainfall be less dry than a hotter place that gets the same amount of rain?

_____

_____

_____

INVESTIGATING DIFFERENCES IN CLIMATE *(continued)*

◆ Problem

How can you use the ratio between precipitation and potential evapotranspiration to map different climates?

◆ Materials *(per group)*

soft graphite pencil
colored pencils or crayons, four colors

◆ Procedure

1. Carefully examine the map of Ert, an imaginary continent. The numbers at various locations are the climate ratios for those areas. Notice that Ert is very large, extending toward the poles beyond latitudes 60° N and 60° S. Notice also the extensive mountain range along the west coast, as well as two mountain ranges along the east coast.

2. Remember the following information when you are working on your map:

   • Climate ratios greater than 1.2 are usually in regions at or near the equator. These regions are generally humid.

   • Regions at or near latitudes 30° N and 30° S are generally arid, unless influenced by mountain ranges or other factors. Climate ratios of 0.4 or less are usually found in these regions.

   • Areas at or near latitudes 60° N and 60° S are generally moist but often have climate ratios that vary a lot because of the influence of global wind systems, large bodies of water, and mountain ranges.

   • The lines of two climate types cannot cross. They tend to run parallel to each other and do not form sharp edges or acute angles. Also, these lines must be continuous; that is, they must form closed loops or run off the edges of the continent.

3. Locate the regions on Ert that are most arid and most humid. Find the mountain ranges and lines of latitude.

4. Using a soft graphite pencil, lightly connect points with a 0.4 climate ratio. Notice that two regions have this climate ratio, one in each hemisphere. The 0.4 line in the Southern Hemisphere has been correctly drawn for you.

5. Lightly draw lines connecting points that have a 0.8 climate ratio. Then draw lines connecting points that have 0.0, 1.2, and 1.6 climate ratios.

6. Darken the contour lines and identify the areas as arid, semiarid, humid, or subhumid. For example, regions between lines 0.4 and 0.8 are semiarid. Color each type of region on your map a different color. Add a color key that identifies the climate.

© Prentice-Hall, Inc.

INVESTIGATING DIFFERENCES IN CLIMATE *(continued)*

Ert: A Continent

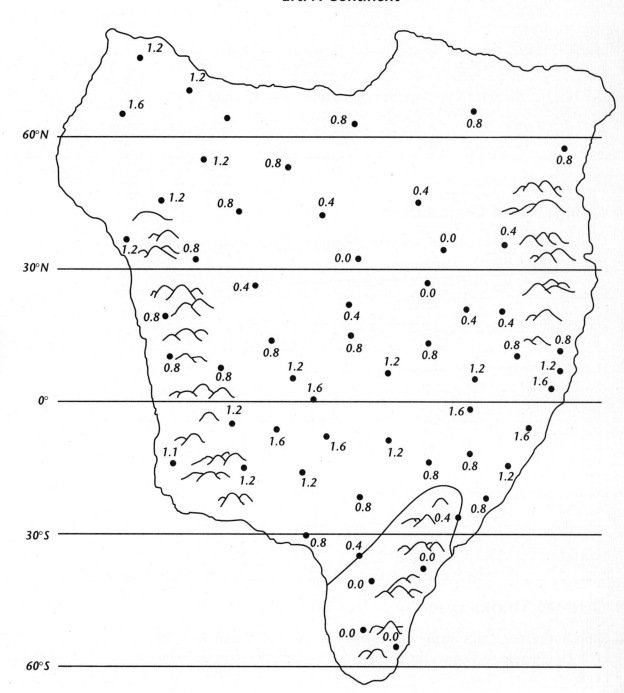

INVESTIGATING DIFFERENCES IN CLIMATE *(continued)*

◆ Observations

1. Describe the general locations of the regions of Ert that are most humid.

_____

_____

_____

2. Describe the general locations of the regions of Ert that are most arid.

_____

_____

_____

◆ Analyze and Conclude

1. How can two regions with the same total yearly precipitation have different climate ratios?

_____

_____

_____

2. How can two regions with the same average yearly temperature have different climate ratios?

_____

_____

_____

3. What relationship exists between latitude and temperature patterns?

_____

_____

_____

◆ Critical Thinking and Applications

1. Suppose the mountains on the west coast of Ert between 0° and 30° S did not exist. How would you expect the climate in those latitudes to be different, if at all?

_____

_____

_____

© Prentice-Hall, Inc.

INVESTIGATING DIFFERENCES IN CLIMATE *(continued)*

2. What areas on Ert would you expect to be the most heavily populated? Give a reason for your answer.

_____

_____

_____

_____

3. In which of the four climatic regions would you prefer to live? Give reasons for your answer.

_____

_____

_____

_____

4. How does the climate of your area in question 2 affect the type of clothing people wear?

_____

_____

_____

The types of plants or animals that are raised for food?

_____

_____

_____

The recreational activities?

_____

_____

_____

The amount of energy consumed?

_____

_____

_____

INVESTIGATING DIFFERENCES IN CLIMATE *(continued)*

◆ **More to Explore**

Imagine that the continent of Ert is located on Earth. Draw on your map the directions of the global winds from above 60° N to 60° S. Also label each latitude line on your map as an area of generally high or low air pressure and wet or dry conditions. Remember that winds flow from high-pressure areas to low-pressure areas. Give reasons for the locations of the most humid and most arid regions of Ert.

4

J-1   **LABORATORY INVESTIGATION**

Constructing a Foucault Pendulum

1

◆ Pre-Lab Discussion

In 1851, Jean Foucault was the first to prove that Earth rotates. He hung a heavy iron ball from a wire 67 m long. He set this pendulum swinging north and south. He knew that a free-swinging pendulum does not change direction. After about 8 hours, however, the pendulum was swinging east and west. Foucault concluded that Earth had rotated beneath the swinging pendulum.

In this investigation, you will make a device that uses the principle behind a Foucault pendulum.

1. Compare and contrast rotation and revolution.

_____

_____

_____

2. Which movement, rotation or revolution, causes day and night? Explain.

_____

◆ Problem

How can you demonstrate that Earth rotates?

◆ Materials *(per group)*

2 ring stands
2 burette clamps
wooden dowel, about 40 cm long
board, at least 45 cm long
thread, about 30 cm
scissors
fishing sinker or several metal washers
    or nuts, 110 g or more
sheet of lined paper
tape
meterstick

◆ Safety   *Review the safety guidelines in the front of your lab book.*

Use caution in handling sharp scissors.

CONSTRUCTING A FOUCAULT PENDULUM *(continued)*

1

◆ Procedure

1. Tape a sheet of lined paper on the middle of the board. The lines should be perpendicular (at 90°) to the length of the board. Then set up the ring stands, clamps, and dowel as pictured in Figure 1.

Figure 1

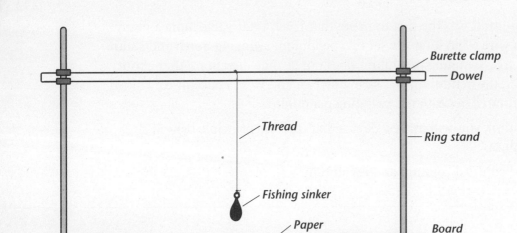

Burette clamp

Dowel

Thread

Ring stand

Fishing sinker

Paper

Board

2. Cut a piece of thread about 30 cm long. Tie the fishing sinker to one end of the thread. Tie the other end of the thread to the center of the dowel so that the sinker can swing freely like a pendulum.

3. Carefully set the pendulum swinging in the direction of the lines on the paper. Draw a two-headed arrow on the paper to show the direction the pendulum is swinging. Label the arrow A.

4. Using two students, slowly turn the whole apparatus clockwise one quarter of a full turn (90°). Be careful not to disturb the swinging of the pendulum.

5. Draw a two-headed arrow on the paper to show the direction the pendulum is now swinging. Label this arrow B. Observe how the direction of the pendulum has changed in relation to the lines on the sheet of paper.

6. Predict how the pendulum swing will compare to the arrows when the students at the ends of the board again slowly turn the whole apparatus clockwise another quarter of a turn (90°). Give a reason for your prediction.

_____

_____

7. Turn the apparatus clockwise 90° and compare the results to your prediction.

© Prentice-Hall, Inc.

CONSTRUCTING A FOUCAULT PENDULUM *(continued)*

◆ Observations

1. Describe how the direction of arrow A differs from that of arrow B.

_____

_____

2. Describe how the direction of the pendulum changed in relation to the lines on the sheet of paper.

_____

_____

_____

◆ Analyze and Conclude

1. If a pendulum was swinging freely on Earth, how would it appear to act if Earth rotated?

_____

_____

_____

2. How would the pendulum appear to act if Earth did not rotate?

_____

_____

_____

3. Think about a playground swing and how it swings with the seat empty and with someone on the seat. Why do you think it is important to use a fairly heavy weight on your pendulum?

_____

_____

◆ Critical Thinking and Applications

1. Describe the changes in geographical direction that a pendulum would appear to undergo if it began swinging north and south.

_____

_____

_____

_____

_____

© Prentice-Hall, Inc.

CONSTRUCTING A FOUCAULT PENDULUM *(continued)*

2. What happens to the swing of a pendulum, or its arc, as the pendulum swings over a period of time?

_____

_____

3. What is the reason for this change? (Hint: Think about what the pendulum weight and string move against.)

_____

_____

◆ More to Explore

Construct a simple working model of a Foucault pendulum. Can this model be used to show Earth's actual rotation? Write a procedure you would follow to answer this question. Have the teacher approve your procedure before you carry out the investigation. Wear your goggles while carrying out your procedure.

J-2   LABORATORY INVESTIGATION

Measuring the Diameter of the Sun

◆ Pre-Lab Discussion

If you look at the full moon in the sky and a golf ball in your hand, they seem to be about the same size. However, you know that they are much different in size. They look about the same to you because they are at much different distances from you. For example, from Earth, the sun and moon appear to be about the same size because the moon is much closer to Earth than the sun is.

How can you measure the size of something as far away from you as the sun is? Although Earth is about 150,000,000 km from the sun, you can still make accurate measurements of the sun's size. In this investigation, you will construct a simple device and use it to collect data that will allow you to calculate the diameter of the sun.

1. What part of the sun do you see when you look at its image?

_____

2. Why must you look at the sun indirectly instead of directly?

_____

_____

◆ Problem

What is the diameter of the sun?

◆ Materials *(per group)*

meterstick
card, 20 cm × 25 cm
card, 10 cm × 15 cm
scissors
tape
square of aluminum foil,
    15 cm × 15 cm
drawing compass or pin

◆ Safety   *Review the safety guidelines in the front of your lab book.*

Use caution in handling sharp objects such as the compass, pin, and scissors. Never look directly at the sun; direct sunlight can damage your eyes.

MEASURING THE DIAMETER OF THE SUN *(continued)*

◆ Procedure

1. Have your teacher cut a slit in each card in the positions shown in Figure 1 so that the meterstick can fit snugly in them.

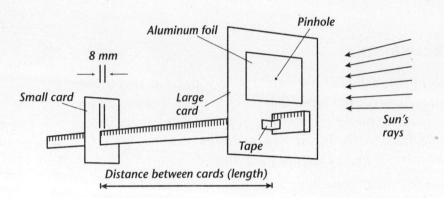

Figure 1

8 mm

Aluminum foil

Pinhole

Small card

Large card

Tape

Sun's rays

Distance between cards (length)

2. Draw two parallel lines exactly 8 mm apart near the center of the small card, as shown in Figure 1.

3. Cut a square hole, about 3 cm × 3 cm, in the larger card and cover it with aluminum foil. Use tape to hold the foil securely in place. Punch a very small hole near the center of the foil with a compass point or a pin.

4. Slide the large card near one end of the meterstick. Set the card perpendicular to the meterstick and tape it in place. Slide the small card on the other end, perpendicular to the meterstick.

5. **CAUTION:** *Never look directly at the sun. Direct sunlight can damage your eyes.* Aim the end of the meterstick with the foil-covered card toward the sun. Move the meterstick until the shadow of the large card covers the smaller card. A bright image of the sun will fall on the smaller card. Move the smaller card along the meterstick until the image exactly fills the space between the two parallel lines.

6. Make sure both cards are still perpendicular to the meterstick. Measure the distance between the two cards to the nearest millimeter. Record the distance and the diameter of the image in the Data Table below.

◆ Observations

Data Table

Distance Between Two Cards	Diameter of Sun's Image

© Prentice-Hall, Inc.

MEASURING THE DIAMETER OF THE SUN *(continued)*

◆ Analyze and Conclude

1. The diameter of the sun's image equals the distance between the parallel lines on the small card. The average distance between Earth and the sun is approximately 150,000,000 km. Using the formula below, calculate the diameter of the sun.

$$\frac{\text{diameter of the sun (km)}}{\text{distance to the sun (km)}} = \frac{\text{diameter of the sun's image (mm)}}{\text{distance between two cards (mm)}}$$

2. The actual diameter of the sun is 1,391,000 km. Using the formula below, determine the percentage of error in your calculated value for the sun's diameter.

$$\text{percentage of error} = \frac{\text{difference between your value and the correct value}}{\text{correct value}} \times 100\%$$

3. What could account for an error in your calculated value for the sun's diameter?

_____

_____

_____

◆ Critical Thinking and Applications

1. How could you use the technique in this investigation to make other astronomical measurements?

_____

_____

_____

_____

© Prentice-Hall, Inc.

MEASURING THE DIAMETER OF THE SUN *(continued)*

2. A camera operates in a way similar to the setup for your experiment. Light through a small hole projects an image onto the film. A common film size is 35 mm. Some film is 11 mm. If the image projected is the size of the film, which size of film must be closer to the hole that projects the image?

_____

_____

3. How might clouds affect the accuracy of your measurement in this investigation?

_____

_____

◆ More to Explore

New Problem What is the diameter of the moon?

Possible Materials
  hole punch
  index card
  meterstick

Procedure

1. Develop a plan similar to the one you used in the investigation to determine the diameter of the moon. (Hint: Because you can observe the moon directly, you can look through a small hole directly at the moon.) Write the steps to your procedure on another sheet of paper. What data will you need to collect? What mathematical formula will you use to calculate the diameter?

2. After your teacher has approved your plan, use your setup and formula to find the diameter of the moon. (The average distance from the moon to Earth is 368,500 km.)

Observations On another sheet of paper, make a data table similar to the one in the investigation in which to record your data.

Analyze and Conclude

1. What is your calculated diameter of the moon?

_____

2. If you were given the diameter of the moon instead of its distance from Earth, how could you find the distance?

_____

_____

_____

J-3   **LABORATORY INVESTIGATION**

Chemical Composition and the Spectrum

◆ Pre-Lab Discussion

Some elements—such as sodium, calcium, strontium, and potassium—are classified as metals because they conduct heat and electricity and have certain other properties in common. Metals often combine with nonmetals to form compounds. For example, the metal sodium will combine with the nonmetal chlorine to form the compound sodium chloride, which is common table salt.

When compounds of certain metals are heated, the metals give off wavelengths of visible light. Each metal gives off wavelengths that are different from the wavelengths produced by other elements.

This light is divided when you use a spectroscope—an instrument that breaks light into its component colors. By using a spectroscope to examine the light from a flame, you can tell whether certain metals are present in the flame. Scientists can learn about stars and other bodies in space by studying the spectrum of the electromagnetic waves each of these objects give off.

In this investigation, you will observe the colors produced by compounds of certain metals when they are heated. You will use a spectroscope to examine the spectrums of several different metals. Then you will design a way to determine what metals are in two unknown solutions.

1. What is a spectrum? How are spectrums useful in studying stars?

_____

_____

_____

_____

2. Can humans see all types of electromagnetic waves? Give a reason for your answer.

_____

_____

◆ Problem

How can astronomers use spectrums to learn about distant stars?

CHEMICAL COMPOSITION AND THE SPECTRUM *(continued)*

◆ Possible Materials *(per group)*

paper towels
Bunsen burner
matches or igniter
hand-held spectroscope
nichrome wire loops with handles,
    one per solution, dipped in
    solutions of calcium chloride,
    strontium chloride, potassium chloride,
    and sodium chloride
colored pencils
nichrome wire loops with handles,
    one per solution, dipped in unknown
    solutions

3

◆ Safety   *Review the safety guidelines in the front of your lab book.*

Wear lab aprons and safety goggles. Use caution when lighting and working around an open flame. Tie back long hair and loose clothing and remove dangling jewelry. Do not touch the nichrome wire loop. Wash your hands after testing each solution, and use paper towels to immediately clean up any spills.

◆ Procedure

Part A: Known Solutions

1. Read through the entire lab before carrying out the procedure.

2. **CAUTION:** *Put on your safety goggles and lab aprons.* Light the burner and adjust it to give a hot, blue flame.

3. Look at the flame through the spectroscope. The slit of the spectroscope should be vertical. Rotate the eyepiece to make a sharp spectrum on the side wall of the spectroscope. Each group member should observe this spectrum.

© Prentice-Hall, Inc.

CHEMICAL COMPOSITION AND THE SPECTRUM *(continued)*

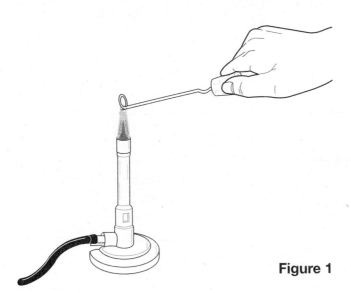

Figure 1

4. CAUTION: *Do not touch the nichrome wire loop. Hold it by the wooden or cork handle at all times. The metal will continue to be hot after it is removed from the flame.* While you are looking at the flame through the spectroscope, have a classmate carefully hold in the top of the burner flame a nichrome wire loop that has been dipped in a calcium chloride solution. See Figure 1. Be sure to look at the flame from the wire loop, not from the burner. In Observations, draw what you see through the spectroscope as the sample burns. Use colored pencils or label the colors that you see. Each group member should observe this calcium spectrum.

5. Repeat Step 4 with nichrome wire loops dipped in solutions of strontium chloride, potassium chloride, and sodium chloride. To avoid contamination, be sure to use a different nichrome wire loop for each solution. In Observations, draw the spectrum for each metal.

Part B: Unknown Solutions

1. Plan how you will find out what metal is in an unknown solution. Will you use the spectroscope? What factors must remain constant? Write down your procedure on a separate sheet of paper.

2. After the teacher has approved your plan, obtain a new nichrome wire loop that has been dipped in a solution of an unknown substance. Use your procedure to find out what metal is in the solution. Draw its spectrum and identify the metal in Observations.

3. Develop a plan to find out what metals are in a second unknown that is a mixture of two of the solutions you tested earlier. Write down your procedure on a separate sheet of paper.

4. Make sure you get the teacher's approval before carrying out your plan. Then repeat Step 2 for the mixture of solutions.

CHEMICAL COMPOSITION AND THE SPECTRUM *(continued)*

◆ Observations

Part A

Spectrums

```
┌────────────────────┐          ┌────────────────────┐
│                    │          │                    │
│                    │          │                    │
└────────────────────┘          └────────────────────┘
```

Spectrum of calcium   *Spectrum of potassium*

```
┌────────────────────┐          ┌────────────────────┐
│                    │          │                    │
│                    │          │                    │
└────────────────────┘          └────────────────────┘
```

Spectrum of sodium   *Spectrum of strontium*

3

Part B

```
┌──────────────────┐
│                  │
│                  │
└──────────────────┘
```

Spectrum of Unknown Solution

Identity of Metal _____

```
┌──────────────────┐
│                  │
│                  │
└──────────────────┘
```

Spectrum of Mixture of Unknown Solutions

Identity of Metals _____

CHEMICAL COMPOSITION AND THE SPECTRUM *(continued)*

◆ Analyze and Conclude

1. Why must you use a different nichrome wire loop for each substance?

_____

_____

2. How did the spectrums of the samples differ?

_____

_____

3. If all the bands you observed were drawn on one band, what would it look like?

_____

_____

_____

4. What might the unknown solution contain? How do you know?

_____

_____

_____

5. When you heated the unknown mixture of solutions, were you able to see the colors of each metal in the flame? Explain your answer.

_____

_____

_____

_____

◆ Critical Thinking and Applications

1. How do the samples resemble stars? How can scientists tell what elements are in a distant star?

_____

_____

_____

_____

_____

CHEMICAL COMPOSITION AND THE SPECTRUM *(continued)*

2. Spectral lines are often called the fingerprints of the elements. Why?

_____

_____

_____

3. When you are heating the nichrome wire loops, what is the responding variable? What is the manipulated variable?

_____

_____

_____

◆ More to Explore

3

Do different types of light bulbs (incandescent, halogen, fluorescent, high intensity, and so forth) have different spectrums? Write a procedure you could follow to answer this question. Your teacher must approve your procedure before you carry out the investigation.

© Prentice-Hall, Inc.

K-1

1

Determining the Density of Liquids

◆ Pre-Lab Discussion

If you've ever carried bags of groceries, you know that some bags have greater mass than others, even though the volumes of the bags are the same. Mass and volume are general properties of all matter. Density is the ratio of mass to volume. The density of a specific kind of matter helps to identify it and to distinguish it from other kinds of matter. Liquids have density, and you determine their densities in grams per milliliter (g/mL).

In this investigation, you will develop a procedure for finding density and use it to determine the density of several liquids. You will compare the densities of liquids by using a wood float.

1. A rock sinks when placed in water. Which is more dense, the rock or the water?

_____

2. Liquid A has a mass of 32 grams and a volume of 20 milliliters. Liquid B has a density of 1.2 g/mL. Will Liquid B float on Liquid A? Explain your answer.

_____

_____

◆ Problem

How can you determine the density of a liquid?

◆ Possible Materials

(per group)

4 graduated cylinders, 100 mL
balance
30 mL ethanol
salad oil
salt water
paper towels
4 wooden dowels, about 6 cm long
glass marker
salt
ruler

DETERMINING THE DENSITY OF LIQUIDS *(continued)*

◆ Safety 〔icons〕 *Review the safety guidelines in your lab book.*

Wear safety goggles and lab aprons. Never have an open flame in the same room as an open container of ethanol. Report any spills of oil or ethanol to the teacher. Ethanol is poisonous.

◆ Procedure

1. Read the entire lab before continuing with the procedure.

2. With your group, design a procedure to find the density of 30 mL of water. Think about what properties of water you need to know to find its density. Your procedure should include keeping the sample of water for Step 6. Write each step of your procedure on a separate sheet of paper.

3. Finish designing the Data Table in Observations to determine the density for water and three other liquids. Add headings and columns to organize the data you will need to find and record. Change the first column if you use other liquids.

4. **CAUTION:** *Wear safety goggles and lab aprons.* After the teacher has approved your plan and Data Table, find the density of the sample of water. What mathematical formula will you use to find density? Record all your data and the density of water in your Data Table.

5. **CAUTION:** *There should be no open flames in the room where you're using the ethanol. Ethanol is a poison, so keep it away from your face.* Use your procedure to find the density of 30-mL samples of ethanol, salad oil, and salt water or other liquids you are using. Record all your data and the density of these three liquids in your data table. **CAUTION:** *Report any oil or ethanol spills immediately.*

6. Set four graduated cylinders side by side, each containing 30 mL of one of the liquids you tested. See Figure 1. Think about their differences in density. Predict how high a wooden dowel will float in each liquid, compared to the other three.

_____

_____

_____

_____

7. On a separate sheet of paper, write a procedure for testing your prediction. Have the teacher approve your plan, and then carry it out.

DETERMINING THE DENSITY OF LIQUIDS *(continued)*

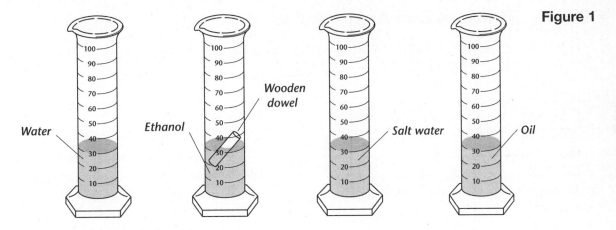

Figure 1

Water · Ethanol · Wooden dowel · Salt water · Oil

◆ Observations

Data Table

Liquid	
Water	
Ethanol	
Salt water	
Oil	

◆ Analyze and Conclude

1. List the four liquids that you used in this experiment, in order of increasing density.

_____

_____

2. Were your predictions accurate? Make a statement that compares the density of a liquid to how high a wooden dowel will float in it.

_____

_____

_____

DETERMINING THE DENSITY OF LIQUIDS *(continued)*

◆ Critical Thinking and Applications

1. Which has the greater mass, 1 L of water or 1 L of ethanol? Explain your answer in terms of density.

   _____

   _____

   _____

2. Which takes up a greater volume, 1,000 g of water or 1,000 g of ethanol? Explain your answer in terms of density.

   _____

   _____

   _____

3. Which is more dense, 1 mL of water or 50 L of water? Give a reason for your answer.

   _____

   _____

   _____

4. Predict what would happen if you poured into one beaker all the liquids used in this lab.

   _____

   _____

   _____

◆ More to Explore

Does the amount of salt in water affect the liquid's density? Write a procedure you would follow to answer this question. Have the teacher approve your procedure before you carry out the investigation. Use your results to explain why it is easier for a person to float in the Great Salt Lake than it is to float in a freshwater lake. Wear your safety goggles and apron and wash up afterwards.

K-2   **LABORATORY INVESTIGATION**

Changes in a Burning Candle

◆ Pre-Lab Discussion

What do you observe as you watch a candle burning? You see a bright flame and feel the heat. You may notice an odor if it is a scented candle. As you watch, the candle becomes smaller until, eventually, it is just a small stub. Some changes that occur are physical, and others are chemical. In this investigation, you will determine the physical and chemical changes in a burning candle.

In one part of the investigation, you will test for carbon dioxide, using limewater. Limewater is a mixture of water and calcium hydroxide that turns cloudy when carbon dioxide is added.

1. What is a physical change?

_____

_____

_____

2. What is a chemical change?

_____

_____

_____

◆ Problem

What physical and chemical changes does a candle undergo as it burns?

◆ Materials *(per group)*

large birthday candle
matches
shallow metal dish
150-mL beaker
paper towel
500-mL Erlenmeyer flask
25 mL of limewater solution
solid rubber stopper
tongs

© Prentice-Hall, Inc.

CHANGES IN A BURNING CANDLE *(continued)*

◆ Safety   *Review the safety guidelines in the front of your lab book.*

Use caution when working around an open flame. Tie back long hair and loose clothing. Keep the limewater away from your eyes. If you get some in your eyes, immediately tell the teacher and rinse your eyes for 15 minutes.

◆ Procedure

1. Light a candle and allow two or three drops of the melted wax to fall on the center of the metal dish. Press the candle upright onto the melted wax before the wax hardens. If the candle burns too low during the following steps, repeat this step with a new candle.

2. Observe the flame of the burning candle for a few minutes. Observe what is burning and where the burning takes place. Note the different regions of the flame. Record your observations in the Data Table.

3. Fill a 150-mL beaker with cold tap water, dry the outside, and use tongs carefully to hold it 3 cm to 5 cm above the candle flame for about 10 seconds. Record your observations.

4. Pour tap water into the metal dish to a depth of about 1 cm. Quickly lower a 500-mL Erlenmeyer flask over the candle so that the mouth of the flask is below the surface of the water. See Figure 1. Leave the flask in place for about a minute. Record your observations.

5. Hold the flask by its neck and lift it out of the water. **CAUTION:** *Lift the flask by its neck because the base of the flask may be hot.* Turn it upright, and add about 25 mL of limewater. Stopper the flask and swirl the solution for about a minute. Record your observations.

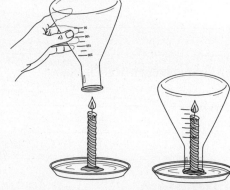

Figure 1

◆ Observations

Data Table

Procedure	Observations
Candle burning (Step 2)	
Beaker above flame (Step 3)	
Flask over candle (Step 4)	
Limewater in flask (Step 5)	

CHANGES IN A BURNING CANDLE *(continued)*

◆ Analyze and Conclude

1. Which of the changes that you observed were physical?

_____

_____

_____

2. Which of the changes that you observed were chemical?

_____

_____

_____

3. One of the requirements for combustion is fuel. From your observations, what are the other requirements? Explain.

_____

_____

_____

_____

4. What are the two chemical products of combustion of the candle? How do you know?

_____

_____

_____

_____

◆ Critical Thinking and Applications

1. Why was water needed when the Erlenmeyer flask was placed over the candle?

_____

_____

_____

_____

CHANGES IN A BURNING CANDLE (continued)

2. You can use an equation to describe a chemical reaction. For a one-way reaction, the part of the equation to the left of the arrow gives the ingredients, and the part of the equation to the right of the arrow gives the products. For example, an equation for the chemical reaction that produces mayonnaise is

Eggs + Vinegar + Salad Oil → Mayonnaise.

Write an equation for the combustion of a candle in oxygen. Hint: There are two ingredients and two products.

_____

_____

◆ More to Explore

New Problem What is actually burning when a candle burns?

Materials
two candles
matches
clay

Safety Follow the same cautions as in the lab when working around an open flame. Wear your safety goggles and apron.

Procedure

1. Set each candle in a lump of clay to hold up the candle. Light one of the candles.

2. Light the second candle and hold the flame about 2 cm to 4 cm to the side of the first candle. Gently blow out the first candle flame, then quickly move the flame of the second candle into the smoke from the first candle. Do not allow the second candle flame to touch the wick of the first candle.

Observations Record what happens when you move the flame of the second candle into the smoke of the first.

_____

Analyze and Conclude Which part of the candle burned? What is the evidence for your answer?

_____

_____

_____

K - 3   LABORATORY INVESTIGATION

Finding Average Mass

◆ Pre-Lab Discussion

Atoms are made up of protons, neutrons, and electrons. The neutron and proton have approximately the same mass, and both masses are very large compared to the mass of the electron. An atom's total mass is the sum of the masses of all the protons and neutrons inside it. Since each proton and each neutron is assigned a mass of 1 atomic mass unit, a particular atom's mass is always a whole number. So why is the mass of the atom in the periodic table *not* a whole number? Atoms of an element all have the same number of protons but can have different numbers of neutrons. The atomic mass in a periodic table is the average mass of all the atoms of an element.

How do you figure out the atomic mass of an element? It's like finding the average mass of all your textbooks. Each book has a different mass. To get the average mass, you add the masses of the books and then divide the total mass by the number of books. In this investigation, you will devise a procedure to determine the average mass of another group of objects.

1. Why must each atom of an element always have the same number of protons?

_____

_____

2. The total mass of ten quarters is 55 grams. What is the average mass of a quarter?

◆ Problem

What is the average mass of an object in a group of similar objects?

◆ Possible Materials *(per group)*

balance
pennies or other small objects
forceps
watch glass

◆ Safety *Review the safety guidelines in the front of your lab book.*

FINDING AVERAGE MASS *(continued)*

◆ Procedure

1. Read through the entire lab before starting the investigation.

2. Working with a partner, plan a way to find the average mass of an object in a group of those objects. Consider the number of objects and their shape. What equipment will you need to measure the mass of each object? Will you need equipment to contain the objects?

3. Decide how to use the Data Table to record each object and its mass. Find the mass of at least ten objects to the nearest 0.1 g.

4. Write your procedure on a separate sheet of paper. Have the teacher approve your procedure before you carry out the investigation.

◆ Observations

Data Table

3

Object	Mass
1	
2	
3	
4	
5	
6	
7	
8	
9	
10	

◆ Analyze and Conclude

1. Add up the masses of all the objects.

FINDING AVERAGE MASS *(continued)*

2. Calculate the average mass.

3. Make a bar graph showing how many of the objects have identical mass. Use increments of 0.1 g in your graph.

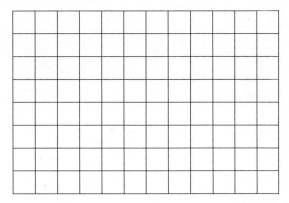

4. Were there more objects with masses greater than the average or with masses less than the average?

_____

_____

5. All the objects look identical. Why do you think some of the objects have more mass than others, although they are all the same size?

_____

_____

_____

_____

◆ Critical Thinking and Applications

1. If you repeated this lab, what might you change in your procedure?

_____

_____

2. A small group of neon atoms has the following masses: 20% have 21 atomic mass units (amu) and 80% have 20 amu. What is the average mass of the neon atoms? Show your calculations.

© Prentice-Hall, Inc.

FINDING AVERAGE MASS *(continued)*

3. How does the mass you found in Question 2 compare to 20.1797 amu reported for neon in the periodic table?

_____

4. Do you think that the atomic mass for neon in the periodic table is more exact and closer to the true value than the answer to Question 2? Give a reason for your answer.

_____

_____

_____

_____

◆ More to Explore

New Problem Would you get the same average mass if you used fifty of the same objects as you did when you used ten of these objects?

Possible Materials Use fifty of the objects you used in the previous lab.

Procedure Predict whether the average masses will be the same, greater, or less. On a separate sheet of paper, write a procedure you would follow to test your prediction. Have the teacher approve your procedure before you carry out the investigation.

Observations Make a data table and record your observations on a separate sheet of paper.

Analyze and Conclude

1. Compare the average mass for the fifty objects to the average mass of ten objects. Was your prediction accurate? If not, give a reason for the inaccuracy.

_____

_____

2. Does finding the average mass of fifty objects produce a more correct value than finding the average mass of ten objects? Give a reason for your answer.

_____

_____

_____

Name ______________________ Date __________ Class ______________

K-4 **LABORATORY INVESTIGATION**

Testing Unsaturated Cooking Oils

◆ Pre-Lab Discussion

The nutrition labels on packages of food tell you how much saturated fat is in a serving. Why should you care? Fats are made mostly of saturated fatty acids. Research shows that unsaturated fatty acids are better for your health than saturated fatty acids are. Oils, which are usually liquid at room temperature, are made mostly of unsaturated fatty acids. If you are health conscious, you might choose to cook with oils rather than with solid fats.

Figure 1 shows the difference between molecules of saturated and unsaturated fatty acids. Unsaturated fatty acids have at least one double bond between two carbon atoms. Saturated fatty acids have only single bonds between carbon atoms.

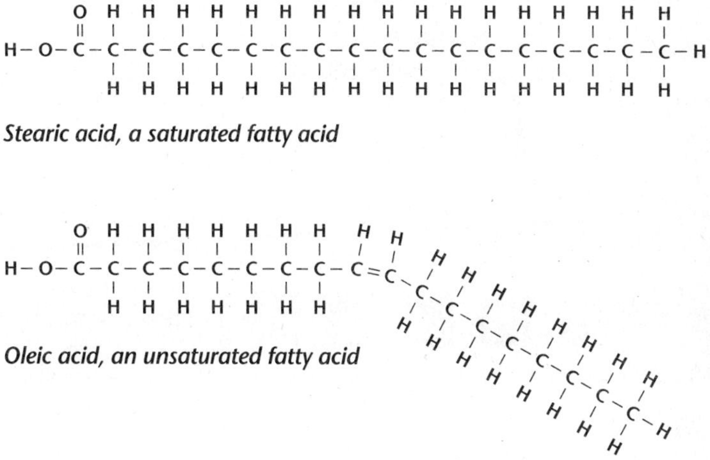

Stearic acid, a saturated fatty acid

Oleic acid, an unsaturated fatty acid

Figure 1

How can you find out how unsaturated the fatty acids in a fat or an oil are? You can mix the chemical iodine with the fat or oil. As iodine reacts with the molecules of unsaturated fatty acids, it loses its color. The more iodine that disappears, the more unsaturated fatty acid is in the fat or oil. When the iodine no longer changes color, the reaction is complete.

In this investigation, you will determine the relative amount of unsaturated fatty acid in some cooking oils.

1. How does a saturated fatty acid differ from an unsaturated fatty acid?

____

____

2. What is the connection between saturated fats and cholesterol?

____

____

4

TESTING UNSATURATED COOKING OILS *(continued)*

◆ Problem

How can you tell how unsaturated an oil is?

◆ Materials *(per group)*

10 test tubes
10 stoppers for test tubes
test-tube rack
balance
several vegetable oils, such as
    corn, olive, sunflower,
    safflower, and soybean oil
tincture of iodine
3 plastic droppers
glass-marking pencil
paper towels

◆ Safety   *Review the safety guidelines in the front of your lab book.*

Handle tincture of iodine carefully; it will stain your skin and clothes. Clean up any spills immediately and notify the teacher.

◆ Procedure

1. You will be given one oil to test. Label 10 test tubes with the name of the oil. Number them 1 through 10. The number tells you how many drops of iodine to add to each test tube.

2. Add 20 drops (1 mL) of oil to each test tube. Record the color in the Data Table.

3. **CAUTION:** *Wipe up any spilled iodine immediately, especially on the outside of the test tube and stopper.* Add one drop of iodine to the first test tube and put the stopper on. Shake the test tube while holding the stopper and carefully observe the reaction of the oil and iodine. Record your observations in the Data Table.

4. Now add 2 drops of iodine to the test tube marked 2. Stopper it, shake it, and observe.

5. Add the corresponding number of drops to the remaining test tubes in order. Shake each test tube thoroughly to mix the contents.

6. Allow the test tubes to sit with stoppers on in the test tube rack overnight. The next day observe any color changes. On a separate piece of paper, record the color change for each test tube in a chart.

7. Record in your Data Table the lowest number of drops of iodine used where the color remained.

TESTING UNSATURATED COOKING OILS *(continued)*

8. Provide your results to your teacher so they may be shared with your class-mates. Enter the data from one additional oil into your Data Table.

9. Clean up the equipment with soapy water. Wash your hands as well.

◆ Observations

Data Table

	Oil _____	Oil _____
Color before adding iodine		
Color and other observations after adding iodine (first day)		
Color after iodine color stops changing (second day)		
Drops of iodine needed for permanent color change		

◆ Analyze and Conclude

1. Why did the oil react with the iodine?

_____

_____

_____

_____

2. Which of the oils is the most unsaturated? Give evidence to support your conclusion.

_____

_____

_____

_____

TESTING UNSATURATED COOKING OILS *(continued)*

◆ Critical Thinking and Applications

1. The iodine was orange when added to the oil. Why did the color disappear?

_____

_____

_____

_____

2. Is the iodine-oil reaction a physical change or a chemical change? Give a reason for your answer.

_____

_____

3. Why did the iodine color remain when the reaction was complete?

_____

_____

_____

4. How can you use the data from this lab to improve your health?

_____

_____

_____

_____

◆ More to Explore

Do the relative amounts of unsaturated fatty acids from your tests agree with the relative amounts on the nutrition labels for the oils? On a separate sheet of paper, make a data table that compares the two sets of figures. Discuss why the relative amounts are or are not comparable.

L-1

The Law of Definite Proportions

1

◆ Pre-Lab Discussion

Many compounds made of exactly the same elements have different physical and chemical properties. For example, carbon dioxide (CO_2) and carbon monoxide (CO) are both gases made of carbon and oxygen. Yet CO_2 is a virtually harmless gas found in the body and in the atmosphere, while CO is deadly when inhaled in sufficient amounts.

The law of definite proportions explains the differences between these two carbon-oxygen compounds. This law states that the elements in a compound always occur in the same ratio by mass. In other words, a CO molecule consists of only one carbon atom and one oxygen atom. A CO_2 molecule consists of one carbon atom and two oxygen atoms. The different numbers of oxygen atoms make these two compounds different from each other.

In this investigation, you will compare the physical and chemical properties of water and hydrogen peroxide, both of which consist of hydrogen and oxygen.

1. What is a ratio?

_____

_____

2. What are some signs of a chemical reaction?

_____

_____

3. How does a catalyst affect a chemical reaction?

_____

_____

4. What happens during a decomposition reaction?

_____

_____

© Prentice-Hall, Inc.

THE LAW OF DEFINITE PROPORTIONS (continued)

◆ Problem

How can two compounds consist of the same elements yet have
different properties?

◆ Materials (per group)

2 test tubes
test-tube rack
glass marker
graduated cylinder, 10 mL
hydrogen peroxide, 3% solution
manganese dioxide
2 wood splints
matches
tongs

◆ Safety   *Review the safety guidelines in the front of your lab book.*

Hydrogen peroxide and manganese dioxide are both poisonous. Keep them away
from your face, and wash your hands thoroughly after using these compounds.
Wear safety goggles and lab aprons throughout the activity.

◆ Procedure

1. **CAUTION:** *Put on your safety goggles and lab apron. Hydrogen peroxide is a
   poison. Keep it away from your face.* Label one test tube H_2O (water) and the
   other H_2O_2 (hydrogen peroxide). Measure 5 mL of each liquid and pour it into
   the appropriate test tube.

2. Observe the physical properties of each compound and record your observations in the Data Table provided on the next page.

3. **CAUTION:** *Tie back long hair and loose clothing, in case you need to use a flame.
   Manganese dioxide is a poison.* Put a small amount of manganese dioxide on
   the tip of a wood splint and add a little of this chemical to each test tube. If
   you see evidence of a chemical reaction, light the unused wood splint with a
   match. Blow out the flame, so that the wood is glowing at the edges. Using
   tongs, insert the glowing splint into the test tube(s) in which a chemical reaction is occurring. Record your observations in the Data Table.

4. Wash your hands when you're finished with the lab.

THE LAW OF DEFINITE PROPORTIONS *(continued)*

◆ Observations

Data Table

Compound	Physical Properties	Evidence of Chemical Reaction to Manganese Dioxide
Water (H_2O)		
Hydrogen peroxide (H_2O_2)		

◆ Analyze and Conclude

1. Compare the physical properties of water and the hydrogen peroxide solution.

_____

_____

2. Compare and contrast the molecular formulas for the two compounds.

_____

_____

3. State a hypothesis to explain why water and hydrogen peroxide have different chemical properties.

_____

_____

◆ Critical Thinking and Applications

1. Hydrogen gas burns. Oxygen gas does not burn but supports the burning of other materials. What seemed to burn in the splint test? What gas did the chemical reaction in this activity produce? How do you know?

_____

_____

2. In this activity, manganese dioxide is a catalyst and is not permanently changed by any chemical reaction in which it is involved. Consider your observations and the role that manganese dioxide plays in a reaction. State a hypothesis about what happened during any chemical reaction that took place.

_____

_____

© Prentice-Hall, Inc.

THE LAW OF DEFINITE PROPORTIONS (continued)

1

3. The atomic mass number of hydrogen is 1.0. The atomic mass number of oxygen is 16.0. What is the ratio by mass of hydrogen to oxygen in water? In hydrogen peroxide?

_____

4. How does the law of definite proportions explain why water and hydrogen peroxide have different properties, although they consist of the same elements?

_____

_____

◆ More to Explore

New Problem Do hydrogen peroxide and water react differently in bleach?

Materials You will need hydrogen peroxide, water, bleach, 2 test tubes, a test tube holder, and a medicine dropper.

Safety Wear safety goggles and aprons. Bleach can damage your clothes. It is also a poison, so keep it away from your face. Wash up after the experiment is done.

Procedure Put a test tube in a holder. Put a few drops of bleach in the test tube. Hold the test tube away from you and add a few drops of hydrogen peroxide. Make sure the tube is not pointed at anyone. Record your observations below. Predict what will happen if you repeat this investigation using water instead of hydrogen peroxide. Test your prediction.

Observations

Hydrogen peroxide and bleach:

Water and bleach:

Analyze and Conclude

1. Why do you think hydrogen peroxide and bleach reacted as they did?

_____

_____

2. How could you find out if bleach is used up in the reaction with hydrogen peroxide or if it is a catalyst?

_____

_____

_____

L-2   LABORATORY INVESTIGATION

Testing for Hard Water

◆ Pre-Lab Discussion

Hard water is a common problem for many households. It can form chemical deposits that clog water pipes and damage water heaters and boilers. What causes hard water? No natural water source is 100% pure water. All sources contain other chemicals, such as calcium and magnesium compounds. These compounds form ions in water. Ions are single atoms or groups of atoms that carry an electric charge. The total amount of ions present in water is a measure of the hardness of the water.

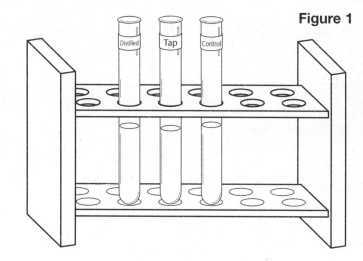

Figure 1

When you add soap to hard water, the ions combine with the soap and form scum. Because some soap is being used to produce scum, fewer suds form. Therefore, you need to use more soap when you shower or wash your clothes. You can tell from the amount of soap suds how hard the water is.

In this investigation, you will test water and rate its hardness.

1. How does soap make it possible for water and oil to mix?

_____

_____

2. Why are soap and the ions in hard water attracted to each other to form scum?

_____

_____

_____

◆ Problem

How can you determine if water is hard?

TESTING FOR HARD WATER *(continued)*

◆ Possible Materials *(per group)*

distilled water
tap water
3 or 4 test tubes
test-tube rack
graduated cylinder
plastic dropper
100-mL beaker
bar soap
liquid hand soap
standard sample of hard water

2

◆ Safety   *Review the safety guidelines in the front of your lab book.*

Always clean up spilled water to prevent falls.

◆ Procedure

1. Read the entire lab before starting your investigation.

2. Working with a partner or group, plan how to test the hardness of water. Consider the following:

   • What water will you test?

   • What will you use as a control?

   • Use soap to test for hardness. What will you look for as evidence of hardness? Be sure to use the same amount of soap for each sample.

   • What observations will you record? You can either use the Data Table in Observations or develop your own data table on a separate sheet of paper.

3. Once you have decided what samples you will test, predict which sample will be the hardest and which the least hard. Give reasons for your predictions.

   _____

   _____

   _____

   _____

4. Write your procedure on a separate sheet of paper. Have the teacher approve your procedure before you carry out the investigation. Remember to wear your safety goggles and apron.

© Prentice-Hall, Inc.

TESTING FOR HARD WATER *(continued)*

◆ Observations

Data Table

Water Type and Soap	Observations	
	Just After Mixing	10 min After Mixing
Distilled water		
Tap water		
Control		

◆ Analyze and Conclude

1. How does the soap show that water is hard?

_____

_____

_____

2. List samples in order of hardness, from most to least.

_____

3. How do your results differ from your prediction? Explain what your results mean.

_____

_____

_____

TESTING FOR HARD WATER *(continued)*

◆ Critical Thinking and Applications

1. Did suds form in all the test tubes? If not, why?

_____

_____

2. The control contained calcium chloride dissolved in distilled water. What ions are present in the control?

_____

_____

2

3. What are the disadvantages of using hard water to do laundry?

_____

_____

_____

_____

4. What do you have to do to turn hard water into soft water?

_____

_____

_____

◆ More to Explore

Check the labels of some laundry detergents and soaps and list the ingredients. Note any special directions about using the detergent. Use a chemical reference book to find out more about these chemicals. How does getting clothes clean in hard water differ from doing so in soft water? Write a procedure you could use to test your hypothesis. Have the teacher approve your procedure before you carry out your investigation. Remember to wear your safety goggles and apron.

L-3   **LABORATORY INVESTIGATION**

Determining Solubility

◆ Pre-Lab Discussion

Solubility is how much of a solid can dissolve in a liquid. Suppose, for example, you stir salt (the solute) into a glass of water (the solvent) a little at a time. The salt dissolves until the saltwater solution is saturated. After that, added salt crystals will no longer disappear.

Now suppose you took an identical glass of water and made a saturated solution of sugar. You could stir in a lot more sugar than salt before the solution becomes saturated. In fact, you could tell the two samples apart by observing how much of each dissolves in the same amount of water. The water has to be the same temperature, however, or your results would not be comparable. The amount of sugar that could dissolve in cold water is different than the amount that can dissolve in the same amount of warm water.

In this investigation, you will determine the amount of a solute that can dissolve in water at different temperatures.

1. What is a solution?

_____

_____

2. What is a saturated solution?

_____

_____

3. How do you know when a solution is saturated?

_____

_____

◆ Problem

How can you determine the solubility of a substance in water?

◆ Materials (per group)

small piece of paper, about	2 test tubes
15 cm × 15 cm	thermometer
balance	hot plate
25 g potassium nitrate	two 250-mL beakers
water	ice
10-mL graduated cylinder	spatula
tongs	

© Prentice-Hall, Inc.

3

DETERMINING SOLUBILITY *(continued)*

◆ Safety   *Review the safety guidelines in the front of your lab book.*

Handle the thermometer carefully. If it breaks, tell the teacher. Use tongs or an oven mitt when handling hot objects.

◆ Procedure

1. The teacher will assign you a high and a low temperature to use in the lab.

2. Use a balance to find the mass of the small sheet of plain paper. In the Data Table, record the mass of the paper.

3. Adjust the balance so that it registers 25 g more than the mass of the paper alone. Slowly and carefully add potassium nitrate to the paper until the balance is again level. In this way, you have poured out 25 g of potassium nitrate. Record this amount in the Data Table. Add and record the total mass of the paper and potassium nitrate.

4. Pour 10 mL of water into a test tube. Put the test tube in a half-filled beaker of water. Place the beaker on the hot plate. See Figure 1. Insert a thermometer in the test tube. You will need to hold the thermometer so that the end is in the water but not touching the bottom.

5. Heat the test tube in the water bath over the hot plate until the water reaches the high temperature assigned to you. **CAUTION:** *Use tongs to hold the thermometer in the test tube.* Try to maintain this temperature during the next step by adjusting the dial on the hot plate.

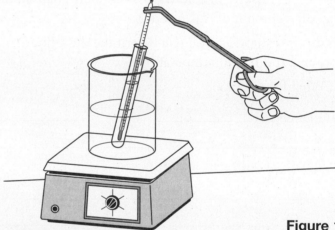

Figure 1

6. Use as spatula to put a small amount of the 25 g of potassium nitrate into the test tube. Stir carefully with the thermometer. If the potassium nitrate dissolves completely, add a little more. Continue adding small amounts of potassium nitrate until no more dissolves and a few small grains settle to the bottom of the test tube. Now you have a saturated solution.

7. In the Data Table, record the exact temperature of the solution when it has become saturated.

8. Find the mass of the paper and the remaining potassium nitrate. Subtract this amount from the mass before dissolving to find the amount of potassium nitrate you used. Record the amount used in the Data Table.

DETERMINING SOLUBILITY *(continued)*

9. Half-fill a beaker with ice. Pour 10 mL of water into another test tube. Set the test tube on the ice. Insert a thermometer so that the end is in the water but not touching the bottom. Cool the water until it reaches the second temperature assigned to you. Try to maintain this temperature during the next step by periodically removing the test tube from the ice.

10. Repeat steps 6–8.

11. Report your data to the teacher, who will compile all the information obtained by the class. In this way, you will find out how much potassium nitrate dissolves in 10 mL of water over a wide temperature range.

12. Graph the class's results on the grid provided in Observations.

◆ Observations

Data Table

Mass of paper	
Mass of potassium nitrate	
Mass of paper and potassium nitrate before dissolving	
Temperature of heated solution when saturated	
Mass of paper and potassium nitrate after saturation	
Mass of potassium nitrate used to saturate	
Temperature of cooled solution	
Mass of paper and potassium nitrate before dissolving	
Mass of paper and potassium nitrate after saturation	
Mass of potassium nitrate used to saturate	

DETERMINING SOLUBILITY *(continued)*

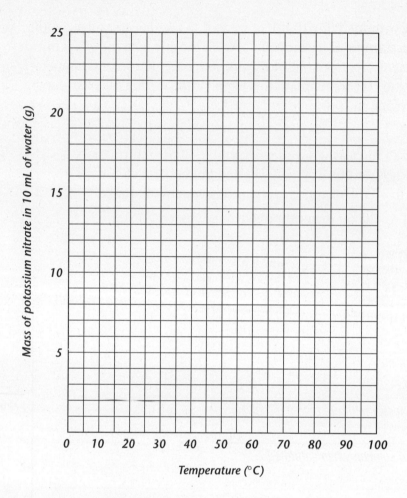

◆ Analyze and Conclude

1. What effect does temperature have on the amount of potassium nitrate that can dissolve in a given amount of water?

_____

_____

2. From your graph, predict how much potassium nitrate would dissolve in 10 mL of water at 60°C.

_____

3. How much potassium nitrate do you think could dissolve in 100 mL of water at 60°C? Show your calculations.

DETERMINING SOLUBILITY *(continued)*

4. What temperature would 10 mL of water have to be for 14 g of potassium nitrate to just dissolve completely?

_____

◆ Critical Thinking and Applications

1. If the temperature of a saturated solution of potassium nitrate dropped, what would you see?

_____

_____

_____

2. Based on the graph, how much potassium nitrate do you think would dissolve in 190 mL of water at 100°C? Show your calculations.

3. Suppose you measured the solubility of potassium nitrate only at 10°C and at 90°C. Would this affect the accuracy of your solubility graph? Give a reason for your answer.

_____

_____

_____

_____

4. If 10 mL of a saturated solution of potassium nitrate cooled from 60°C to 10°C, how much potassium nitrate would be on the bottom of the test tube? Show your calculations.

DETERMINING SOLUBILITY *(continued)*

◆ More to Explore

New Problem What is the solubility of sodium chloride under the same conditions as in this lab? Does its graph differ from the graph for potassium nitrate?

Materials Use the same equipment as in this lab.

Safety Handle the thermometer carefully. If it breaks, tell your teacher. Use tongs or an oven mitt when handling hot objects. Wear your safety goggles and apron.

Procedure Decide how, if at all, you should adjust the previous procedure to solve this new problem. Have the teacher approve your procedure before you carry out the investigation.

Observations Plot the data on the same graph in Observations.

Analyze and Conclude

1. How does the solubility graph for sodium chloride compare to the graph for potassium nitrate?

_____

_____

2. Use your graph to find the temperature at which sodium chloride and potassium nitrate have the same solubility.

_____

L-4

Separating Plastics

◆ Pre-Lab Discussion

Schools, stores, and sports arenas make special containers available for disposal of aluminum cans. Trash collectors pick up recyclable materials separated from the rest of the trash.

More and more, people are recycling resources so they can be used again. Along with metals, glass, and paper, a variety of plastics can be recycled. If you look at a soft-drink bottle, plastic wrap, a cottage-cheese container, and a plastic pipe, you can see some of the different properties plastics can have. Because of these differences, plastics must be separated by type before recycling. Often a number in a triangle on the bottom of the item indicates the type of plastic, as shown in Data Table 1 below.

Data Table 1: Recyclable Plastics

Plastic	Some Uses	Recycling Code	Products Made from Recycled Plastic
Polyethylene terephthalate (PETE)	Soft-drink bottles, detergent containers	(1)	Carpets, skis, paintbrushes, fiberfill
High-density polyethylene (HDPE)	Milk jugs, some grocery bags, crates	(2)	Piping, toys, fencing, garden furniture
Polyvinyl chloride (PVC)	Shampoo bottles, credit cards, shrink wrap	(3)	Fencing, flooring, piping, wiring insulation
Low-density polyethylene (LDPE)	Food wrap, trash bags, some grocery bags	(4)	Trash bags, insulation
Polypropylene (PP)	Drinking straws, caps, lids	(5)	Batteries, industrial parts
Polystyrene (PS)	Fast-food containers, disposable cups and plates, egg cartons, meat trays, packing material	(6)	Office equipment, insulation

© Prentice-Hall, Inc.

SEPARATING PLASTICS *(continued)*

Plastic containers can take up a lot of space, so waste-handling facilities prefer to shred them as they arrive. Unfortunately, shredding makes separating the plastic more difficult because identifying codes get lost. In this investigation, you will find a way to separate these pieces of different types of plastic by comparing their densities. Remember that less dense materials float in more dense materials, and more dense materials sink in less dense materials.

1. Plastic is a type of polymer. What is a polymer?

_____

_____

_____

2. Explain the difference between a natural polymer and a synthetic polymer.

_____

_____

_____

_____

◆ Problem

How can different types of shredded plastic be separated?

◆ Materials *(per group)*

sheet of paper
2 or 3 pieces of polystyrene
2 or 3 pieces of PETE (polyethylene terephthalate)
2 or 3 pieces of HDPE (high-density polyethylene)
2 or 3 pieces of polypropylene
2 plastic or paper cups, 8-oz
water
100-mL graduated cylinder
forceps
isopropyl (rubbing) alcohol 91%
tablespoon
plastic spoon

◆ Safety   *Review the safety guidelines in your lab book.*

© Prentice-Hall, Inc.

SEPARATING PLASTICS *(continued)*

◆ Procedure

1. Fold a sheet of paper in fourths. Unfold the paper. Write the name of a different type of plastic from the materials list in each of the four sections.

2. Get two or three pieces of each type of plastic. When you are not using them, keep the plastic pieces on their section of the paper to help you keep track of their identity.

3. Write a description of each plastic in Data Table 2.

4. Predict which plastic is the most dense and which is the least dense. Give reasons for your predictions.

_____

_____

_____

_____

5. Add 100 mL of water to one cup. Put two or three pieces of polystyrene in the water. Use a spoon to gently stir the water. Push the pieces underwater as you stir. Record in Data Table 2 whether the polystyrene floats in water.

6. Use forceps to remove the plastic from the water. One type at a time, test the other plastic samples to see whether they float in water. Record your results in Data Table 2.

7. Add 100 mL of rubbing alcohol to the other cup. **CAUTION:** *Do not get alcohol near your mouth or eyes. Be sure no open flame is anywhere in the room when you are using alcohol.*

8. Repeat steps 5 and 6, using the alcohol instead of water to test any samples that floated in the water.

9. Return to the cup containing the water. Add one piece of each type of plastic that floated on the water but sank in the alcohol.

10. Add one tablespoonful of the alcohol from Step 7 to the water, then stir.

11. Keep adding alcohol, one tablespoon at a time, to the cup until one of the samples sinks. Keep track of how many tablespoons of alcohol were added. Record this information in Observations question 1 and your results in Data Table 2.

12. Rinse the plastic pieces in water and give them to the teacher to recycle. Pour the alcohol-water mixture down the drain, accompanied by plenty of water. Return any unused alcohol to the teacher.

SEPARATING PLASTICS *(continued)*

◆ Observations

Data Table 2

Plastic	Description of Plastic	Floated or not, if tested		
		In Water	In Alcohol	In Mixture

1. How many tablespoons of alcohol did you add in steps 10 and 11 before one piece of plastic sank? What type was it?

_____

_____

◆ Analyze and Conclude

1. Why wasn't it necessary to test all the plastics with the alcohol (in Step 8) and the alcohol-water mixture (in steps 9–11)?

_____

_____

_____

_____

2. Rank the following from least dense to most dense: water, alcohol, water-alcohol mixture. Give a reason for your answer.

_____

_____

_____

_____

SEPARATING PLASTICS *(continued)*

3. Rank the plastics you tested from least dense to most dense. Give reasons for your answer.

_____

_____

_____

_____

◆ Critical Thinking and Applications

1. Were your predictions in Step 4 correct? What difficulties did you face in making a prediction?

_____

_____

_____

_____

2. Describe a procedure that a recycling center could use to separate small pieces of different types of plastic.

_____

_____

_____

_____

3. Think about the densities of gold, water, and soil. Explain how panning for gold uses differences in density.

_____

_____

_____

_____

4. Metals are extracted from ores that are mined. A limited amount of ore is available, so it's important to recycle metals and conserve ore. Plastics, on the other hand, are human-made. Why is it important that they be recycled?

_____

_____

_____

_____

SEPARATING PLASTICS *(continued)*

◆ More to Explore

Look at the plastic coding system in Data Table 1. Examine plastic items around your home. Which types of plastic do you dispose of most often? Contact a local recycling operation and find out which of these plastics it collects and recycles. If your community doesn't recycle all types of plastics, find out why not.

4

© Prentice-Hall, Inc.

Measuring Speed

◆ Pre-Lab Discussion

Perhaps you've heard about the race between the tortoise and the hare. The hare was a fast runner but kept taking breaks because it was so sure of winning. The tortoise could only walk but never took a break. The hare lost the race.

These two racers demonstrate the difference between speed at one particular instant and average speed. To find a person's speed, you need an accurate measurement of the distance he or she travels and how long it takes the person to cover the distance.

In this investigation, you will design and use a plan to find the average speed of a pedestrian.

1. What is the formula used to calculate speed?

_____

2. If you calculated the average speed of a runner in a marathon, would the runner be moving at that speed at every point in the race? Give a reason for your answer.

_____

_____

◆ Problem

How can you find the average speed of a pedestrian?

◆ Possible Materials *(per group)*

tape measure or meterstick
masking tape
3 stopwatches

◆ Safety 🔬 *Review the safety guidelines in the front of your lab book.*

Don't get in the way of the people whose speed you are measuring. Don't create hazards in the walkway.

MEASURING SPEED (continued)

◆ Procedure

1. Read through the entire lab now.

2. Develop a procedure to find out how fast pedestrians move. Consider the following variables and questions as you develop your procedure.

- Choose a place that gets a lot of pedestrian traffic. It should have room for you to work without getting in the subjects' way.

- How long should the course be?

- How will you mark the beginning and end of the course?

- When does a subject officially enter the course and leave it?

- How will you get accurate beginning and ending times for the course?

- How many people will you need to do the timing?

- Include a way to check whether the pedestrian's rate is variable or constant. For example, you could have timers at the quarter mark, halfway point, and at the three-quarters mark. A fourth person could signal all the timers to begin timing, and each would stop their stopwatch as the pedestrian passed by.

Write your procedure on a separate sheet of paper.

3. Decide what data you will need to collect. You should gather enough data to be able to show whether the subject speeds up or slows down. Time at least 5 subjects. Adjust the Data Table on the next page so that you can use it with your procedure. You may want to add columns and headings.

4. After the teacher has approved your plan and data table, go ahead with the experiment. Practice your timing technique before trying to record data. You may need to adjust the length of the course.

5. After you collect your data, answer the questions in Observations.

◆ Observations

1. Which pedestrian had the fastest average speed over the entire course? What was it?

_____

2. Which pedestrian had the slowest average speed over the entire course? What was it?

_____

MEASURING SPEED *(continued)*

Data Table

Course Length: _____

Subject		Total Time (s)	Average Speed (m/s)

© Prentice-Hall, Inc.

◆ Analyze and Conclude

1. Did any of the pedestrians speed up while walking the course? How do you know?

_____

_____

_____

2. Did any of the pedestrians slow down while walking the course? How do you know?

_____

_____

_____

MEASURING SPEED *(continued)*

◆ Critical Thinking and Applications

1. How accurate do you think the measured times are? Suggest a method that would allow you to get more accurate results in this experiment.

_____

_____

_____

2. Would the results of your investigation have been different if you had timed vehicles on a street rather than people walking? Would it have been easier or more difficult to get accurate results? Give a reason for your answer.

_____

_____

_____

_____

_____

3. If you were going to repeat the investigation using vehicles, would you be more likely to get accurate results with a longer course or a shorter course? Give a reason for your answer.

_____

_____

_____

◆ More to Explore

Do you know what your average walking speed is? It probably varies, depending on circumstances, such as whether you're late or early for school. How could you use your walking speed to measure distance? On another sheet of paper, write a procedure you would follow to answer this question. Include a way to check the accuracy of your measurements. Have the teacher approve your procedure before you carry out the investigation. How could you improve the accuracy of your measurements?

M-2 LABORATORY INVESTIGATION

Weight and the Force of Gravity

◆ Pre-Lab Discussion

If you've ever seen astronauts floating in a spacecraft, you've observed that mass and weight are different properties. The astronauts' mass doesn't change, but their weight decreases so much that they appear to float.

Mass and weight are certainly different, yet they are related. The mass of an object is the amount of matter it contains. You can use a balance to measure mass. The weight of an object is the force of gravity on its mass. To measure weight, you can use a spring. Because weight is the downward force of gravity on an object, a weight on a spring stretches the spring. The greater the weight of the object, the more the spring stretches.

If known masses are attached to a spring, you can use the amount of stretch (weight) to compare the weights of the unknown masses. In this investigation, you will measure how much a spring stretches with different numbers of washers. You will use these data to find the relationship between mass and weight.

1. What is gravity?

_____

2. How would your mass and weight change if you went to the moon, which has much less mass than Earth?

_____

_____

◆ Problem

How can you measure the force known as weight?

◆ Materials *(per group)*

ring stand	clamp
large ring	2 large paper clips
spring	15 washers
meterstick	100-g mass

WEIGHT AND THE FORCE OF GRAVITY (continued)

◆ Safety   *Review the safety guidelines in the front of your lab book.*

Wear safety goggles during this activity. To prevent slips or falls, immediately pick up any dropped washers.

◆ Procedure

1. Attach the ring to the ring stand and hang the spring from it. Clamp the meterstick to the ring stand, so that the 100-cm mark is on the tabletop and the spring is close to, but not touching, the meterstick. Bend the large paper clip into an S and hang it on the bottom of the spring. See Figure 1.

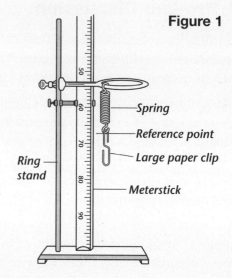

Figure 1

2. Note the number on the meterstick, to the nearest tenth of a centimeter, that is just even with the bottom of the spring. Record this reference point in Data Table 1.

3. Hang 5 washers on the paper clip and note the number on the meterstick that is just even with the bottom of the spring. Record this number in Data Table 1.

4. Repeat Step 3 with 10 washers and with 15 washers on the paper clip.

5. If you removed washers five at a time, predict whether the spring's length will be the same or different from its length when you added washers. Give a reason for your prediction.

_____

_____

6. Remove 5 washers. Note the number on the meterstick that is just even with the bottom of the spring. Record the number in Data Table 1. Do this twice more, removing 5 washers each time.

7. To find the change in the length of the spring, find the difference between each particular meterstick reading and the previous reading. Calculate this change to complete Data Table 1.

8. Note the reference point, as you did in Step 2. Record this number in Data Table 2.

9. Hang a 100-g mass from the spring and note the number on the meterstick that is just even with the bottom of the spring. Record this number in Data Table 2. Calculate and record the change in length of the spring.

© Prentice-Hall, Inc.

WEIGHT AND THE FORCE OF GRAVITY *(continued)*

◆ Observations

Data Table 1

Number of Washers	Reading of Meterstick (cm)	Stretch Length (cm) (Change in Length of Spring Compared to Previous Measurement)
0		
5		
10		
15		
10		
5		
0		

Data Table 2

Reference point (cm)	
Meterstick reading with 100-g mass (cm)	
Change in length of spring (cm)	

◆ Analyze and Conclude

1. Use the grid at the right to graph your results in Data Table 1. Label the vertical axis *Stretch length (cm)* and the horizontal axis *Number of washers.*

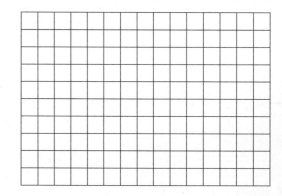

2. How much did the length of the spring change as each group of 5 washers was added?

_____

3. How much did the length of the spring change as each group of 5 washers was removed?

_____

WEIGHT AND THE FORCE OF GRAVITY *(continued)*

4. How do your answers to questions 2 and 3 compare? Explain why they are the same or different.

_____

_____

5. How does the shape of your graph illustrate your answers to questions 2 and 3?

_____

_____

◆ Critical Thinking and Applications

1. What forces act on the objects you attach to the spring?

_____

_____

2. In terms of force, explain why the spring stretched as more washers were added.

_____

_____

_____

3. In Data Table 2, you put a 100-g mass on the spring and recorded the amount the spring stretched. From your graph, you know that mass and stretch length increase together at a steady rate. Use this information to calculate the mass of 5 washers. What is the mass of 1 washer?

4. Why do you think a spring balance might give different results at different times?

_____

_____

◆ More to Explore

Does an object weigh more, less, or the same under water as it does in air? Write a procedure you would follow to answer this question, and predict the results. Have the teacher approve your procedure before you carry out the investigation. Was your prediction correct? If not, do some research to find out why you had surprising results.

M-3   LABORATORY INVESTIGATION

Raising a Sunken Ship

◆ Pre-Lab Discussion

Why does a ship float? Ships float because they are buoyant. Buoyancy is related to the density of the ship. A ship will float if its density is less than the density of the water in which it floats.

Many ships carrying valuable cargo have sunk over the centuries. Some went down because great holes in their hulls let in water that destroyed their buoyancy. Suppose you have been hired by a salvage operation that has discovered a sunken ship. The ship is not too badly damaged, and the salvage crew hopes to raise it intact. The rumor is that this vessel was carrying valuable cargo when it went down 100 years ago. You might make a lot of money if you could get the vessel to the surface of the ocean. In addition, the historical significance could be great. You have some ideas on how to raise the ship, but you need to try them on a model first.

In this investigation, you will try to raise a model of a sunken ship.

1. Define density.

_____

_____

2. How can a ship that weighs many tons float when the metal it is made of would sink if in a solid block?

_____

_____

_____

_____

◆ Problem

How can you change the buoyancy of a ship sunk in deep water so that it floats to the surface?

RAISING A SUNKEN SHIP *(continued)*

◆ **Possible Materials** *(per group)*

soda can or other container
    that will float when empty
aquarium or large bucket
handheld air pump
plastic or rubber tubing,
    various lengths
tongs or forceps
tape
clay
balloons
string
plastic straws
balance
graduated cylinder, 100 mL

◆ **Safety**   *Review the safety guidelines in the front of your lab book.*

Always wear safety goggles. To prevent slips or falls, immediately wipe up any
water spilled on the floor.

◆ **Procedure**

1. Observe the can at the bottom of the container of water. The can represents the
   sunken ship. Working with a partner or in a group, decide on a plan to float
   the can. Because the sunken ship is supposed to be in very deep water, you may
   not touch the can with your hands or put your hands in the water until the can
   is at the surface. You may only use the tools and materials listed above to get
   the can to float. What property of the can has to change before it will float?

   _____

2. Write down your selected procedure on a separate sheet of paper. Have the
   teacher approve your procedure before you carry out the investigation. Follow
   your procedure to float the can.

3. After the can floats to the surface, remove the can from the water and dry
   it. Find the mass of the empty can and record it in the Data Table on the
   next page.

4. Fill the can with water and find the mass of the filled can. Record the value.

5. Measure the volume of the water in the can, using a graduated cylinder. If the
   amount of water is more than 100 mL, measure the first 100 mL, empty the
   graduated cylinder, and measure the remaining water. Add the numbers and
   record the volume in the Data Table.

RAISING A SUNKEN SHIP *(continued)*

◆ Observations

Data Table

Mass of empty can		g
Mass of can plus water		g
Volume of water		mL

◆ Analyze and Conclude

1. If the volume of the water in the can is 350 mL, what is the volume of the can when it is empty (that is, contains only air)?

_____

2. Calculate the density of the can when it is empty.

3. Calculate the density of the water-filled can.

4. How do the densities of the empty can and the water-filled can compare to the density of water, which is 1.0 g/mL?

_____

_____

_____

_____

RAISING A SUNKEN SHIP *(continued)*

◆ Critical Thinking and Applications

1. Would you expect the empty can to float? Give a reason for your answer.

_____

_____

_____

2. Use the data you collected on mass and volume to explain why the water-filled can sank.

_____

_____

_____

3. Would you expect a can that is half-filled with water to float? Use the data that you collected on mass and volume to solve this problem.

4. Calculate the maximum amount of water that the can could hold and still float. (Hint: To barely float, the can and water must have a density slightly less than the density of water, which is 1.0 g/mL.)

◆ More to Explore

Consider how you would raise an artifact from the sea floor, such as a 225-kg cannon or a 5,000-kg section of the *Titanic*. What problems would you encounter? Write a procedure you would follow to answer this question. Present your procedure to the class and compare it to other students' ideas.

LABORATORY INVESTIGATION

Pulleys as Simple Machines

◆ Pre-Lab Discussion

Pulleys are simple machines that lift objects in a variety of ways. The simplest kind of pulley is a grooved wheel around which a rope is pulled. Pulleys can change the direction of an applied force. For example, a pulley fixed to the top of a flagpole lets you raise a flag *up* by pulling *down*.

A combination of fixed and movable pulleys is a pulley system, or block and tackle. A pulley system multiplies input force to lift heavy objects. Pulley systems are commonly seen on construction sites.

In this investigation, you will use different pulley systems and determine the mechanical advantage of each.

1. Define the mechanical advantage of a machine.

_____

_____

2. Why is a pulley considered a machine?

_____

_____

_____

◆ Problem

How do pulleys help raise objects? How can you find the actual mechanical advantage of a pulley or pulley system?

◆ Materials *(per group)*

2 single pulleys
2 double pulleys
nylon fishing line, 1 m
ring stand
large ring
1,000–g spring scale
500-g mass

◆ Safety *Review the safety guidelines in the front of your lab book.*

PULLEYS AS SIMPLE MACHINES *(continued)*

◆ Procedure

1. Calibrate the spring scale so that it reads zero when no masses are attached to it.

2. Find the weight of the mass you are using by attaching it directly to the spring scale. Record this weight in the Data Table in Observations as the output force for all the pulley arrangements.

3. Set up a single fixed pulley as shown in Figure 1. Pull down on the spring scale to lift the mass. The reading on the scale shows the amount of input force needed to lift the mass. Record this number in the Data Table.

4. Set up a single movable pulley as shown in Figure 2. Lift the mass by pulling up on the spring scale. The reading on the scale shows the amount of force needed to lift the mass. Record this number in the Data Table.

5. Set up the single fixed and single movable pulley system shown in Figure 3. Measure the amount of force needed to lift the mass and record it in the Data Table.

6. Set up the pulley systems shown in figures 4 and 5. For each pulley system, measure the amount of force needed to lift the mass and record it in the Data Table.

7. Calculate the actual mechanical advantage for each pulley and record it in the Data Table.

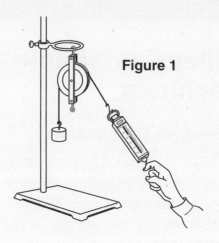

Figure 1

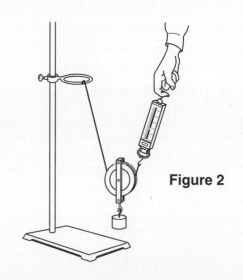

Figure 2

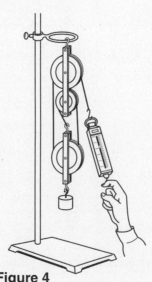

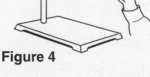

Figure 3

Figure 4

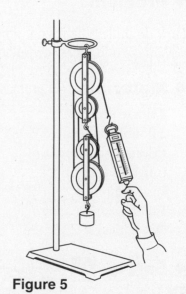

Figure 5

PULLEYS AS SIMPLE MACHINES *(continued)*

◆ Observations

Data Table

Pulley Arrangements	Output Force (O)	Input Force (I)	Actual Mechanical Advantage (O ÷ I)
Single fixed			
Single movable			
Single fixed and single movable			
Double fixed and single movable			
Double fixed and double movable			

◆ Analyze and Conclude

1. Was there a difference in the mechanical advantages you calculated for the single fixed pulley and the single movable pulley? Give a reason for your answer.

_____

_____

_____

2. As you added pulleys to the system, what happened to the amount of input force needed to raise the mass?

_____

_____

3. What factors determine the mechanical advantage of pulley systems?

_____

_____

◆ Critical Thinking and Applications

1. If a simple machine has a mechanical advantage of 1, input force is not multiplied. Which type of pulley has an ideal mechanical advantage of 1? What is the practical use of this pulley?

_____

_____

© Prentice-Hall, Inc.

PULLEYS AS SIMPLE MACHINES *(continued)*

2. To determine the ideal mechanical advantage of a pulley or pulley system without calculations, count the number of sections of rope that support the weight. The end section, which is attached to the spring scale, counts as a supporting section *only when pulled upward.* Using figures 1 through 5, determine the number of supporting rope sections for each type of pulley.

    a. Figure 1: _____   **c.** Figure 3: _____   **e.** Figure 5: _____

    b. Figure 2: _____   **d.** Figure 4: _____

3. Do the values from question 2 agree with the actual mechanical advantage calculated for the Data Table? Why or why not?

_____

_____

_____

4. Draw an arrangement of two double pulleys that would give you a mechanical advantage of 6.

5. When using any simple machine, you never get something for nothing. Although the amount of input force needed to lift a mass is usually less in a pulley system, something else increases. What must increase as the input force decreases?

_____

6. Explain your answer to question 5 in terms of work input and work output.

_____

_____

_____

◆ More to Explore

In this investigation, you calculated mechanical advantage by dividing the output force by the input force. How could you use distances moved by the output and input forces to calculate mechanical advantage? Write a procedure you would follow to answer this question. Have the teacher approve your procedure before you carry out the investigation. How do these mechanical advantages compare with the ones you calculated earlier? Is one method better than the other for calculating mechanical advantage?

M - 5   **LABORATORY INVESTIGATION**

Winding Up With Wind

◆ Pre-Lab Discussion

Wind power is an ancient energy source. The earliest ships used the wind to carry them across seas. The first windmills were built in Persia (now Iran) in the sixth century A.D. They raised water from rivers. Later, windmills were used to turn a large stone wheel that ground grains.

Today, huge windmills, or wind turbines, generate electricity. The wind turbines are grouped in clusters called wind farms. Most wind farms are in California, located in windy mountain passes. California wind farms produce enough electricity to power all the homes of San Francisco. By the middle of the twenty-first century, experts think wind power could supply up to one-fifth of the electricity used in the United States.

In this investigation, you will design blades for a windmill, build a model windmill, and measure its power output.

1. What kind of energy does wind have? Give a reason for your answer.

_____

2. How do you calculate power?

_____

_____

◆ Problem

How can you design a windmill and test its power output?

◆ Possible Materials *(per group)*

windmill base	thumbtacks
electric fan	string
scissors	cloth
poster board	sandpaper
cardboard	thread
balsa wood	paper clips
white glue	stopwatch
masking tape	meterstick
transparent tape	balance
pushpins	plastic straw

WINDING UP WITH WIND *(continued)*

◆ **Safety** *Review the safety guidelines in the front of your lab book.*

Keep your fingers and other objects away from the moving blades of the fan.

◆ Procedure

Part A: Design Blades

1. Brainstorm a list of features that you need to consider in designing windmill blades. Look at pictures of different types of windmills, both old and modern in design. See Figure 1.

2. Choose the materials you will use for your windmill blades.

3. Design the blades for your windmill. (Hint: Consider the tilt of each blade.) On a separate sheet of paper, draw and describe how you will construct the blades and attach them to the windmill base. Have the teacher approve your design.

4. Construct your windmill blades and attach them to the base.

5. Try out the windmill, using an electric fan for wind. Hold the windmill about 30 cm from the fan.

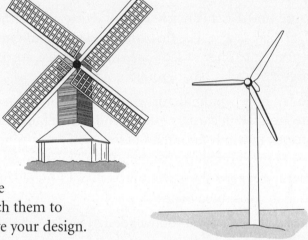

Figure 1

Part B: Measure Power Output

6. Tape a piece of thread, about 75 cm long, on your windmill's spool. Attach a paper clip to the other end of the string, as shown in Figure 2.

7. Place your windmill at the edge of your lab bench so that the paper clip is suspended in air. See if your windmill can lift the paper clip by winding up the thread on the spool.

8. Add more paper clips until you reach the maximum capacity for your windmill.

9. Measure the length of the thread, from the spool to the top of the paper clips. Record this length in the Data Table on the next page. Use a stopwatch to time how long it takes to lift the paper clips. Record the time.

10. Remove the paper clips and find their mass. Record the mass in the Data Table.

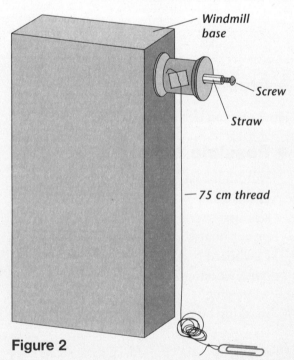

Windmill base

Screw

Straw

75 cm thread

Figure 2

© Prentice-Hall, Inc.

WINDING UP WITH WIND *(continued)*

◆ Observations

Data Table

Length of thread	
Time for paper clips to be lifted	
Mass of paper clips	

◆ Analyze and Conclude

1. Calculate the potential energy that the paper clips gained when they were lifted. Use the formula

Gravitational potential energy =
Mass (g) × Gravitational acceleration (980 cm/s^2) × Height (cm).

Divide your results by 10,000 and the units of your result will be mJ (millijoule, a thousandth of a joule).

2. Calculate the power that gave the paper clips this energy. Use the formula

Power = Work (mJ) ÷ Time (s).

The units of your result will be mW (milliwatt, a thousandth of a watt).

3. Did your design work well? Which features of your design do you think were most important?

_____

_____

_____

_____

WINDING UP WITH WIND (*continued*)

◆ Critical Thinking and Applications

1. Was gravitational potential energy the only kind of energy that the paper clips got from the windmill? Give a reason for your answer.

_____

_____

_____

_____

2. Look at the fan you used in the investigation, especially at its blades. Could it be used for a windmill? How could you prove this?

_____

_____

_____

_____

3. In terms of energy conversion, what is the difference between an electric fan and a windmill that generates electricity?

_____

_____

_____

_____

◆ More to Explore

Try to improve your windmill by changing one feature of your design. Have the teacher approve your new design before you build it. Construct your new design and test your windmill as you did before. Compare your new results to those of your original design. Which generated more power?

© Prentice-Hall, Inc.

M-6

Combustion Heat of a Candle

◆ Pre-Lab Discussion

During combustion, fuel burns, which produces heat and light. The combustion heat of a candle is the heat released when a candle burns. You can measure the amount of heat released by using a calorimeter. The calorimeter holds water and measures changes in the water's temperature. You heat the water with a candle and can calculate the combustion heat of the candle by using the mass and the temperature change of the water.

In this investigation, you will find out how much heat it takes to raise the temperature of a certain amount of water and what the combustion heat of candle wax is.

1. Why do you think that water is used in the calorimeter?

_____

_____

_____

2. Do all candles have the same combustion heat? Give a reason for your answer.

_____

_____

_____

◆ Problem

What is the combustion heat of a candle?

◆ Materials *(per group)*

bottle and can opener	large can, open at both ends
small can, open at one end	matches
thin wooden dowel	metric ruler
ring stand and ring	balance
candle	water
can lid	graduated cylinder, 100 mL
Celsius thermometer	ice cubes

6

COMBUSTION HEAT OF A CANDLE (continued)

◆ Safety   *Review the safety guidelines in the front of your lab book.*

Handle the thermometer carefully. If it breaks, tell the teacher. Use tongs or an oven mitt when handling hot objects. Always wear safety goggles when heating objects. Be careful of raw, sharp edges on the cans and can lid.

◆ Procedure

1. Insert the wooden dowel through the two holes in opposite sides of the small can. Hang the small can by the dowel on a support ring, as shown in Figure 1.

2. Attach the unlit candle to a small can lid or tray with a few drops of melted wax. Record the combined mass of the candle and the can lid to the nearest 0.1 g. Record this value in the Data Table on the next page.

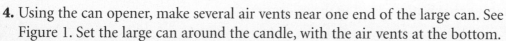

Figure 1

3. Set the unlit candle under the hanging can. Adjust the ring so that the bottom of the can is 5 cm above the top of the candle. Remove the small can from the ring stand and take the wooden dowel out.

4. Using the can opener, make several air vents near one end of the large can. See Figure 1. Set the large can around the candle, with the air vents at the bottom.

5. Use the graduated cylinder to fill the small can approximately half full of water. In the Data Table, record the volume of water you use.

6. Measure the temperature of the water in the small can. Cool the water with some ice enclosed in a plastic bag until the temperature drops 10° to 15°C below its initial temperature. Remove the bag of ice. In the Data Table, record the temperature of the water after cooling to the nearest 1°C.

7. **CAUTION:** *Be extremely careful when lighting and working with an open flame. Put on goggles and tie back long hair and any loose clothing.* Insert the wooden dowel through the holes in the small can. Light the candle. Immediately hang the can of water on the ring.

8. Stir the water gently with the thermometer and observe the temperature change.

9. When the water temperature is about the same number of degrees above its initial temperature as it was below when the ice was added, blow out the candle.

10. Continue observing the water temperature. In the Data Table, record the highest temperature reached by the water. Calculate the change in water temperature (the difference between the cooled water and the heated water).

11. Find the mass of the candle and the lid after burning and record it in the Data Table. Calculate the mass of candle that burned.

12. Repeat steps 5–11. Compare your two sets of results. Note that the mass of the candle and lid before burning in Trial 2 is the same as the mass of the candle and lid after burning in Trial 1.

6

© Prentice-Hall, Inc.

COMBUSTION HEAT OF A CANDLE *(continued)*

◆ Observations

Data Table

	Trial 1	Trial 2
Mass of candle and lid before burning		
Mass of candle and lid after burning		
Mass of candle burned		
Volume of water in can		
Temperature of water after cooling		
Temperature of water after heating		
Change in temperature		

◆ Analyze and Conclude

1. Use the specific heat of water to calculate the amount of heat absorbed by the can of water. Use the following formula:

   Heat (in joules) = Volume of water (mL) × Temperature change (°C) × 4.18 J/g°C × 1 g/mL water

2. Calculate the combustion heat by dividing the heat that the can of water absorbed by the mass of the candle burned.

3. Do you think the water absorbed all of the heat released by the candle? Give a reason for your answer.

   _____

   _____

◆ Critical Thinking and Applications

1. A candle has a mass of 30 grams. How much heat will be released when the candle burns to one-third its original height? Use the combustion heat of wax from question 2 in Analyze and Conclude. Show your calculation. (Hint: How many grams of wax burned?)

6

COMBUSTION HEAT OF A CANDLE *(continued)*

2. How many joules would it take to heat 1000 mL of water at 25°C to a temperature of 30°C? Show your calculation.

3. How many grams of candle wax would be needed to heat the water in the previous question? Show your calculation. (Hint: Use the combustion heat of wax from question 2 in Analyze and Conclude.)

4. Based upon this investigation, describe how you could determine the energy content of foods.

_____

_____

◆ More to Explore

New Problem If the small can contained a different liquid, such as a soft drink, would the heat required to raise the temperature be the same?

Possible Materials Decide which liquid you will use. Use materials as in the previous lab.

Safety Handle the thermometer carefully. If it breaks, tell the teacher. Use tongs or an oven mitt when handling hot objects. Always wear safety goggles when heating objects.

Procedure Develop a procedure to measure the combustion heat of the candle, using the new liquid. Write the steps on a separate sheet of paper. Have the teacher approve your procedure before you carry out the investigation.

Observations On a separate sheet of paper, make a data table like the one in the lab, in which you record your observations.

Analyze and Conclude

1. Compare the heat required to raise the temperature of the new liquid to the heat required to raise the temperature of water. Would you expect the two values to be the same?

_____

_____

2. If the new liquid is not water, would you use the value 4.18 J/g°C as the specific heat?

_____

_____

N-1

Electromagnetism

◆ Pre-Lab Discussion

When charges move in an electric current, they create a magnetic field. It's possible to make an electromagnet with a magnetic field that is stronger than any permanent magnet. The magnetic field of an electromagnet is produced by the current in the wire and the magnetized core. You can also turn an electromagnet on or off, which makes it a useful tool. The drawback is that an electromagnet is useless without a supply of electricity.

In this investigation, you will make an electromagnet and find out what affects the strength of its magnetic field.

1. How is an electromagnet different from a regular magnet?

_____

_____

2. How could you use an electromagnet?

_____

_____

◆ Problem

What affects the strength of an electromagnet?

◆ Materials *(per group)*

dry cell, D cell or larger
5 iron nails, 10 cm long
small piece of aluminum foil
penny
nickel
dime
other test objects
bell wire, 2 m with ends stripped
15–20 paper clips

© Prentice-Hall, Inc.

ELECTROMAGNETISM *(continued)*

◆ **Safety** ⚠ *Review the safety guidelines in the front of your lab book.*

Computer disks, audiotapes, videotapes, and watches can be ruined by strong magnets. Keep them away from the lab area.

◆ Procedure

1. Hold the five nails in a bunch. Touch the bunch of nails to each test object to check for magnetic attraction between the nails and the object. Record your results in the Data Table.

2. Hold the five nails together and neatly wrap about 25 cm of wire around them in a single layer. See Figure 1. Do not overlap the coils. Leave about 50 cm of wire at one end and about 125 cm of wire at the other end.

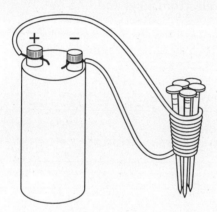

Figure 1

3. Attach the shorter end of the wire to one terminal of the dry cell.

4. Momentarily touch the 125-cm end of the wire to the other terminal of the dry cell. **CAUTION:** *Do not operate the electromagnet for more than a few seconds at a time. Otherwise it will rapidly use up the dry cell's power.* When the electromagnet is on, test each material for magnetic attraction. Record your results in the Data Table.

5. Give the electromagnet power again and find out how many paper clips it can hold. Record the number in the Data Table. Disconnect the longer end of the wire from the dry cell.

6. Use the 125-cm end of the wire to wrap another 25 cm of wire around the nails. You should have a single layer of windings. Repeat Steps 4 and 5.

7. Wind a second layer of wire over the first winding, using the 100-cm end of wire. You should have about 50 cm of unwound wire remaining.

8. Repeat Steps 4 and 5.

9. Take apart the electromagnet. Use just two nails to make an electromagnet with two layers of wire windings. Repeat Steps 4 and 5.

ELECTROMAGNETISM *(continued)*

◆ Observations

Test	Object	Attraction
Five nails alone Number of paper clips held =		
Five nails, 25 cm of wire Number of paper clips held =		
Five nails, 50 cm of wire Number of paper clips held =		
Five nails, two layers of wire Number of paper clips held =		
Two nails, two layers of wire Number of paper clips held =		

◆ Analyze and Conclude

1. Which materials did the electromagnet attract? Which materials did the electromagnet not attract?

_____

_____

ELECTROMAGNETISM (continued)

2. Why were some objects attracted by the electromagnet? Why were other objects not attracted?

_____

_____

1

3. How did increasing the number of turns of the wire affect the strength of the electromagnet? Why did it have this effect?

_____

_____

_____

4. How did removing some of the nails affect the strength of the electromagnet? Why did it have this effect?

_____

_____

◆ Critical Thinking and Applications

1. List the common properties of the materials attracted to the magnet.

_____

_____

2. Why are magnets a hazard for audiotapes, videotapes, and computer disks?

_____

_____

_____

3. Explain how you might construct an electromagnet that could hold more paper clips than your electromagnet in this lab was able to hold.

_____

_____

◆ More to Explore

Consider what goes into an electromagnet and enhances the magnetic field. How can you increase or decrease the strength of an electromagnet without making any changes to the arrangement of wire or nails? Write a procedure you would follow to answer this question. Have the teacher approve your procedure before you carry out the investigation.

© Prentice-Hall, Inc.

N-2   LABORATORY INVESTIGATION

Building Electric Circuits

◆ Pre-lab Discussion

An electric circuit allows the flow of electrons from a power source to make a complete round trip back to the power source. Every circuit has a source of electrical energy, a device that is run by electrical energy such as a lightbulb, and a switch. In a series circuit, only one path is available for electrons to flow through. In a parallel circuit, two or more paths are available for the electrons to flow through. In this investigation, you will construct several series and parallel circuits, and then measure and compare their current and voltage.

1. What instrument can you use to measure the current in an electric circuit?

_____

2. What instrument can you use to measure the voltage in an electric circuit?

_____

3. How is current related to voltage in electric circuits? (Hint: Think of Ohm's law.)

_____

_____

◆ Problem

How do current and voltage compare between two types of circuits—a parallel circuit and a series circuit?

◆ Materials *(per group)*

3 small bulbs with sockets
1.5-V dry cell
17 connecting wires
ammeter, 0–1A range
voltmeter, 0–3V range
knife switch

◆ Safety   *Review the safety guidelines in the front of your lab book.*

Wear safety goggles throughout the activity. Be careful when handling electric circuits to avoid shocks.

© Prentice-Hall, Inc.

BUILDING ELECTRIC CIRCUITS *(continued)*

◆ Procedure

Part A: A Parallel Circuit

1. Use the dry cell, connecting wires, and knife switch to connect the three bulbs in parallel. See Figure 1. Be sure to connect the bulbs to the dry cell and knife switch exactly as shown. Each of the round dots represents a connection between two wires. Make sure the knife switch is open. The switch connects to the negative terminal of the dry cell. When you have finished, have the teacher check the circuit.

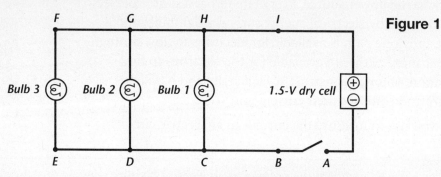

Figure 1

2. Close the switch and record your observations in Data Table 1.

3. Unscrew bulb 2. Record your observations in the same data table.

4. Retighten the bulb. Open the switch. Measure the total voltage of the circuit by placing the voltmeter as shown in Figure 2. Using the two remaining wires, connect the positive terminal of the voltmeter to position I, and connect the negative terminal of the voltmeter to position B. Momentarily close the switch to see if the needle deflects to the right. If the needle deflects to the left, reverse the voltmeter connections. Close the switch and record the total voltage (V_T) in Data Table 2. Open the switch.

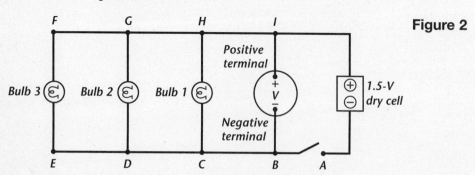

Figure 2

5. Measure the voltage across bulb 1 by connecting the positive terminal of the voltmeter to position H and the negative terminal of the voltmeter to position C. Close the switch and record the voltage (V_1) in Data Table 2. Open the switch.

© Prentice-Hall, Inc.

BUILDING ELECTRIC CIRCUITS *(continued)*

6. Measure the voltage across bulb 2 by connecting the positive terminal of the voltmeter to position G and the negative terminal to position D. Close the switch and record the voltage (V_2) in Data Table 2. Open the switch.

7. Measure the voltage across bulb 3 by connecting the positive terminal of the voltmeter to position F and the negative terminal to position E. Close the switch and record the voltage (V_3) in Data Table 2. Open the switch and remove the voltmeter.

8. Measure the total current by removing the connecting wire between positions H and I and attaching the positive terminal of the ammeter to position I and the negative terminal of the ammeter to position H. See Figure 3. Momentarily close the switch. If the needle deflects to the left, open the switch and reverse the ammeter connections. Close the switch and record the total current (I_T) in Data Table 2. Open the switch.

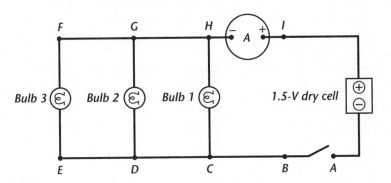

Figure 3

9. Disconnect the ammeter and replace the connecting wire between positions H and I. Disconnect the wire at position H that leads to bulb 1. Do not disconnect the wire at the lamp. Connect the negative terminal of the ammeter to the wire that is connected to the lamp. Connect the positive terminal of the ammeter to position H. See Figure 4. Close the switch and record the current (I_1) through bulb 1 in Data Table 2. Open the switch, disconnect the ammeter, and reconnect the wire to position H.

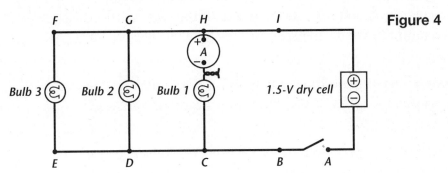

Figure 4

BUILDING ELECTRIC CIRCUITS *(continued)*

10. Disconnect the wire from bulb 2 at position G. Do not disconnect it at the bulb. Connect the negative terminal of the ammeter to the wire and the positive terminal of the ammeter to position G. Close the switch and record the current (I_2) through bulb 2 in Data Table 2. Open the switch, disconnect the ammeter, and reconnect the wire to position G.

11. Disconnect the wire from bulb 3 at position F. Do not disconnect it at the bulb. Connect the negative terminal of the ammeter to the wire and the positive terminal of the ammeter to position F. Close the switch and record the current (I_3) through bulb 3 in Data Table 2. Open the switch, disconnect the ammeter, and reconnect the wire to position F.

Part B: A Series Circuit

1. Connect the three bulbs in series by removing the connecting wires between positions G and H, between positions E and D, and between positions C and B. Insert a connecting wire between positions E and B. Your circuit should now look like Figure 5. Have the teacher check your circuit. Close the switch and record your observations in Data Table 1.

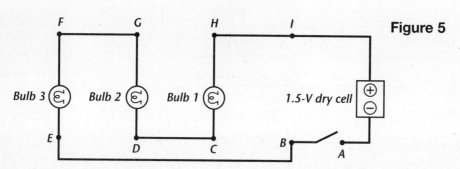

Figure 5

2. Unscrew bulb 2 and record your observation in the same data table. Retighten the bulb and open the switch.

3. Connect the positive terminal of the voltmeter to position I and the negative terminal of the voltmeter to position B. Close the switch. If the switch deflects to the left, reverse the voltmeter connections. Record the total voltage (V_T) in Data Table 2. Open the switch.

4. Connect the positive terminal of the voltmeter to position H and the negative terminal of the voltmeter to position C. Close the switch. Record the voltage (V_1) across bulb 1. Open the switch.

5. Connect the positive terminal of the voltmeter to position D and the negative terminal of the voltmeter to position G. Close the switch. Record the voltage (V_2) across bulb 2. Open the switch.

BUILDING ELECTRIC CIRCUITS *(continued)*

6. Connect the positive terminal of the voltmeter to position F and the negative terminal of the voltmeter to position E. Close the switch. Record the voltage (V_3) across bulb 3. Open the switch and remove the voltmeter.

7. Measure the total current by removing the connecting wire between positions H and I and connecting the positive terminal of the ammeter to position I and the negative terminal of the ammeter to position H. Close the switch. If the needle deflects to the left, reverse the ammeter connections. Record the total current (I_T) in Data Table 2. Open the switch, remove the ammeter, and replace the connecting wire between positions H and I.

8. Disconnect the wire from bulb 1 at position C. Do not disconnect this wire at the bulb. Connect the positive terminal of the ammeter to the wire and the negative terminal of the ammeter to position C. Close the switch and record the current (I_1) through bulb 1. Open the switch, disconnect the ammeter, and reconnect the wire to position C.

9. Disconnect the wire from bulb 2 at position G. Do not disconnect this wire at the bulb. Connect the positive terminal of the ammeter to the wire and the negative terminal of the ammeter to position G. Close the switch and record the current (I_2) through bulb 2. Open the switch, disconnect the ammeter, and reconnect the wire to position G.

10. Disconnect the wire from bulb 3 at position E. Do not disconnect this wire at the bulb. Connect the positive terminal of the ammeter to the wire and the negative terminal of the ammeter to position E. Close the switch and record the current (I_3) through bulb 3. Open the switch, disconnect the ammeter, and reconnect the wire to position E.

◆ Observations

Data Table 1

Circuit	Switch Closed	Bulb 2 Unscrewed
Part A: Parallel		
Part B: Series		

BUILDING ELECTRIC CIRCUITS (continued)

Data Table 2

Circuit	Voltage (volts)				Current (amps)			
	V_T	V_1	V_2	V_3	I_T	I_1	I_2	I_3
Part A: Parallel								
Part B: Series								

2 ◆ **Analyze and Conclude**

1. Add the currents I_1, I_2, and I_3 in the parallel circuit. Is the total current, I_T, approximately equal to the sum of the three individual currents in the parallel circuit?

2. Add the voltages V_1, V_2, and V_3 in the parallel circuit. Is the total voltage approximately equal to the sum of the individual voltages in the parallel circuit?

3. In the parallel circuit, how does the total voltage compare with the individual voltages?

_____

4. Add the currents I_1, I_2, and I_3 in the series circuit. Does the total current approximately equal the sum of the individual currents in a series circuit?

5. How does the total current compare with the individual currents in a series circuit?

_____

6. Add the voltages V_1, V_2, and V_3 in the series circuit. Is the total voltage approximately equal to the sum of the individual voltages in a series circuit?

© Prentice-Hall, Inc.

BUILDING ELECTRIC CIRCUITS *(continued)*

◆ Critical Thinking and Applications

1. In which circuit would a burned-out bulb cause all the other bulbs to go out? Why?

_____

_____

_____

2. Voltage is the force, or "push," that gets electrons moving. Based on your data, explain why the bulbs in a series circuit burn dimmer than the bulbs in a parallel circuit.

_____

_____

_____

3. What would happen to the current in a parallel circuit if all the bulbs were not the same size?

_____

_____

_____

◆ More To Explore

You have been given the job of designing the electrical circuits to supply the power to a house. You have the following information.

House Electrical Requirements

Room	Number of Lights Needed	Circuit Breaker Number
Kitchen	4	1
Bathroom	1	2
Laundry	1	2
Family room	2	3
Bedroom	1	3

You must design the correct circuits to accommodate the needs of the house. In each circuit, identify the position of lights in the circuit and identify the presence of a circuit breaker by a switch. (Hint: Each circuit breaker is wired in parallel with the house power supply and all the other circuit breakers. Also, all lights in a particular circuit must be in parallel.)

BUILDING ELECTRIC CIRCUITS *(continued)*

Use the information in the table of electrical requirements to determine the number of lights in each circuit and to find out how many series and parallel circuits are needed for the house.

Make a drawing of your circuits and locate all the lights in the circuit. Identify the circuit breakers with switches in the drawing.

2

1. How many circuits are in the house? What kind are they?

   _____

   _____

   _____

2. Assume that you have a working model of the circuit and that all the lights are on. What happens when you open each circuit-breaker switch?

   _____

   _____

3. As a designer, why would you not want all of the lights in the house to be connected in series?

   _____

   _____

   _____

   _____

4. Under what circumstances would all of the lights in the house go out?

   _____

   _____

   _____

© Prentice-Hall, Inc.

Electricity From a Lemon

◆ Pre-lab Discussion

Chemical reactions can generate electricity. That's how an electrochemical cell works. Cells and batteries can be made from different kinds of materials. As you have read, Alessandro Volta produced the first battery by stacking zinc and silver plates with moist paper between them.

In this investigation, you will build a simple electrochemical cell using a lemon and two types of coins. You will determine if your cell works by testing to see if the needle of a voltmeter moves when you complete a circuit that includes your electrochemical cell.

1. What are the components that make up an electrochemical cell?

_____

_____

2. What is the difference between a wet cell and a dry cell?

_____

_____

3. A voltmeter needle will deflect when current flows through it. How can you make the needle deflect more?

_____

_____

_____

◆ Problem

How can you make an electrochemical cell using a lemon and two coins?

◆ Possible Materials (per group)

coins of different types
sandpaper, steel wool,
　　or metal cleaner
lemon
scissors

small cardboard box
voltmeter
bell wire
tape

© Prentice-Hall, Inc.

ELECTRICITY FROM A LEMON (*continued*)

◆ Safety   *Review the safety guidelines in the front of your lab book.*

Always wear safety goggles. Be careful when handling scissors or any strong chemicals, such as metal cleaner. Wash your hands after using chemicals.

◆ Procedure

1. Read the entire lab before starting your investigation.

2. Design an electrochemical cell using the materials listed or similar materials. As you design the electrochemical cell, consider the following questions.
   - What metal or metals will you use for the electrodes?
   - Should the electrodes be made of the same or different metals?
   - Do you need to do anything to prepare the electrodes?
   - What will you use for an electrolyte?
   - Does the electrolyte need any special preparation?
   - How will you insert the electrodes into the electrolyte?
   - How should the electrodes be oriented in relation to each other?
   - How far apart should the electrodes be?

   On a separate sheet of paper, draw your design and show it to the teacher for approval. Then build your electrochemical cell.

3. Prepare your voltmeter so that you can see if your electrochemical cell generates a current. Consider these questions.
   - Where should you place the voltmeter in relation to the electrochemical cell?
   - How will you complete your circuit?
   - How will you turn the current on and off?

4. Prepare your lemon to act as an electrolyte by gently rolling it back and forth on a table or bench to release the juice inside.

5. To insert electrodes into the lemon, use scissors to carefully make two parallel slits in the lemon skin. In the left column of the Data Table, record what you used for electrodes.

6. Complete your circuit using your electrochemical cell and the wires. Observe any movement of the voltmeter needle including the direction and amount of movement. Record your observations in the right column of the Data Table.

7. If your electrochemical cell worked, go on to Step 8. If it did not work, consider how you could change your electrochemical cell and try again.

8. Reverse the connecting wires of your electrodes. Again observe and record any movement of the compass needle.

ELECTRICITY FROM A LEMON *(continued)*

◆ Observations

Data Table

Electrodes	Wire Connections	Observations of Compass

◆ Analyze and Conclude

1. What are the components of an electrochemical cell? Which of these correspond to the items used in this experiment?

_____

_____

_____

2. Why was the voltmeter important in this experiment?

_____

_____

3. Did your lemon electrochemical cell generate electricity on your first attempt? If so, what made it work? If not, how did you change your cell to make it work?

_____

_____

_____

_____

ELECTRICITY FROM A LEMON *(continued)*

4. With a working electrochemical cell, what happened to the voltmeter when you reversed the wires? Why does this happen?

_____

_____

◆ Critical Thinking and Applications

1. Did you make a wet cell or a dry cell? Explain your answer.

_____

_____

2. You may have found that scrubbing or cleaning the coins was an important factor in whether your electrochemical cell worked. How did cleaning the coins help your electrochemical cell work?

_____

_____

_____

3. How might using an old, dried-out lemon have affected your experiment? Explain.

_____

_____

_____

◆ More To Explore

How can you increase the strength of the current to get the voltmeter needle to move even more? Consider what was needed to generate the electric current and think about how these factors could be enhanced. Form a hypothesis and write a procedure for testing your hypothesis. Have the teacher approve your procedure before you carry out your investigation. Be sure to wear your safety goggles and apron.

N-4   **LABORATORY INVESTIGATION**

Constructing a Simple Computer Circuit

◆ Pre-Lab Discussion

Computers use combinations of off-on switches to perform their various functions. A circuit that is closed and through which current flows is said to be "on" and represents the number 1. A circuit that is open and through which current does not flow is said to be "off" and represents the number 0.

In this investigation, you will construct an electric circuit that will show base-10 numbers as binary (base 2) numbers.

1. What is the binary system?

_____

_____

_____

_____

2. How do you know if a number is 0 or 1 in a binary electric circuit?

_____

_____

◆ Problem

How can off-on switches model how a computer circuit converts base-10 numbers to binary numbers?

◆ Materials (per group)

three 1.5-V bulbs with sockets
1.5-V dry cell
3 knife switches, single pole–single throw
knife switch, double pole–single throw
connecting wires
pegboard
machine screws
12 clips or screws for connecting wires

CONSTRUCTING A SIMPLE COMPUTER CIRCUIT *(continued)*

◆ Safety   *Review the safety guidelines in the front of your lab book.*

The amount of electricity you will be using in this lab cannot hurt you. If you feel components of a circuit getting warm, open the circuit. Examine it carefully for a short circuit.

◆ Procedure

1. Connect the bulbs, switches, and dry cell on the pegboard as shown in Figure 1. Note that you must use a double-pole switch for switch 3, so that it can be connected to both bulb 1 and 2.

2. Have the teacher check your circuit before you proceed.

3. Switches 1, 2, 3, and 4 correspond to the base-10 numbers 1, 2, 3, and 4. Close switch 1 and record in the Data Table which bulbs are on and which remain off. For example, if only the middle bulb is on, record off, on, off.

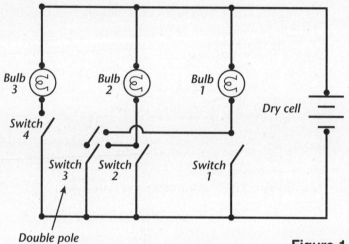

Figure 1

4. Open switch 1.

5. Close switch 2 and record which bulbs are on and which remain off.

6. Open switch 2.

7. Close switch 3 and record which bulbs are on and which remain off.

8. Close switch 3

9. Close switch 4 and record which bulbs are on and which remain off.

10. Open switch 4.

◆ Observations

Data Table

Switch Closed	Bulb 3	Bulb 2	Bulb 1
1			
2			
3			
4			

CONSTRUCTING A SIMPLE COMPUTER CIRCUIT *(continued)*

◆ Analyze and Conclude

1. Use the data in your Data Table to help you show base-10 numbers as binary (base 2) numbers. In the table below, for base-10 numbers 1, 2, 3, and 4, record "1" if a bulb is lit and "0" if a bulb is off. For example, if only the middle switch is lit, record 010. Examine the pattern and then complete the table for base-10 numbers 5, 6, and 7.

Base-10 Number	Binary Number
1	
2	
3	
4	
5	
6	
7	

2. Your circuit models only how a computer shows the first four base-10 numbers as binary numbers. How could you show the following base-10 numbers as binary numbers using your circuit: 5, 6, 7? If time permits, try these numbers on your circuit.

_____

_____

_____

_____

◆ Critical Thinking and Applications

1. What is the largest base-10 number your circuit can show? Give a reason for your answer.

_____

_____

_____

_____

CONSTRUCTING A SIMPLE COMPUTER CIRCUIT *(continued)*

2. How would you have to modify your circuit to go beyond the number from question 1?

_____

_____

3. What number do you get if you add the binary numbers 101 and 001? Write your answer as a binary number.

_____

_____

4. What is the base-10 value of the binary number 111101?

_____

◆ More to Explore

Write a hypothesis that explains how the bulb circuit you used for the lab relates to the operation of a computer that uses binary numbers to represent 256 characters. Begin by considering how many bulbs would be needed to accommodate all of the characters used by the computer. Then devise a way to get all of these characters represented by the fewest binary digits. (Hint: Try to find a pattern instead of writing out all the binary numbers.)

If you were to attempt to represent all of the characters using a bulb circuit, what is the minimum number of bulbs that would be needed?

_____

Look at a computer keyboard. Why do you think that it's necessary for a computer to use so many binary numbers?

_____

_____

© Prentice-Hall, Inc.

Making Waves

◆ Pre-Lab Discussion

The speed of a wave is how far the wave travels in one unit of time. The speed also equals the wavelength multiplied by the wave's frequency. If you know any two of the quantities in the speed formula—wavelength, frequency, or speed— you can calculate the third.

In this experiment, you will model waves and investigate the relationship of the frequency and length of the wave to its speed.

1. Write the equation for the speed of a wave.

_____

2. Define wavelength.

_____

_____

3. If a wave travels 6 m in 2 s, what is its speed?

If the same wave has a frequency of 10 Hz, what is its wavelength?

◆ Problem

How does a wave's speed relate to its frequency and wavelength?

◆ Materials *(per group)*

meterstick	string
ruler	graduated cylinder, 100-mL
masking tape	water
plain brown paper	stopwatch or clock with a second hand
paper cup	marker
pencil	

◆ Safety *Review the safety guidelines in the front of your lab book.*

To prevent slips or falls, immediately wipe up any water spilled on the floor.

MAKING WAVES (*continued*)

◆ Procedure

1. Work with two other students. Measure off 4 m on the floor. Mark the starting and end points with masking tape. Lay the brown paper on the floor between the two marked points.

2. Poke a tiny hole in the bottom of a cup with a pencil point. Poke two larger holes near the top of the cup on opposite sides.

3. Thread a string through the holes near the top of the cup and attach the string to the pencil. See Figure 1. The pencil acts as a handle that lets the cup swing freely.

4. Read Steps 5–9 before continuing with the investigation.

5. Have a classmate stand at the end point with a stopwatch or a clock with a second hand. That student will time how long it takes the second student to walk the measured distance.

6. Stand behind the starting point and hold the pencil ends so the cup can swing freely.

7. Have a second classmate hold the cup while plugging the bottom hole with one finger. That student should fill the cup with 100 mL of water and hold the cup 5 cm to one side, so that the cup will swing from side to side when it is released.

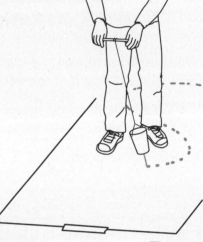

Figure 1

8. When the first student gives a signal, he or she should start the stopwatch, and the second student should let go of the cup. At the same time, walk at a steady pace along the marked distance, holding the pencil away from your body. As you walk, the cup will swing from side to side, and the water will drain through the hole. The water will trace a wave on the paper.

9. When you reach the end point, the first student should stop the stopwatch. In the Data Table provided on the next page, record the time it took to walk the 4 m. Properly dispose of any water remaining in the cup.

10. If necessary, use the marker to retrace the wave on the paper. Measure the wavelength and count the number of crests in 4 m. Record these values in the table.

11. Calculate the frequency of the wave—the number of complete waves per second. Round off your number to the nearest complete wave. Record this value in the table.

12. Predict whether you would have more or fewer crests if you repeated the experiment while walking faster. Give a reason for your prediction.

_____

_____

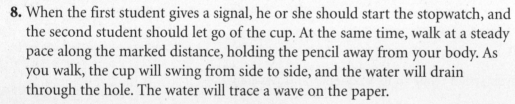

© Prentice-Hall, Inc.

MAKING WAVES *(continued)*

13. Check your prediction by repeating Steps 5–11, but at a faster pace than in the first trial. Record your results in the Data Table.

14. Predict whether you would have more or fewer crests if you repeated the experiment while walking slower than at first. Give a reason for your prediction.

_____

_____

15. Check your prediction. Record your results in the Data Table.

◆ Observations

Data Table

Trial	Time (s)	Wavelength (m)	Waves in 4 m	Frequency (Hz)
1				
2				
3				

◆ Analyze and Conclude

1. Calculate the speed of each wave from the distance traveled and the time.

2. Calculate the speed of each wave from the frequency and the wavelength.

3. Compare the speeds you calculated for Questions 1 and 2.

_____

4. Compare the frequencies and the wavelengths of each wave. What would happen if the frequency increased?

_____

© Prentice-Hall, Inc.

MAKING WAVES (*continued*)

◆ Critical Thinking and Applications

1. Was your first prediction in the Procedure correct? Explain why the number of crests changed.

_____

_____

_____

2. If you made more crests over a given distance by walking at a different speed, did the wavelength increase? Why or why not?

_____

_____

_____

3. Blue light has a higher frequency than red light. Does blue light travel faster than red light in the same medium? Give a reason for your answer.

_____

_____

_____

_____

_____

◆ More to Explore

New Problem What would happen to the speed of the wave if you repeated the experiment with waves that have a greater amplitude?

Possible Materials Use the materials from this lab.

Safety To prevent slips or falls, immediately wipe up any water spilled on the floor.

Procedure Develop a procedure to solve the problem. Think about how you could increase the amplitude of the waves. Write your procedure on a separate sheet of paper. Have the teacher approve your procedure before you carry out the investigation.

Observations On a separate sheet of paper, make a data table similar to the one in this lab to record your observations.

Analyze and Conclude What effect did changing the wave's amplitude have on its speed?

© Prentice-Hall, Inc.

O-2

Tuning Forks

◆ Pre-Lab Discussion

If you could live in outer space, you'd have a very quiet life. Why is that?

The energy of a sound wave disturbs the molecules in a medium, making them rock back and forth in time with the wave frequency. When the disturbance reaches your ears, you hear sound. When the vibrations are very fast, you hear a high-pitched sound. When the vibrations are slow, the pitch is low. Sound can also travel through solids and liquids. The speed of the sound depends on the temperature, the elasticity, and the density of the medium. If there's no medium, as in the vacuum of outer space, there's no sound.

In this investigation, you will use two tuning forks that vibrate at the same frequency. You will test how sound affects and is affected by different media, different speeds, and interference.

1. What does sound do to the surrounding medium?

_____

_____

_____

_____

_____

_____

2. What property of a sound wave changes as it gets louder?

_____

_____

◆ Problem

How does sound interact with a medium?

◆ Materials *(per group)*

2 tuning forks, 320 Hz
beaker, 400-mL
water
rubber band
resonance box

© Prentice-Hall, Inc.

TUNING FORKS *(continued)*

◆ Safety *Review the safety guidelines in the front of your lab book.*

Be careful when you strike the tuning forks against an object. Strike them against unbreakable objects (such as the heel of your shoe) and with just enough force to start them vibrating.

◆ Procedure

Work with a partner. Take turns performing each of the six tests below and note any differences between your observations. Read through all six tests before you perform them. Always strike the tuning fork against the heel of your shoe.

1. **Vibration in a medium:** Strike a tuning fork and insert the prongs into a beaker of water. Observe what happens. In the Data Table provided on the next page, record your observations.

2. **Similar vibration:** Strike a tuning fork and bring it within a few centimeters of a second tuning fork with the same frequency. Bring the second tuning fork to within a few centimeters of your ear. Observe what happens. Record your observations.

3. **Resonance:** Strike a tuning fork and note the loudness of the sound. Strike the tuning fork again and touch the base of its stem to the top of the resonance box. Note the loudness of the sound. Record your observations.

4. **Interference:** Strike a tuning fork and bring one of the prongs to within 2 or 3 cm of your ear. Slowly rotate the tuning fork completely. Carefully note any change in the loudness of the sound. Record your observations.

5. **Beats:** Fasten a rubber band securely on the middle of one prong of a tuning fork. See Figure 1. Using a second tuning fork of the same frequency, strike both forks. Touch the bases of the stems of the forks on the resonance box. If the sound is constant, reposition the rubber band and try again. Carefully note the sound emitted by the forks. Record your observations.

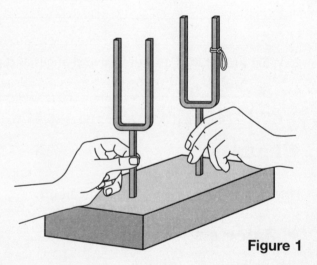

Figure 1

6. **Moving source:** Make sure you have plenty of room to swing your arm to the side. Strike a tuning fork extra hard. Rapidly move the tuning fork in a wide arc from your side to over your head. Note and record what you hear. Repeat this experiment with your partner standing several meters away. Does your partner observe any difference in sound at a greater distance? Record your observations and those of your partner.

TUNING FORKS *(continued)*

◆ Observations

Data Table

Test	Loudness Change	Pitch Change	Effect
Vibration in a medium			
Similar vibrations			
Resonance			
Interference			
Beats			
Moving sound			

◆ Analyze and Conclude

1. Did the loudness of the sound change in some tests? If so, give examples and explain why the loudness changed.

_____

_____

_____

_____

2. How did the pitch change in the moving-source test? Explain this observation.

_____

_____

_____

_____

3. Why did you experiment with two tuning forks that vibrate at the same frequency?

_____

_____

_____

_____

TUNING FORKS (continued)

◆ Critical Thinking and Applications

1. How does one vibrating object make another object vibrate, when they're not touching? What is true of both objects' vibrations when this happens?

_____

_____

_____

2. Why does sound get louder with the use of the resonance box?

_____

_____

_____

_____

3. How are beats produced by two similar tuning forks?

_____

_____

_____

_____

4. Bats bounce sound waves off objects to get information about prey and obstacles. If a bat makes a constant-frequency sound and the sound bounces back with a different frequency, what does that change tell the bat about an object?

_____

_____

◆ More to Explore

How might a change in the resonance box affect the sound that you heard from the resonance test? For example, what would happen to its resonance if the box were a different size or shape? What if it were filled with a gas other than air or a liquid medium? Choose one of the following variables:

- size of resonance box
- shape of resonance box
- substance within resonance box

Write a procedure you would follow to test that variable. Include a hypothesis about how that variable affects the sound from the box. Have the teacher approve your procedure before you carry out the investigation.

O-3   **LABORATORY INVESTIGATION**

In the Heat of the Light

◆ Pre-Lab Discussion

Fluorescent and incandescent lights use
electricity to produce light in two different
ways. However, the two types of light bulbs have some common characteristics
that let you make comparisons between them. They each give off a specific
amount of light, called luminosity, or light output, which is measured in lumens.
They each use energy at a certain rate, a characteristic called power, which is
measured in watts. They each last for about a certain amount of time, often called
the average life of the bulb, which is measured in hours of use. This kind of information, plus the costs of power and of the light bulb, can help you determine
which type of bulbs you should buy.

In this investigation, you will compare the light given off and the power used by
incandescent and fluorescent light bulbs.

1. Compare the way that incandescent and fluorescent light bulbs work.

_____

_____

_____

_____

◆ Problem

How do fluorescent and incandescent bulbs that produce
the same amount of light compare in their use of energy?

◆ Materials *(per group)*

cardboard carton (approximately
   25 cm × 25 cm × 30 cm)
masking tape
15- and 60-watt incandescent bulbs
light socket
black electrical tape
thermometer

aluminum foil
graph paper
15- and 25-watt fluorescent bulbs
bulb packaging for 15-watt fluorescent
   and 60-watt incandescent bulbs
scissors
watch or clock with second hand

IN THE HEAT OF THE LIGHT *(continued)*

◆ **Safety**   *Review the safety guidelines in the front of your lab book.*

Use caution in handling scissors. Handle the thermometer carefully. If it breaks, tell the teacher. Be careful not to touch a light bulb while it is on or shortly after turning it off. In Part A, look at the lighted bulbs for only a few seconds at a time.

◆ Procedure

Part A: Investigating the Brightness of Light Bulbs

1. If you compare a 15-watt fluorescent bulb and a 15-watt incandescent bulb, do you think one would be brighter, or would they look about the same? How would the brightness of a 25-watt fluorescent bulb compare with that of a 60-watt incandescent bulb? On a separate sheet of paper, write a prediction about the brightness of each of these four light bulbs, ranking them in order from brightest to least bright.

2. In a darkened room, compare the brightness of a lighted 15-watt fluorescent bulb and of a 15-watt incandescent bulb. Which bulb is brighter?

_____

3. In a darkened room, compare the brightness of a 25-watt fluorescent bulb and of a 60-watt incandescent bulb. Which bulb is brighter?

_____

4. Observe any other combinations needed to test your prediction.

_____

_____

Part B: Comparing Energy Use by Bulbs of the Same Brightness

1. Prepare a Data Table like the one shown on the next page. Then your teacher will give you a carton with two holes cut out. One hole will be large enough for a light socket. The other hole will be large enough for a thermometer.

2. Use aluminum foil to line the inside of the carton, including the two long flaps on top. Use masking tape to hold the foil in place. Use scissors to create two holes in the foil to match the holes in the carton.

3. Fasten a sheet of foil across part of the carton as a divider. It will shade the thermometer from direct light while still allowing air to circulate in the carton. See Figure 1 on the next page.

© Prentice-Hall, Inc.

IN THE HEAT OF THE LIGHT *(continued)*

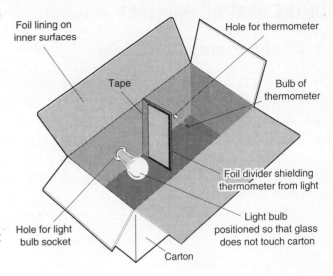

Foil lining on inner surfaces

Hole for thermometer

Tape

Bulb of thermometer

Foil divider shielding thermometer from light

Hole for light bulb socket

Light bulb positioned so that glass does not touch carton

Carton

4. Insert a light socket through the large hole, and seal it in place with black electrical tape. If necessary, support the socket outside the carton so it is stable.

5. Examine the labels on a 60-watt incandescent bulb and its packaging. In the Data Table, record the number of watts, lumens, and predicted hours of life.

6. Insert the incandescent bulb into the socket. Make sure the light bulb does not touch any part of the cardboard or aluminum foil. Test the bulb to make sure it works, and then turn it off.

7. Insert a thermometer through the other hole in the carton. Wait about one minute, and then observe the temperature inside the carton. Record that temperature for Time 0 in the first column in the Data Table.

8. On a separate sheet of paper, write a prediction about the amount of temperature change you expect when the light is turned on.

9. Close the carton so that the foil-covered lids are on the inside. Turn on the light, and for 10 minutes, record the temperature in the Data Table every half minute.

10. Turn off the light, and open the carton. **CAUTION:** *Do not touch the hot light bulb or its base.* Allow the bulb and its base to cool down for at least two minutes. When the light is cool, and the temperature of the carton reaches the original temperature, carefully remove the light bulb.

11. Repeat Steps 5 through 10 using a 15-watt fluorescent light bulb.

◆ Observations

Using the Data Table below as a model, on a separate sheet of paper create a complete Data Table. Include rows for 21 entries, one every half minute, for a total of 10 minutes.

Data Table

	Incandescent Bulb ___ Watts ___ Lumens ___ Hours of Life	Fluorescent Bulb ___ Watts ___ Lumens ___ Hours of Life
Time (min)	Temperature (°C)	Temperature (°C)
0		
0.5		

Continue for 21 rows.

IN THE HEAT OF THE LIGHT (continued)

◆ Analyze and Conclude

1. Make a graph of your data, placing time on the horizontal axis and temperature on the vertical axis. Which light bulb heated up the inside of the box more? Explain.

_____

_____

2. Which bulb gave off more light for the amount of energy used? How do you know?

_____

_____

_____

◆ Critical Thinking and Applications

3

1. Which gives off more visible light, a 15-watt fluorescent bulb or a 15-watt incandescent bulb? What happens to the energy that is not given off as visible light?

_____

_____

2. In people's homes, incandescent bulbs commonly use 60 to 100 watts. Fluorescent bulbs only use between 15 and 25 watts. Why do you think this is so?

_____

_____

More to Explore

You can use the information from this lab along with information about costs to determine which light bulbs to buy. For example, the cost to operate a light bulb is about 10 cents per kilowatt hour. That equals $0.0001 for each watt for one hour. Assume that a 15-watt fluorescent bulb costs $15.00, and the 60-watt incandescent bulb costs 50¢. Assume that you will use each type of light bulb about 4 hours per day.

1. Determine the average cost of operating a 15-watt fluorescent bulb for one year.

2. Determine the average cost of operating a 60-watt incandescent bulb for one year.

3. If you consider the initial cost of the bulbs, the cost of operating them, and their average lifetimes, which bulb is less expensive to use? Explain your reasoning and show your work.

O-4   **LABORATORY INVESTIGATION**

Plane-Mirror Images

◆ Pre-Lab Discussion

When light strikes an object, the light can be reflected, absorbed, or transmitted. When the reflected light from an object strikes a mirror, the light reflects off the coating, and an image forms in the mirror. The image formed by a plane, or flat, mirror seems to be exactly like the object. But is the image really an exact copy of the object? And how does a mirror produce an image?

In this investigation, you will see how a plane mirror forms an image and how that image compares with the object.

1. What is an image?

_____

_____

2. When you look in a plane mirror, what size image do you see? How far away does the image appear to be?

_____

_____

_____

◆ Problem

How is an image produced by a plane mirror?

◆ Materials *(per group)*

cardboard (approximately 30 cm × 30 cm)
unlined paper
small mirror and support
metric ruler
3 straight pins
protractor

◆ Safety 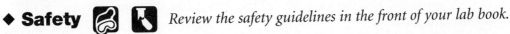 *Review the safety guidelines in the front of your lab book.*

Handle the mirror carefully. If it breaks, tell the teacher. Do not pick up broken glass.

PLANE-MIRROR IMAGES (continued)

◆ Procedure

1. Lay the paper on the cardboard. Stand the mirror in the center of the paper and draw a line along the edge of the mirror. Stick a pin in the paper and cardboard about 4 cm in front of the mirror. Draw a small circle around the pin position and label it "Object." See Figure 1.

2. Bend down so that your head is near the lower right corner of the paper. Look at the mirror with one eye closed and observe the image of the pin. Do not look at the real pin. Stick a pin in the paper so that it hides the image of the pin in the mirror. Draw a small circle around the pin position and label it "1."

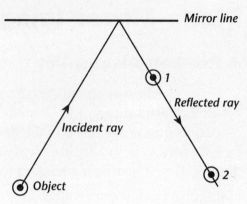

Figure 1

3. From the same position on the right-hand side of the paper, stick a second pin in the paper so that it hides the real pin at position 1 and the image of the object pin. Draw a small circle around the pin position and label it "2."

4. Remove the pins from positions 1 and 2. Use them to repeat steps 2 and 3 from the lower left corner of the paper. Draw circles around these pin positions and label them "3" and "4."

5. Remove the mirror and all of the pins. Using the ruler, draw a solid line through pin positions 1 and 2 and extend it as far as the mirror line. This line represents a reflected ray. Draw a line from the object position to the point where the reflected ray leaves the mirror. This line represents the incident ray. Label each ray and draw an arrow on the ray to show its direction.

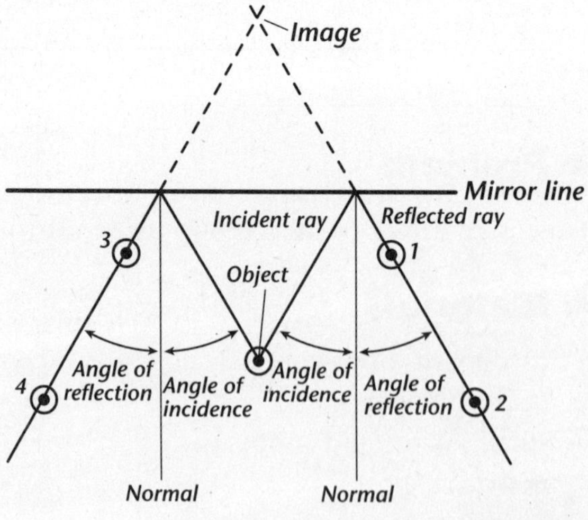

6. Repeat Step 5 for positions 3 and 4.

7. Draw a line perpendicular to the mirror line at each of the two points where the incident rays and the reflected rays touch. These lines are the normals. See Figure 2. Label and measure the angle of incidence and the angle of reflection for the rays coming from the left and right corners of the paper. Record your measurements in the Data Table.

Figure 2

8. Using the ruler, draw two dashed lines extending the two reflected rays beyond the mirror line. Continue your dashed lines just beyond the point where they cross. This point is the position of the image of the pin in the mirror. Label this point "Image."

Include your completed drawing when you hand in this lab to the teacher.

PLANE-MIRROR IMAGES *(continued)*

◆ Observations

Data Table

	Angle of Incidence	*Angle of reflection*
Left-side rays		
Right-side rays		

◆ Analyze and Conclude

1. At what distance is the object from the mirror line?

_____

2. At what distance is the image from the mirror line?

_____

3. Compare the distance of the object and of the image from the mirror.

_____

4. Compare the measures of the angle of incidence and the angle of reflection for the rays from the left side of the paper.

_____

5. Compare the measures of the angle of incidence and the angle of reflection for the rays from the right side of the paper.

_____

◆ Critical Thinking and Applications

1. Follow the path of an incident ray and its reflected ray. If the incident ray enters from the left, toward what direction does the reflected ray leave? If the incident ray enters from the right, toward what direction does the reflected ray leave?

_____

2. Based on your answer to Question 1, how does the image compare with the object?

_____

_____

© Prentice-Hall, Inc.

PLANE-MIRROR IMAGES *(continued)*

3. If the angle of incidence were not equal to the angle of reflection, would that affect the image's appearance? Give a reason for your answer.

_____

_____

4. Why does the image seem to be inside or behind the mirror?

_____

_____

_____

_____

◆ More to Explore

New Problem How do convex and concave mirrors form images?

Possible Materials Consider which materials you can use from the previous part of this lab. What else will you need?

Safety Handle the mirrors carefully. If they break, tell the teacher. Do not pick up broken glass.

Procedure Develop a procedure to solve the problem. Write your procedure on a separate sheet of paper. Have the teacher approve your procedure before you carry out the investigation.

Observations On a separate sheet of paper, make a data table like the one in the previous part of this lab in which to record your data.

Analyze and Conclude

1. How do the images formed by these curved mirrors compare to the actual objects?

_____

_____

_____

_____

2. Suggest some practical applications for these mirrors.

_____

_____

_____

Common SI Units

Measurement	Unit	Symbol	Equivalents
Length	1 millimeter	mm	1000 micrometers (μm)
	1 centimeter	cm	10 millimeters (mm)
	1 meter	m	100 centimeters (cm)
	1 kilometer	km	1000 meters (m)
Area	1 square meter	m^2	10 000 square centimeters (cm^2)
	1 square kilometer	km^2	1 000 000 square meters m^2)
Volume	1 milliliter	mL	1 cubic centimeter (cm^3 or cc)
	1 liter	L	1000 milliliters (mL)
Mass	1 gram	g	1000 milligrams (mg)
	1 kilogram	kg	1000 grams (g)
	1 ton	t	1000 kilograms (kg) = 1 metric ton
Time	1 second	s	
Temperature	1 Kelvin	K	1 degree Celsius (°C)

Metric Conversion Tables

When You Know	Multiply by	To Find			
		When You Know	Multiply by	To Find	
inches	2.54	centimeters	0.394	inches	
feet	0.3048	meters	3.281	feet	
yards	0.914	meters	1.0936	yards	
miles	1.609	kilometers	0.62	miles	
square inches	6.45	square centimeters	0.155	square inches	
square feet	0.093	square meters	10.76	square feet	
square yards	0.836	square meters	1.196	square yards	
acres	0.405	hectares	2.471	acres	
square miles	2.59	square kilometers	0.386	square miles	
cubic inches	16.387	cubic centimeters	0.061	cubic inches	
cubic feet	0.028	cubic meters	35.315	cubic feet	
cubic yards	0.765	cubic meters	1.31	cubic yards	
fluid ounces	29.57	milliliters	0.0338	fluid ounces	
quarts	0.946	liters	1.057	quarts	
gallons	3.785	liters	0.264	gallons	
ounces	28.35	grams	0.0353	ounces	
pounds	0.4536	kilograms	2.2046	pounds	
tons	0.907	metric tons	1.102	tons	

When You Know		
Fahrenheit	subtract 32; then *divide* by 1.8	to find Celsius
Celsius	multiply by 1.8; then *add* 32	to find Fahrenheit

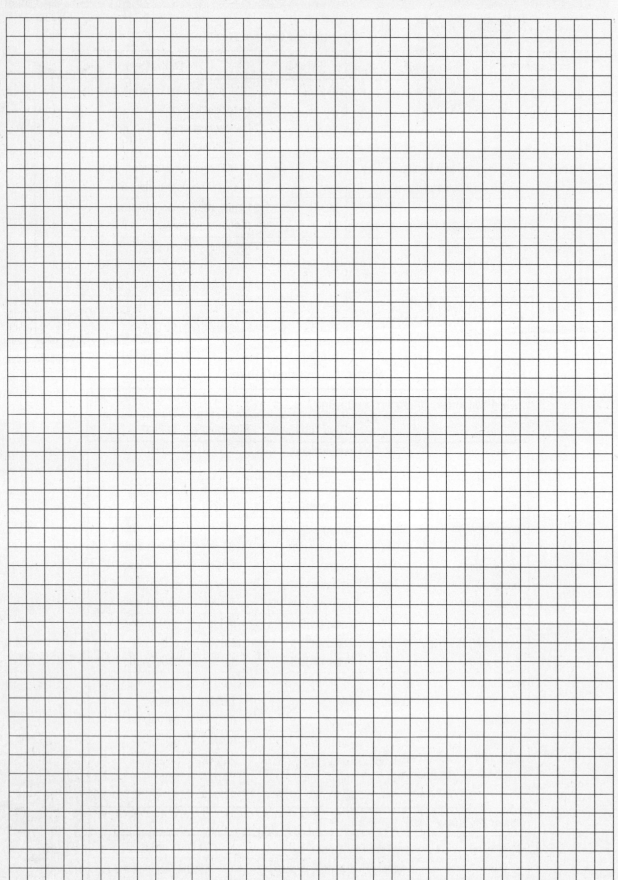